Thomas S. Shenston

A Jubilee Review of the First Baptist Church, Brantford, 1833 to

1884

Thomas S. Shenston

A Jubilee Review of the First Baptist Church, Brantford, 1833 to 1884

ISBN/EAN: 9783337161637

Printed in Europe, USA, Canada, Australia, Japan

Cover: Foto ©ninafisch / pixelio.de

More available books at **www.hansebooks.com**

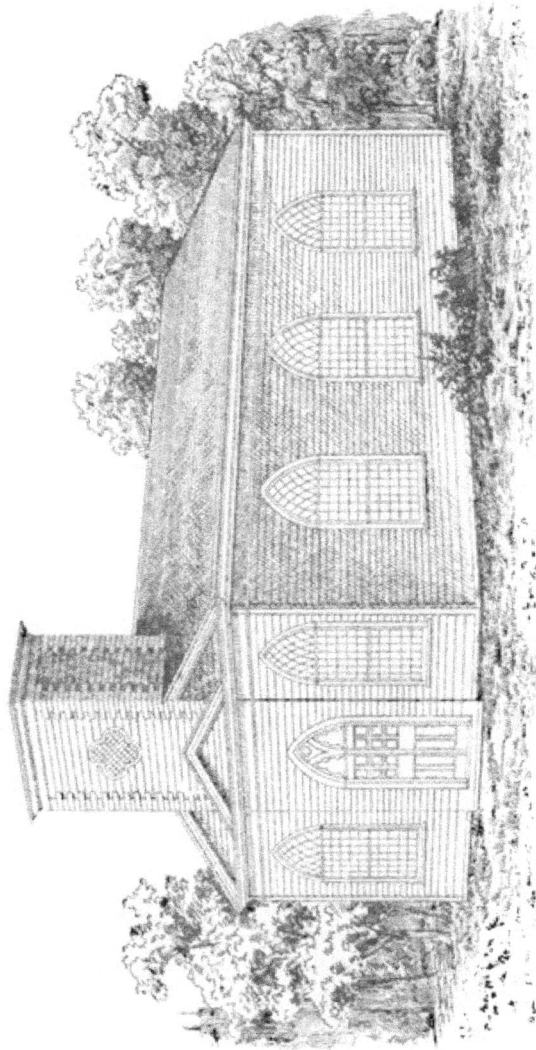

THE FIRST BRANTFORD BAPTIST CHAPEL, ERECTED IN 1834.

"The best Baptist Chapel in all this region of Country."

—*Rev. Wm. Rees. March 1, 1841.*

Sold to Messrs. Smith & Wade for $1,200, December, 1854.

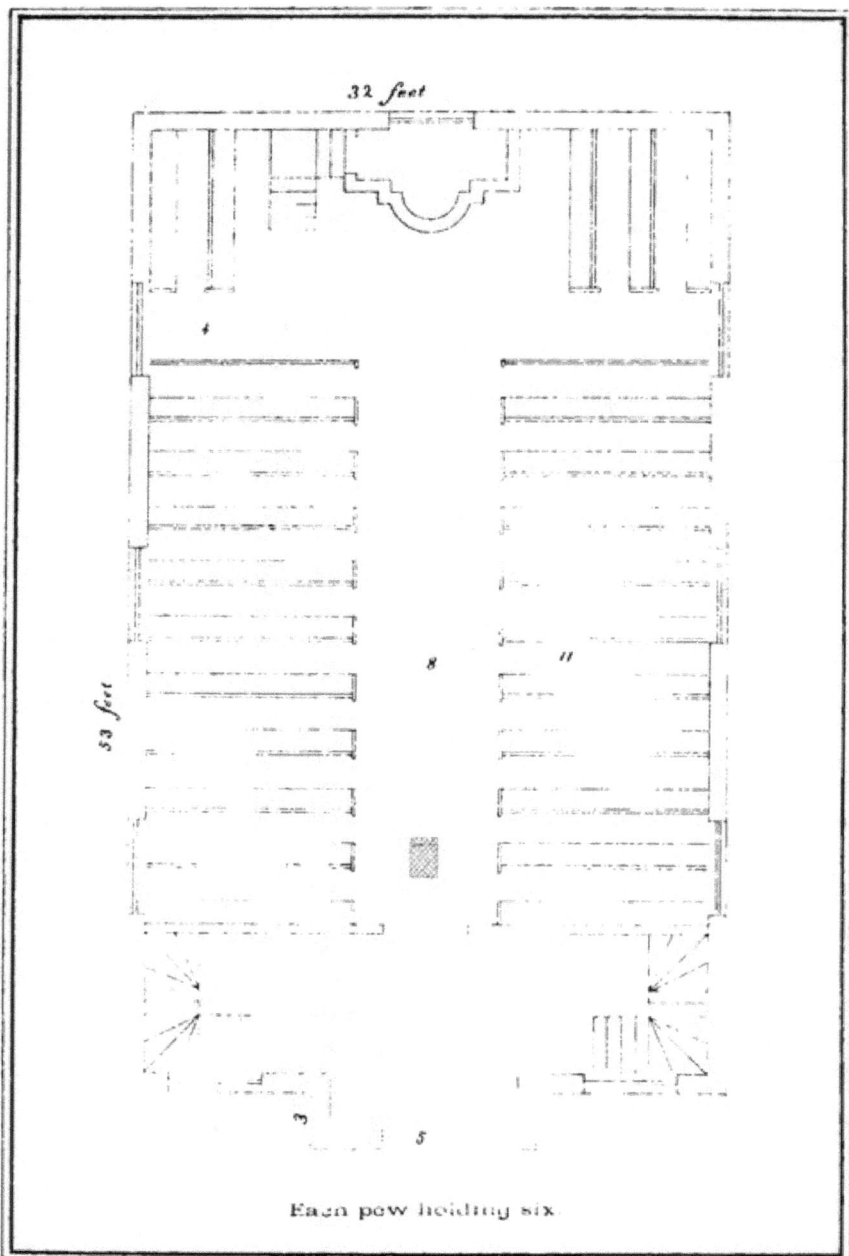

32 feet

53 feet

4

8

11

3

5

Each pew holding six.

A JUBILEE REVIEW

OF THE

FIRST BAPTIST CHURCH

BRANTFORD

1833 - TO - 1884

BY

THOMAS S. SHENSTON.

"That search may be made in the book of record of thy fathers so shall they find" that "Hitherto hath the Lord helped us." "Nevertheless I have somewhat against thee." (*Ezra* iv., 15. *I Samuel* vii., 12. *Rev.* ii., 4).

Toronto:
BINGHAM & WEBBER, PRINTERS,
1890.

INTRODUCTION.

W HAT I did for the county of Oxford in 1852 by the publication of the "*Oxford Gazetteer*": and the Baptist Foreign Missionary Society of Ontario and Quebec in 1888 by the publication of the "*Telegu Scrap Book*," I am now aiming to do for the First Baptist Church of Brantford in 1890 by the publication of this history. My object in each case has been to preserve from oblivion, facts and figures before they are lost beyond recovery. To collate such facts has been no small task, in consequence of the absence of anything like systematic records. It is supposed that the First Baptist Church has kept correct records of its numerous business meetings, but such, unfortunately, is far from being the case. Nor can anyone be very much surprised at the imperfect and perfunctory manner this duty has been discharged, when it is considered that its church meetings have been at irregular intervals, and often without any previous notice. As a consequence, the member of the church who may, for the time being, be acting as church clerk, is necessarily often absent when such meetings are held. On two occasions a period of over a year intervened without any minute having been made of the many business meetings which must have been held during that time. Consequently, in many cases, the first intimation obtained from the minute-book that a party is a member is the appearance of his or her name in connection with some delegation, or as mover of a resolution. How any such first became members of the church the books furnish no means of ascertaining.

It is proposed (as the name of the book implies) to record such of the church's first fifty years' transactions as may be thought useful and interesting to its present and future members. Some readers may possibly take exception to the recording of so many trifling matters lacking general interest, and also to the style in which they are given. I beg to remind all such that the work has been produced solely for the use of the First Baptist Church of Brantford, and virtually for no one else. It is purely a family matter to which strangers are not invited, or even expected to criticise.

T. S. SHENSTON.

BRANTFORD, 1890.

BRANTFORD.

EFORE making any statements relating to the First Baptist Church of Brantford, it will be only proper to say a word or two with respect to the village of Brantford itself. "*The Royal Calendar*" for 1826 says :—"The largest towns are York (now Toronto) and Kingston, of which Kingston is the most populous, containing 2,800 inhabitants. Many other towns are growing into note, of which the following are the principal : "—Here follows a list of thirty, with Brantford within two of the bottom. In this year I find that in Upper Canada there were forty-two post offices, with Brantford being placed the last in the list.

The land now occupied by the now city of Brantford was originally owned by the Six Nation Indians, but was, on the 19th day of April, 1830, surrendered by them to the government. The first lot sold by the government was to William Muirhead, on the 15th October, 1830, being lot eight, on the north side of Colborne street, now owned by Bradford G. Tisdale, Esq. The next one sold was number sixteen on the same side of the same street, to Jedediah Jackson, who proved himself a great friend to the First Baptist Church, and to the Rev. William Rees, its first Pastor. It was in an unfinished frame building on the east part of this lot that the church was first organized. The council was composed of ministerial and lay delegates from the churches in the neighborhood. This part of the lot is now owned by Geo. Foster and Wm. Buck, two staunch Baptists. For several years a "school house," situate where the town hall now stands, was the only public building in the village, and it was used for all manner of public and religious purposes. Smith's "*Canadian Gazetteer*" of 1846 reports thus :—"Brantford is a place of considerable business. * * * It contains seven churches and chapels, namely : Episcopalian, Presbyterian, Catholic, Methodist, Baptist and Congregational. Population nearly 2,000." When, in 1833, the Baptist Church was formed, there would be a population of about 400 or 500 — not more.

REV. WILLIAM REES

PASTOR FROM DECEMBER, 1855, TO JANUARY 1st, 1862.

The above is copied from a likeness taken when about
thirty-two years of age.

ELDER REES was a Welshman, and born in 1804. His
parents were Episcopalians. In his youth he promised
God that he would serve Him when he became a man.
Previous to his conversion for months he was in great distress
of mind, and came to the light while on his knees. For several days he was full of unspeakable joy. It was at this time

that it was impressed deeply on his mind that it would be "woe" to him if he preached not the Gospel His first wife was a Miss Edwards, a most devoted Christian woman, who had been brought to a knowledge of the truth as it is in Jesus through his instrumentality. He died at St. Catharines, May 4th, 1888. aged 84 years. When he came to Canada, for lack of means to bring them all out, he left his wife and baby daughter behind in Wales. She came out some time afterwards, and died in Boston, county of Norfolk, while her husband was in England soliciting money for the Brantford chapel. All who had any personal acquaintance with her speak exceedingly well of her. A correspondent in the *Baptist Magazine* for May, 1841, says:—"Elder Rees is the ablest minister in Upper Canada."

On the 1st November, 1851, Elder Rees wrote from Brantford a letter which appeared in the *Baptist Magazine*, published in Montreal, and from which I quote the following extract :

"I came here on the 31st August, 1833, as it appeared to me, by the direction of Divine Providence. There was no Baptist Church in this village. Never did I feel so much alone in the world, and so entirely destitute of human consolation; yet I felt that God was with me, and His blessed promise afforded me support. That dear old father, Elder Mabee, came and labored with me for two days in the power and love of the Gospel. The preaching was plain, solemn and affectionate : the prayers short and fervent. The meetings were indeed solemn. There was no gust of passion, no enthusiastic excitement : true, now and then was heard the deep sigh, while the tears of penitence rolled profusely from many eyes, unaccustomed to weep under the sound of the Gospel. In a few weeks, we trust, there were at least eight souls translated from the kingdom of darkness into the Kingdom of God's dear Son.

"On the 23rd of December, 1833, according to previous arrangement, a church of twenty-six members, including myself, was regularly constituted. Elder Crandall preached the organization sermon, Elder Pickle gave the right hand of fellowship, and Elder Mabee gave the charge. * * * For the first year we were under the necessity of meeting in small and uncomfortable buildings, and from house to house ; and, sometimes, on the borders of the Grand River in the depth of winter. There I had the pleasure of baptizing many willing converts. Some of these seasons were affecting beyond the power of language to describe. Now we have here a good edifice, it being the best Baptist meeting house I have seen in all this region of country, occupied by a church of eighty members. Their standing in society is quite equal to that of any denomination in the place."

Elder Rees would often expound the Scripture at considerable length on the banks of the Grand River on baptismal occasions, when the weather permitted.

Under date May 5th, 1881, Mrs. Daniels, the oldest daughter of Elder Rees, and formerly a most active member of the church, thus wrote to me:

"As regards my father's reasons for choosing Brantford. As he passed over the Grand River, on his first visit to Brantford, he looked into its clear water, and exclaimed: 'Oh! what a grand place for a Baptist Church.' He proceeded onward, and reached Paris, weary and footsore, and begged for a night's lodging of the late Hiram Capron, which was readily granted. The next morning he was so sick that he was unable to raise his head from his pillow. For two whole months he was sick in that house, and received the best attention, and occupied the best room in the house. The Caprons learned to love him, and when he was able to leave, Mr. Capron gave him a suit of broadcloth, and led out a beautiful young horse with a new saddle and bridle, and said to my father: 'These are yours.' Pa said. 'No, I cannot accept them as a *gift*, but please *sell* them to me.' Mr. Capron made answer, 'Take them, and pay me for them when you are richer than I am.' Mr. C. also offered to give father a lot and a $1,000 chapel if he would remain in Paris. Pa's answer was, 'My dear friend. I have consecrated my life and energies, both of soul and body, to God on the banks of the Grand River at Brantford; and there I really *must* go.' Notwithstanding it was very painful to deny so kind a friend as he had made in Paris.

"I have often heard my dear father say that, as he rode into Brantford that day, his heart was joyous, and as light as air. On his arrival, he went to the trustees of the only schoolhouse in Brantford, and begged leave to preach therein, which was readily granted. With his own money he purchased some candles and a broom, and fitted up the schoolhouse for preaching. Pa's preaching soon began to create no small stir; and the schoolhouse was refused to him. Father, nothing daunted, procured a barrel, on which he stood, and hundreds gathered around him to hear him proclaim Christ crucified."

The writer can well imagine Elder Rees on his first arrival sitting on the bank of the Grand River, and gliding into a reverie, and holding with himself a mental debate somewhat like this :—"Here I am, a stranger, and in a strange land, ten weeks' travel from my native land, home, and loved ones. I have come here in obedience to what I think is Christ's command. I have been preaching, as far as I know, the identical Gospel He commanded to be preached to the whole world: but apparently with but little success. Oh, that some of my hearers would 'believe on the Lord Jesus Christ.' There are, I find, two churches here already, but all those who believe on Christ through their instrumentality are not baptized in accordance with Christ's distinct and positive command. Is it right for me, under such circumstances to remain here? Ought I not, rather, to go to some place where Christ is not preached at all?

'Guide me, O Thou great Jehovah,
Pilgrim through this barren land.'

I have passed through St. Catharines, Queenston, Hamilton
and Ancaster, and found Pedo-Baptists in each of those
villages; and they are also, I learn, in the villages of Guelph,
London, Chatham, etc.; consequently, if I decide not to
locate in any village where there are Pedo-Baptists, and all
other Baptist ministers should follow my example, it would be
virtually abandoning the best parts of the province to Pedo-
Baptists. The Baptists greatly erred in allowing others to get
a foothold in all those places before them. A town like this
will soon require more than the present two churches. Other
Pedo-Baptists will not hesitate to locate here, whenever it may
suit their convenience; and they will not ask any question as
to the propriety of their coming. Then why should I hesitate?
I cannot but think that it is my duty to establish a Baptist
Church in this growing village; and I pray God that He may
qualify me for the work, and bless abundantly my labors."
I judge from the conversations I have had with him that some
such thoughts as these, no doubt, occupied his mind during
his first visit to Brantford.

Elder Mabee, beyond all doubt, was the first one to administer the ordinance of baptism in Brantford village; and it
was some time in the year 1833, being a few months before
the organization of the church; those thus baptized becoming
members at the time of its organization by Elder Rees and
some additions were soon after made.

The place where this baptism was performed, I am told,
was in the Grand River, some few rods below the present iron
bridge. When the candidates and spectators were gathered
on the shore of the river, I can imagine Elder Mabee address
ing them thus: "I am now about to administer the ordinance
of baptism by immersion for the first time in this village on a
profession of faith in the Lord Jesus Christ by the candidates
When John the Baptist was engaged in a similar work he
chose a place, the Bible tells us, of 'much water,' as you see I
have done. The dear candidates have said, virtually, to me,
what the eunuch did to Philip 'See, here is water, what doth
hinder me to be baptized?' My answer has been the same as
Philip's, "If thou believest on the Lord Jesus Christ, thou
mayest!" Their answer being the same as that of the eunuch,
I am about to go down into the water with them, and there
'bury them with Christ in baptism.'"

Deacon Pilsworth, the first church clerk, February 21st,
1881, wrote me thus in answer to some questions I had
asked of him :—

"My father, self, and dear wife arrived in Brantford in June, 1832. One day in the following year, my father came into the house, and with gladness told us that a Baptist minister was going to preach in the old school house in the market square, which was then the only place where religious meetings were held. My father was a Baptist, and so was my mother before her death. My wife's parents also were Baptists, consequently we were all most anxious to hear the new minister preach. When we got to the schoolhouse, Elder Rees had just finished sweeping the floor and was lighting the candles; and Elder Mabee was walking up and down the floor singing. After a while there was a good attendance, and the minister commenced. Elder Mabee opened by singing, prayer, and reading the scriptures, and Elder Rees preached a good sermon. We considered it a great treat. Elder Rees was being aided by some missionary society of New York, and as he was often passing through the village, he would leave appointments to preach, and we always made it a point to attend. In 1833 he expressed regret that such a nice village should be without a Baptist Church, and commenced to labor among the people with that end in view, and very frequently called on us. About the first baptized, I think, were Miles Shaw and his wife; then a few others, then myself and wife, and then John Hammill. These were all baptized near the present iron bridge by Elders Pickle and Mabee. It was in the winter of 1833, and the ice required to be cut. I find by a memorandum I have by me, that the pews were priced March 5th, 1835, as follows: $6, $8, and $10, leaving a few free. At times, two parties wanted the same pew, and that occasioned difficulty. In all such cases, we let the highest bidder have it. We were a united and loving band. Elder Rees possessed great energy, was most affectionate towards all the members with but few failings. For a time he boarded with Mr. Shaw, and then with Surveyor Robinson, when his wife and daughters came out. He then purchased lot number three on the south side of Chatham Street, and built a house thereon."

I find that the patent for this lot issued to Elder Rees, December 2nd, 1846. In November 8th, 1847, Mr. Rees sold this house and lot to Bradford G. Tisdale, Esq., who has owned it ever since, and resided therein until he moved into his present fine brick residence on Nelson Street. Bro. Pilsworth goes on to say :—

"Elder Rees never gave his reasons for leaving Brantford or moving to Simcoe. He left with the best of feeling on both sides. In spite of all our poverty, opposition, and trials, these were the happiest days of my life. The first Sunday School was organized in January, 1841, in the gallery of the old wooden church, and your brother aided thereat. The first collection made, amounted to £2 10s. 6d. Among the first scholars were, Thomas and Sarah Spencer, Wm. and Jane Buck, John and Ellen Jackson, James Tutt, Roger Cropp and sometimes Alfred Watts.

"Among those who belonged to the church at its formation were, Deacon McDiarmid and wife, and Mrs. Hammill. We continued to hold our meetings in the same building as long as we could, and then from house to house. Consequently, often on a Saturday night we had to build a pulpit and make seats. I can well recollect some of the early members. They were, Hugh Devinney and wife, Dora Devinney, Ellen Devinney, Mr. Nice, Betsey Nice, John Brinning, Mrs. Woods and son, John Jackson and wife, Mrs. Michael Brown, Mrs. Ebenezer Roy, William Jackson and wife, Elizabeth Clement and James McMichael and wife.

To this list I may add that of John Winch, who wrote me a letter a year ago from Brandon, in which he says :—

"In the spring of 1837, I resided in Brantford ; during that time I became acquainted with the Whithams, Pilsworths, Moyles, Bucks and Elder Rees, who succeeded in knocking the validity of baby baptism out of my head. I had been taught infant baptism from my infancy, but I then saw it to be one of the worst delusions of the age in which we live. I look on those practising it as treading on the last law of the Lord which He strictly commands us to obey."

Deacon Pilsworth writes further :—

"The lot on which the chapel was built was given by Mr. James Biggar, and the other was purchased some time afterwards."

REV. WILLIAM REES

WHEN EIGHTY YEARS OF AGE.

1833.

THE first entry made in the First Church minute-book is dated *December 23rd, 1833*, the day after the church was formed; at which it was resolved:—That the Covenant meetings should be held on the third Saturday in each month, the Communion on the Sabbath following. Prayer meeting every Tuesday evening, and Church meeting on the first Friday in each month.

1834.

Some ten years since one of the oldest members of the church wrote me thus:—"In June, 1834, Elder Rees and self, by orders of the church, attended an Association held with a church sixteen miles from Hamilton on the road running to York." (Toronto).

DECEMBER 25TH (Christmas day.) Among others who were baptized this day were Sister Buck (now living) and Brethren Keelar (printer) and Webster.

1835.

No other entry is made till 2nd October, being a period of twenty-one months without any account of the Church's doings.

[It has been out of my power to fill up this long interval in the Church's history.]

At this meeting Brother Thomas Pilsworth was appointed Church Clerk; John Bryning and wife were received by letter from the Townsend Church.

DECEMBER 4TH. John Bryning and wife were granted letters to unite with the Townsend Church. Further, it was *resolved* that a balance of $1.35 due to Deacon Hazleton was to be paid him, and that Brother Whitham be allowed $1.00 per week for "supplying the fire, opening the Church, and keeping it clean." During the year 1835 there are minutes of only ten meetings made.

1836.

JANUARY 1ST. At this meeting Elder Rees was to make inquiry as to members residing in Paris. 2nd—"Brother Hopkins shall inquire into the situation of Nancy Shaw," and "Brother Hopkins shall assist the Deacons in accomplishing the domestic affairs of the Church."

MARCH 4TH. "It was ordered that Brethren McMichael, Robinson and Buck shall serve three months as Sunday School teachers."

APRIL 1ST. At this meeting it was "*Resolved* to send Elder Rees to attend a Council in Blenheim, to be held on the fifth of the month;" also "to cross-cut the balance with Brother Shaw;" and, it was found that a balance of fourteen cents was due to Brother Shaw. I trust the poor fellow got it without a law suit!

JUNE 2ND. At this meeting the Pastor, Brethren McDiarmid, Hazelton, Pull and Buck, were appointed delegates to attend the Association meeting at Townsend; and it was *resolved* "that application for aid be made to New York to support the Pastor."

JUNE 24TH. At this meeting it was *resolved* "that Brethren Pilsworth, Robinson and Buck, be tried for twelve months as Deacons." Brother Pilsworth was also requested to go to Townsend, to solicit aid in supporting the Pastor.

In the July number of the *Baptist Magazine*, published in Montreal, Elder Rees writes that during the year he had "done thirty-two weeks and four days missionary labor."

1837.

SEPTEMBER 8TH. Elder Rees, Brethren McDiarmid and Joseph Pilsworth, were appointed to attend the Townsend convention.

NOVEMBER 1ST. *Resolved:* "that we make new exertions to support the ministry: and that a public collection be taken up each month."

Nearly all the meetings in this year related mainly to the reception or discipline of members.

1838.

FEBRUARY 6TH. *Resolved,* "that Deacon McDiarmid shall endeavor to collect the subscriptions in Townsend towards the support of our Elder."

Elder Rees appears to have visited England this year in order to collect funds for the chapel. In connection with this visit I find £3 18s. 9d. marked, but what connection there may be between the same and the visit, I have been unable to ascertain.

1839.

JUNE 7TH. Elder Rees, Brethren McDiarmid, Pilsworth, Martin, McColl and McMichael, were appointed delegates to attend the Association to be held in Townsend.

DECEMBER 7TH. It was *resolved* "that the Pastor, Elder Rees, be paid $300.00 a year."

1840.

JANUARY 18TH. It was *resolved* "to make an effort to collect money sufficient to paint the meeting-house."

APRIL 18TH. It was *resolved* "to allow Brother Jackson £1 10s. for cleaning and attending to the meeting house for three months, and Brother Pilsworth fifteen shillings for his three months' care of the house, and that Brother Jones collect from the County members for ministerial support."

JUNE 13TH. The Pastor, Brethren McDiarmid, Pilsworth, Martin, McColl, Benedict, Jones and Read, were appointed delegates to attend "The Association,"—where held is not stated.

In this same year, in the *Missionary Register* for September 8th I find a statement from Brother Pilsworth "that the membership for this year was eighty-two; sixteen having been added by baptism, five by letter, five excluded, and one died."

DECEMBER 18TH. It was *resolved* "that of whatever is lacking towards our Pastor's support, each Brother, so far as he is able, shall pay an equal share."

At this meeting, a certain Brother (whose name is mentioned) was excluded "for neglect of duty, and a *capital* crime." The *Missionary Register* for October, 1840, gives the number of members of the Brantford Church as sixty-seven, and baptized during the year, two.

1841.

In the *Missionary Register* of March 1st, 1841, elder Rees writes : —" January 1st was observed as a day of fasting and prayer for the conversion of sinners, and the spread of the Gospel in Canada." In the same magazine under date June 4th, he writes :—" Now we have a good edifice erected— the best Baptist meeting-house I have seen in all this region of country occupied by a church of eighty members. * * * I leave the church in perfect friendship. * * * On the 13th of December, (1840) I had the pleasure of baptizing seven young converts. A large multitude assembled

on this occasion to witness the administration of this Divine
ordinance, it being the fourth time in this town during five
months.   On the east side of the Grand River, the candidates
were one by one led down into the water, and there buried by
baptism."

AUGUST 1ST.   A Brother was required to give his reasons
for reducing the amount he had been giving towards Ministerial support.

OCTOBER 17TH.   Pastor Rees, Brother Pilsworth, Brother
Martin and Brother Buchan, were appointed a committee to
select a suitable Pastor for the church.

NOVEMBER 1ST.   Elder Rees wrote that it was his intention to leave Brantford in January 1842.   Some party writing
in the *Canadian Baptist* magazine, Montreal, under date May
24th, says :—" I left Woodstock and reached Elder Mabee's
about eight o'clock, when I again joined Elder Rees who had
gone before me to preach the preceding night.   I was glad to
meet this good *old man* again."

NOVEMBER 7TH.   The Pastor, and Brethren Stephen
Jones and Charles Pickle, were appointed delegates to meet
with the Beverly Church for consultation regarding Samuel
Read's appointment to the Gospel Ministry.

DECEMBER 5TH.   "*Resolved* that Brethren Martin, Whitham and Pilsworth, be a committee to draft a letter of dismission for Elder Rees and wife, to join the Simcoe Church."
   The following is an extract from the letter of dismission
granted to William Rees and Eliza Rees.   "Among all the
dismissions which we have been called upon to execute none
have perplexed our wisdom more than to do justice to the
parties concerned.   Elder Rees, as a Pastor, is one of those
talented individuals that is seldom to be met with in this
section of the country.
   "As to Mrs. Rees we have no hesitation in saying that she
is possessed of those spiritual qualifications that fully fit her for
the situation : and any more recommendation of ours would
only detract from her worth."
   Rev. Newton Bosworth, (F.R.A.S.), of Paris, was invited
to preach on the last Sabbath of the year, "and be paid ten
shillings."
   Brother Smith was recommended to improve his talents
"whenever he is called upon to do so."

December 26th. Fellowship was withdrawn from another Brother who had been guilty of "a capital crime."

Elder Rees, during his ministry of eight years, baptized seventy-eight persons. When he left, the Church was owing him $200, which he had advanced on the chapel, and which was to be paid in a year, and the deed obtained.

1842.

January 2nd. Brethren Pilsworth, Stephen Jones and Hector Dickie, were appointed trustees. The deed of the church being in the name of Pastor Rees, who had advanced £50 thereon. *Resolved*, "That the church give their joint notes for the sum of £50, payable in one year with interest, in order to receive the deed, which amount was to be paid by subscription."

February 5th. Brother Read was requested to supply for "one Sabbath in each month, till a Pastor is secured."

March 6th. Brethren Pilsworth, Whitham and Martin, were appointed "delegates to attend a council in Tuscarora, for the purpose of organizing a church among the Indians."

April 9th. The Rev. Mr. Winterbotham had written to the Church from England, respecting the pastorate, and an answer was sent him.

It was resolved to secure the services of the Rev. N. Bosworth, and pay $2.00 for each Sabbath.

June 5th. Brethren McDiarmid, Martin and Whitham were appointed "to meet in council respecting some difficulty between the Burford and Township of Brantford Churches." "Brethren McDiarmid, Martin, Pilsworth, Jones, Dickie, Pickle, and Devinney, were appointed delegates to attend the Association at Townsend."

July 16th. The hand of fellowship was withdrawn from a certain Brother "for committing a capital crime."

August 20th. Brethren McDiarmid and Martin were appointed delegates to atted a meeting appointed by the Association to meet in the 2nd Charlotteville Church.

The following are extracts from a long "Statement."

"*   *   A minister in England, in whose mind had long lingered a desire to come to Canada, had written to the Deacons through the medium of Giles Hartley, a member of this church, proposing to come out, if they thought proper   *   *   if the church would wait two months until they might have an opportunity of hearing him, and forming an opinion of his gifts and doctrines.   *   *   The said minister, John Winterbotham, sailed from England, July 30th, and arrived in Brantford on the 17th of September, Saturday, and preached on the following day.   *   *   The church gave him a unanimous call, which he accepted.   *   *   would pay a remuneration for his services, just as the Lord prospered them.   The church intended to act on the voluntary principle, but he might expect at least $200.00 per annum   *   *   no covenant was drawn up   *   *   recognition January 3rd, 1843.   Mr. Winterbotham wrote to an old friend—Mr. Cockshutt—to know the state of the country   *   *   induced him to write to the Deacons; this letter was brought to a prayer meeting, when the church was seeking direction from the Lord.   *   *   Although shipwrecked, he was guided in safety to his destination here.   *   *   At the first settlement, a few chosen ministers were invited to come and take part in the services.   On the 3rd January, 1843, the meeting took place.   Elders Bosworth, McConnell, and Landon were present and and engaged severally in the services of the day, which were delightful and soul-refreshing.   Elder McConnell preached from Hebrews 3, 1; Elder Bosworth asked the usual questions.   *   *   Elder Landon pointed out the relation between Pastor and people, and the duties of church members."

NOVEMBER 19TH.   Mrs. Buchan, Sen., and Mr. and Mrs. Buchan, Jr., together with John Evans, received letters of dismission in order that they might aid in forming a church in Paris.

DECEMBER 17TH.   "Rev. J. Winterbotham and Brethren Martin and Dickie are appointed delegates to attend a Council at Blenheim."

1843.

Of the meetings held during this year we find nothing of special interest recorded : we therefore pass them by.

1844.

JUNE 24TH.   The thanks of the church were sent "to the Beamsville Church, for the donation of $30.00 to apply on the church debt."

AUGUST 10TH.   "The Pastor and Deacons are delegated to attend a Convention to be held in Charlotteville"—for what purpose not stated.

2

AUGUST 20TH.   It was "*Resolved*, that four new Deacons are needed for the pecuniary affairs of the church; and that the 20th of October be the day for the election of them, and by ballot."

OCTOBER 20TH.   "William Moyle, E. Benedict, Hector Dickie and M. Whitham, were elected Deacons; the same to be dedicated on the 10th of next month."

NOVEMBER 10TH.   M. Whitham and E. Benedict declined to accept the office of Deacons.

1845.

JANUARY 15TH.   *Resolved* that "Brethren Pilsworth, Moyle, Whitham, Martin and Bates in the town; Dickie and Jones in Burford and Mount Pleasant; and Benedict and Hartley on the Grand River, collect subscriptions for the support of the Ministry."

JUNE 15TH.   *Resolved* "to drop from the books all members unknown."

It was *resolved* not to send delegates to the Association, until "peace and harmony are more fully restored among the churches."

SEPTEMBER 21ST.   "The Pastor, and Brethren Benedict and Moyle, were appointed delegates to an ordination at St. Catharines on the 24th."   Party to be ordained, not mentioned.

1846.

JANUARY 21ST.   The Pastor and Brother Pilsworth were "appointed a committee to draft rules for the formation of a Missionary Society in connection with the Montreal Missionary Society."

FEBRUARY 20TH.   Brethren Pilsworth and Martin were appointed "to visit such members as were absenting themselves from the meetings of the church."

MARCH 22ND.   *Resolved*, "that a hymn book be got for the pulpit, and one for the church."

REV. JOHN WINTERBOTHAM

PASTOR FROM SEPTEMBER, 1842, TO JUNE, 1850.

MAY 5TH. The Pastor, Brethren Pilsworth, Moyle and Whitham were appointed delegates "to attend an ordination council at Townsend." The party to be ordained not mentioned.

JUNE 6TH. The Pastor and four Deacons were appointed delegates to attend the "Grand River Association, with instructions, in case of any trouble, not to participate therein."

JULY 4TH.   Brethren Giles Hartley, James Cowherd, Mrs. Cowherd, Wm. Cannon, Mrs. Cannon and Richard Hartley, were allowed to withdraw in order to form a church "down the river."

SEPTEMBER 5TH.   The Pastor was requested to visit the "Brethren 'down the river,' to ascertain who may be considered church members."

OCTOBER 3RD.   It was *resolved* that "Rev. A. Cleghorn preach Sabbath after next and take up a collection."

1847.

MAY 29TH.   The Pastor, Brethren Moyle, Martin and Whitham, were appointed as delegates "to attend the Association to meet at Vittoria."

JUNE 5TH.   The meeting-house had been used for some purpose by which several members felt aggrieved.   It was therefore *resolved* "that three more trustees be elected, and the chapel used for such purposes only as the Pastor and a majority of the trustees approved."

JUNE 20TH.   *Resolved* that Brethren Pilsworth, Jackson and Buck, be a committee to "ventilate the chapel by next Sunday."
An effort was made to purchase the lot on the north side of the chapel.

JULY 3RD.   An effort was made to purchase the lot on the south side of the chapel.   Brethren Jackson, Pilsworth and Moyle, were appointed additional trustees.   18s. 1d. ordered to be paid for the expenses attending the ventilation.

AUGUST 12TH.   The Pastor and Deacons were appointed "to frame a scriptural code of rules for our church."

OCTOBER 2nd.   The following rules were submitted :—
1.   Members to be dealt with if absent from Communion three months, etc.
2.   Members to support the church, etc.
3.   Training of children, etc.
4.   Members residing in town, etc.
5.   Absent members to be visited, etc.
6.   Members to attend covenant meetings, etc.

1848.

MAY.—The Pastor, Brethren Pilsworth, Moyle, Benedict, Buck and Broughton, were appointed "delegates to attend the Association at St. George."

SEPTEMBER 3RD. The Pastor, Brethren Moyle, Buck and Edmonson, were appointed delegates to attend the convention at St. George, on the 7th September,

1849.

APRIL 1ST. Pastor Winterbotham gave in his resignation and Brethren Pilsworth, Whitham, Broughton and Moyle, were appointed a committee "to procure present supplies."

APRIL 7TH. *Resolved,* "that we confess before God and each other our want of unanimity, and neglect of Christian duties : also, our general deadness as a Church of Christ, etc."

Resolved, "that we will endeavor, through divine grace, to take our places and engage in all the spiritual duties of religion as members of the Church of Christ, with more punctuality than we have yet done, etc."

Resolved, "that we consider that Mr. Winterbotham, when our Pastor, neg'ected his duty in this respect (visitation) for some time past, etc."

Resolved, "that we, as a church wish to know if Mr. Winterbotham will continue as our Pastor, with the understanding expressed by us on this subject."—Brethren Dickie, Buck, Martin and Chave, were appointed to wait upon Mr. Winterbotham for this purpose.

APRIL 29TH. Brethren Jones and Pilsworth were appointed delegates "to assist in settling Rev. James Cusick over the Tuscarora church." (An Indian.)

MAY 20TH. The committee appointed to wait on Pastor Winterbotham, reported that they "found it impossible to reconcile the difficulties."

JUNE 2ND. *Resolved,* "that, as Mr. Crellin, the agent of the Regular Baptist Union of Canada; has made an appointment to preach here on behalf of the Union, on Sabbath evening next : but, as he has made some remarks detrimental to the character of some of the managers of the Canada Baptist

Missionary Society, with whom we, as a church are connected, we think it only proper that he should be informed that he cannot be allowed to fulfil this appointment until he has made some satisfactory explanation about this matter to the church."

Brethren Winterbotham, Dickie, Moyle and E. Benedict, were appointed "delegates to attend the Grand River Association."

JUNE 26TH. In consequence of some disagreement "a document was handed in to the church signed by thirty-six members, stating that they could not worship with the church, and that they had come to the determination to leave and meet elsewhere, which they have done." The books and funds of the school were, by mutual consent, equally divided.

These members who thus left, met for worship in a building on the south side of Colborne Street, a few lots from the present iron bridge. Elder Cook occasionally preached for them, but they were never organized into a church. July 6th, 1850, these discontents were received back into the church at their own request.

In 1849 there was formed "The Brantford Baptist Ladies' Sewing Society." Its constitution of sixteen long articles is written out very neatly by Mr. George Foster. The second article provides that "the proceeds of the society's labors shall be devoted annually to some object in connection with the Brantford Baptist Church."

Inasmuch as money was paid by this society to the church, meetings must have been held by them prior to 1861, but no minutes can be found of any special work having been done by them.

Of a number of the meetings in 1861, full minutes are made. The first one is as follows : —

"First regular meeting took place at 2 o'clock, p.m., Wednesday, January 30th, 1861. Ladies present fifteen in number, namely :—

Mrs. Shenston,	Mrs. Tisdale
" Whitham,	" Sherwood,
" Jackson,	" Young,
" Broughton,	Miss Rockey,
" Foster,	" Fisher,
" Pilsworth,	" Martin,
" Harrison,	" Cousin.
" Powley,	

"Visitors—Miss Naomi Shenston, also dear little Ruth and Joseph Shenston.

"Mrs. Jackson read a portion of scripture and engaged in prayer.   A. G. Young, Secretary."

The following week there were eighteen in attendance, the next twenty-one, the next twenty-four, and the next twenty-six. There was one, the attendance at which was thirty-six. The names are as follows :—

"Mrs. Tisdale,	Mrs. Buck,
" Shenston,	" Street,
" Whitham,	" Kennedy,
" Morton,	" Jackson,
" Smith,	" Young,
" Sage,	Miss Walrouth,
" Pott,	" Muirhead,
" Geo. Winter,	" Winter,
" Powley,	" West,
" Broughton,	" Rockey,
" Alexander,	" Foster,
" Excell,	" D. Martin,
" Preston,	" M. Maxwell,
" Pilsworth,	" Pilsworth,
" Barker,	" Ormerod,
" Jones,	" Steele,
" Dalrymple,	" J. Martin,
" Foster,	" K. Foster."

The membership of the church is now about double what it then was. Could twice thirty-six (72) be now got together for a similar purpose? I fear not. But why not?

1850.

JANUARY 6TH. Mr. Winterbotham continued his membership, and preached until some permanent arrangements could be made. By a resolution, the thirty who had formerly left were excluded.

FEBRUARY 10TH. A Grande Ligne Mission was held in the chapel, Bro. B. G. Tisdale in the chair. Among the speakers were Rev. Mr. Cleghorn of Paris and A. A. Drummond of Brantford. Collection, $10.25. Collected by the ladies, $30.37.

JUNE ——. The last Sabbath in June, Mr. Winterbotham preached his farewell sermon.

JULY 6TH. "A deputation from the parties who have recently withdrawn from the church, and had been meeting at a house on Colborne Street, bring with them a letter expressing their regret for what they had done, and wishing to be received back into church fellowship."

SEPTEMBER 8TH. It was *Resolved* "to receive these our friends to our communion and fellowship, with the exception of W. C." * * *

NOVEMBER 2ND. "Saturday. Church meeting. Bro. Canfield in the chair. Rev. T. L. Davidson was present. *Resolved*, That the subject under consideration respecting the propriety of immediately inviting Mr. Davidson to become our Pastor be deferred until to-morrow after the Lord's Supper."

NOVEMBER 3RD. "Sunday. After the Lord's Supper the church remained to determine as to giving Mr. Davidson an invitation to become our Pastor, and after some discussion it was unanimously resolved to do so. All the 40 members present voting for it."

"After having duly considered the invitation of the church, Mr. Davidson decided on accepting the call to become our Pastor."

"Mr. Davidson entered on his duties as Pastor the 2nd Sabbath in December, being the 8th of the month.

1851.

On New Year's day, 1851, the writer had business in Brantford which he was unable to finish before the departure of the stage for Woodstock, which was at that time his home. Consequently he was obliged to remain in Brantford over night, and he availed himself of the opportunity thus offered to attend, for the first time, one of the celebrated tea meetings held in connection with the church.

As he entered, the ladies were very busy in a shanty near the door, making ready for the repast. He took his seat on the right hand side of the aisle, in about the centre of the chapel.

Notwithstanding the great height of the pulpit, a temporary gallery had been erected above it for the accommodation of the choir. This gallery was well filled with singers, led by Mr. John W——, who entertained the waiting congregation by fiddling some popular song and dancing tunes. This "vexed the righteous soul" of the late Deacon Wm. Moyle, and he rose to his feet, and, in a mild and dignified manner, objected to such fiddling in the House of God.

This stopped the fiddling with "awful" suddenness, but it did not stop the fiddler, and "you had better believe it" the fiddle box came down with a *whop!*; the fiddle was placed therein with a *whack!*; the lid brought down with a *bang!*, and the fiddler solemnly declared his intention *to do* a lot of naughty things, and to leave undone some very amiable ones.

Elder D. took in "the situation" in a moment, and saw at a glance that "the fat was in the fire." Oh, how he did plead! but all in vain. The fiddle was boxed, the cloak was on the enraged fiddler's back, and he partly down the steps, when he was taken in hand by that champion peace-maker, Wm. Buck. His oil was superior to that of Elder D. He used it lavishly on the troubled waters, and there was a calm, and the fiddling and the singing went off "O.K." for the remainder of the evening, to the relief of all.

JANUARY 3RD. The Rev. T. L. Davidson and wife were received by letter from the Markham Church, and the right hand of fellowship given them by Brother Francis Foster. Brother Thomas Greenell and Sister Harriet Crawford were received, and baptized by Elder Davidson on the following Sabbath, the same being the first baptized by him in Brantford.

FEBRUARY 1ST. *Resolved*, "that the names of any members absenting themselves for one year from the church, without asking for their letters, shall be crossed out of the church book." The Pastor, Brethren Moyle, Benedict and Foster, were appointed delegates to a council to be held with the second Beverley church—for what purpose not stated.

MARCH 1ST. The Pastor, and Brethren Broughton and Edmondson, were appointed delegates to attend a council held with the East Flamboro Church, "to examine an individual." The Sunday school voted $50.00 to the church—one-half towards paying a balance still due Elder Winterbotham, and the other towards the present Pastor's salary.

JUNE 8TH. "The Pastor, Brethren Thos. Evans, John Evans and M. Whitham, were appointed delegates by invita tion of the Second Hamilton church (John Street) to aid in organizing them into a church."

AUGUST 31ST. The Pastor, with Brethren Harris and Devinney, were appointed delegates "to aid in the organization of a church in Waterloo, and one in Beverley."

SEPTEMBER 21ST. The Pastor, Brethren John Evans, McIntosh and Thomas Broughton, were appointed delegates to a convention in Hamilton "in case such a meeting takes place."

OCTOBER 31ST. There was held "a meeting for the purpose of deciding as to whether the Rev. T. L. Davidson should remain as Pastor. * * * After considerable discussion on the subject, it was resolved that he be requested to remain." At the same meeting it was also decided that, instead of the question coming up every year, the pastor should remain till he receive a three months' notice to "vacate."

NOVEMBER 2ND. A vote of thanks was passed to William Buck, for his kindness in making a new drum and pipes for the stove, and assisting to put up the same free of charge.

NOVEMBER 23RD. *Resolved*, that the Rev. Mr. Searle be allowed to preach this evening, and present the claims of the society of which he is the agent, (A. H. M. Society) and take up a collection.

DECEMBER 5TH. It was decided that two more Deacons should be balloted for on the 7th of the month.

DECEMBER 21ST. Deacons elected were, John Jackson and Brother Rainbow.

1852.

JANUARY 4TH. The two new Deacons were ordained.

FEBRUARY 22ND. It was agreed that Rev. James B. Olcott be allowed to preach, and present the claims of Rochester Seminary, next Sabbath.

JUNE 18TH. The Pastor, Brethren Dickie, Moyle, Harris and Jackson, were appointed "delegates to attend the Association"—where held, not stated. A letter was read from Mr. Winterbotham, requesting the payment of the balance still due him; and a committee was appointed to collect the same, if possible.

REV. T. L. DAVIDSON, (D.D.)

Pastor from December, 1852, to March, 1861.

1853.

JANUARY 29TH. A meeting was held "for the purpose of considering the propriety of building a new chapel." A committee was appointed to obtain subscriptions—one-third to be paid when the building is fairly commenced, one-third at the end of three, and one-third at the end of six months, conditional on $2,000.00 being subscribed.

FEBRUARY 20TH. An effort was made by way of subscription to pay £14 0s. 0d. due to the church treasurer.

MARCH 27TH. The Pastor informed the church, "that he had received an invitation from another church, but would not leave unless the church wished him to do so." * * * Some discussion arose. * * * "It was decided to take up the matter on Saturday, April 2nd, at 2 o'clock."

APRIL 2ND. The Pastor was requested to remain by an unanimous vote, "with the same salary as before," No mention is made as to what the "same salary was." ($450.)

APRIL 16TH. Brethren Benedict, C. Edmondson and Wm. Cole, were elected trustees in place and room of those who had ceased to be members of the church.

MAY 9TH. The following were appointed a building committee :—T. S. Shenston, John Maxwell, James McMichael, Francis Foster, John Harris, Christopher Edmondson, Erastus Benedict, Hector Dickie, Rev. T. L. Davidson and William Young. (All have now departed this life, except W. Young and the writer.) This committee was instructed to procure a neat and substantial plan of a house 74 x 47, with a basement, a gallery, and a baptistry in front of the pulpit. * * * To find an eligible site, * * * sell the old chapel, * * * procure tenders for the new chapel," etc. The lot selected and purchased was No. 4, on the west side of West Street. [It was intended to place the chapel some ten feet nearer the road, but at the request of the party residing on the next lot north, and the promise of $200.00, it was moved back the ten feet. No portion of the money was ever received.]

JUNE 5TH. The Pastor, Brethren Dickie, Moyle, Harris, Foster, McDonald and Buck, were appointed delegates to attend the Association—place of meeting not named.

SEPTEMBER 1ST. In compliance with a circular sent to nearly all the regular Baptist Churches in the Province, setting forth the divided state of the denomination, and urging the necessity of union and more general and hearty co-operation in the work of the Lord, a Convention of Ministers and Delegates assembled in the Baptist Meeting House in Brantford. The Brantford delegates were Rev. T. L. Davidson, Rev. John Harris, and Brethren H. Dickie, Wm. Moyle and Wm. Young.

SEPTEMBER 28TH. Died at his residence in Malahide, Elder Reuben Crandell, aged 62 years. Elder Crandell aided in organizing the church in 1833.

1854.

JUNE 2ND. The Pastor, Brethren J. Harris, Wm. Robinson, and G. Cummins, were appointed delegates to attend the Association which met with the Charlotteville Church. The reported number of members 150, baptized during the year, 10.

SEPTEMBER 1ST. The first convention was held this year, the delegates to which, from this church, were, Rev. John Harris, Rev. T. L. Davidson, H. Dickie, Wm. Moyle and William Young.

OCTOBER 1ST. On this day was published the first number of our denominational paper the *Christian Messenger*. It was published by three members of the Brantford Church, namely, Rev. T. L. Davidson, R. W. Sawtell, Editors, and Wm. Winter, Proprietor.

It says :—"During the nine months which have elapsed since the discontinuance of the *Observer*, the greatest discomfort has been felt and expressed in view of the want of a weekly denominational journal to advocate our principles."

DECEMBER 3RD. The choir asked permission to introduce a melodeon into the chapel, and were answered as follows : —" The church concur * * * provided that they do not introduce new music so fast that the congregation cannot keep pace with them, and join in the singing."

The Building committee reported that Messrs. Smith and Wade "would give $1,200 for the old church property, half cash down and half on the 1st of July next."

The church consented to its sale on the terms offered.

DECEMBER 19TH. Wm. Winter, Benjamin McIntosh and Thomas Huskinson were appointed Deacons.

1855.

JANUARY 1ST. *Died*—in the Township of Brantford, at the residence of his daughter, Mr. Hugh Devinney, aged 72 years. For many years he was a member of the Brantford Baptist Church.

The newly elected Deacons were ordained by the laying on of hands by the Pastor and Rev. John Harris.

JANUARY 11TH. " Brethren Wm. Winter and James Cox were added to the building committee, and the said committee urged to push forward the work as fast as possible ;" and that, in order to do so, "they may obtain money for finishing the building either by borrowing the same or furnishing it themselves, for which the church would be responsible."

Resolved—" That all lotteries, golden-gift enterprises, and cake-cutting for money speculation, this church regards as a species of gambling, * * * that while we deeply sympathize with Brother E. * * * in view of his financial embarrassments, they feel it to be their duty, in view of the interest and honor of Christ's cause, to express their most unqualified disapprobation of his conduct in resorting to a lottery for the purpose of extricating himself from his financial embarrassments, * * * doing evil that good may come."

JANUARY 21ST. *Died*—At Delhi, aged thirty years, R. Ann Thompson, fourth daughter of Elder John Harris, of Mount Pleasant, once a member of the Brantford Church. The following is an extract from her published obituary notice :

" The deceased made a public profession of religion by baptism, and was added to the first Townsend Baptist Church at the age of sixteen, and continued her membership with that church till about four years ago when she became, with her husband, a resident of this place, since which time she was a member of the Baptist Church here. During her illness (which lasted for several months at intervals) she was thoughtful and reflective on her future state, and expressed a willingness to die. She entertained but little hope of recovery, yet she was cheerful. The promises of God were cheering to her mind."

FEBRUARY 24TH. A donation visit was paid to Elder Davidson, the proceeds of which were $150.

APRIL 1ST. *Resolved* "that after each monthly communion a collection shall be taken up for the relief of the indigent members of the church." This has been continued ever since.

APRIL 29TH.   *Died* -in Brantford, Mrs. Spencer, the wife of William Spencer, aged 67 years.   The following is an extract from her obituary notice :—

" The deceased was born near Keighley, in Yorkshire, England, and removed with her family to Canada in the year 1832. After residing with her husband and family for four years in Toronto, she removed with them to Brantford, where she resided until the time of her death.

" Mrs. Spencer was a much beloved and much esteemed member of the Baptist Church in Brantford, to which she has belonged since she has lived in the town."

MAY 9TH.   Lot No. 4 on the west side of West Street on which the chapel stands, was purchased from Mr. William Young, and conveyed to Erastus Benedict, Christopher Edmondson, Hector Dickie, William Cole, William Moyle and John Jackson, trustees, all of whom, I believe, have departed this life.

MAY 24TH.   A special subscription taken up "in aid of the poor, indigent and helpless members of the church."

JUNE 3RD.   The Pastor and Brethren W. Winter, Wm. Moyle, F. Hill, F. Foster and William Robinson were appointed delegates to attend the Association. The total number of members reported was 157.   Where the Association was held is not stated.

Dr. Babcock, agent of the American Bible Society, preached and took up a collection in behalf of the said society.

Dr. Babcock made a short address at the baptism of several candidates in the Grand River.

JULY 8TH.   " Fifteen were baptized in the Grand River, in the presence of at least two thousand spectators."

JULY 12TH.   " The Pastor, Elder Davidson, has visited the baptismal waters three times since the meeting of the Association.   On the first of these occasions he baptized two, on the second, four : and last Sabbath, thirteen rejoicing converts were " buried with Christ in baptism " in the presence of about 2,000 spectators.   It was a most interesting and deeply solemn season, and considering the largeness of the number assembled, excellent order was preserved."—*Christian Messenger.*

JULY 19TH.   The Pastor brought the following question before the church :—" Whether this church would recognize and admit a member who was baptized by a Methodist minis-

ter under the following circumstances. The individual referred to was a Baptist in sentiment, and wished to be baptized
by a regular Baptist minister, but her friends prevented her.
They consented to her being baptized by a Methodist minister, and she accordingly submitted. Now, that influence is
extinct, and she wishes to unite with a regular Baptist Church.

"After considerable discussion, it was duly moved and
seconded :—'that this church cannot recognize immersion,
when performed by any other than an ordained Baptist minister in good standing, as a regular christian baptism.' "

In amendment,

"That, while the church cannot recognize baptism, when
performed by a Methodist minister, as regular Gospel baptism,
yet, when the person so baptized is believed to be, and has
been, a christian when so baptized : and was so baptized to
answer a good conscience, and is still satisfied with the
baptism ;—under such circumstances, we believe it would be
the duty of the church to receive, rather than reject, such person so baptized."

After considerable discussion, "the subject was dropped,
and the candidate remains as before."

The new church to be insured for $5,000. Brethren
Jackson and Young were delegated "to get a good, substantial ladder, and fix it at the north end of the chapel."

JULY 26TH. As to the renting of the pews in the new
chapel, after long discussion, it was *Resolved :*—"That the six
rows of pews nearest the door of entrance, shall remain free
seats, for the occupancy of such persons as may be either
unable or unwilling to rent pews." A committee was appointed to place a rental on the remaining pews * * * "that the
entire sum realized shall be sufficient to meet and cover the
annual expenses of the church, including the salaries of the
Pastor and Sexton, insurance, fuel, with a sufficient annual sur-
plus to create a sinking fund for liquidating the church debt.
Committee—"Brethren Winter, Jackson, Young, Cox and
Shenston. Rents to commence on the 1st September."

AUGUST 6TH. John Jackson, S. K. Dollar and Peter
Buck, were appointed a committee to erect a fence on the
south and west sides of the chapel lot.

AUGUST 14TH. Elder Davidson writes me: "In 1852, 20
were baptized ; in 1853, 30 ; in 1854, 7. The total since my

pastorate of four years and eight months is 103. Our actual
present number is 191. Elder Mabee baptized 2 : Elder Rees
71 : unknown, 2 : Elder Winterbotham, 27 : Elders Crellen
and Cleghorn, 3 : and myself, 103, in all, 215."

Writing in the *Christian Messenger* about the chapel
opening, Brother Davidson says : —" it is computed to hold 750
persons, and is the largest but one in Canada belonging to our
denomination. It has been built at a cost of $6,000."

AUGUST 19TH. Sabbath day the new chapel was opened.
The dedication sermon proper was preached in the morning,
at 11 o'clock, by Rev. Martin B. Anderson, LL.D., President
of Rochester University, New York, from John, xv., 12 : which
sermon was published in the *Christian Messenger*, the then
denominational organ.

In the afternoon Rev. J. R. Nesbit, of Paris, Ontario,
preached from 2 Cor. v : 17 : in the evening, Rev. Mr. Anderson, from 1 Cor. xv : 42-43. In the following evening there
was a successful tea-meeting—addresses by Rev. Dr. Anderson, Zenas Freeman and James B. Olcott.

At this meeting a testimonial in the shape of an electro
silver tea service, was presented to Thomas S. Shenston, by the
members of the building committee and others, with an address, to which an answer was made.

AUGUST 25TH. Messrs. Winter, Moyle, Foster and Buck,
were appointed delegates to St. George, to attend the ordination of William Hulbert, on the 5th of September.

Resolved—" That all the seats in the body of the chapel
be rented, and that the former resolution providing for twenty
free seats be repealed."

This day the church meeting was held in the basement
of the new chapel for the first time.

OCTOBER 15TH. Thomas S. Shenston presented a full
report of the building committee, which was accepted, and
the committee discharged and thanked.

OCTOBER 28TH. Sisters Julia Oliver, Martha Burgess and
Mrs. Jex, were baptized. Supposed to have been the first in
the new chapel.

NOVEMBER 4TH. " Brethren T. L. Davidson, William
Winter, Wm. Moyle, F. Foster and E. Benedict, were appointed to sit in council at Boston, Ont., on the 27th of the
3

month, to take part in the examination of Brother Ziba
Canfield for ordination to the work of the ministry."

The Pastor, and Rev. John Harris, Brethren Eli Harris
and William Winter, were appointed delegates "to sit in
council at Delhi, on the 21st inst., for the purpose of examining and ordaining Brother B. H. Rogers to the Gospel
ministry."

DECEMBER 2ND. A somewhat lengthy "proposition,"
drawn up by the Deacons, was read before the church by
Deacon Moyle, the first and last parts of which we here
copy : —

"It has pleased God to smile on our efforts as a church,
not only in temporal, but we hope in spiritual concerns ; and
we think we are speaking correctly when we say, there never
was a time in which more harmony and Christian affection
existed than now among us. * * * Brother T. L. Davidson's
duties are now much more onerous than formerly * * * not
merely by our progress, but by need of pecuniary aid, in such
a manner that his mind may be freed from embarrassment and
anxiety. And we, the Deacons, unanimously beg to suggest
as to the propriety of increasing his salary from $500 to $650
per annum."

A matter of so much importance was "laid over until
next Sabbath."

DECEMBER 9TH. — By an apparently unanimous vote the
increase to the Pastor's salary was carried.

1856.

JANUARY 1ST. The ministers advertised to be present at
our annual tea meeting were—Rev. Wm. Hewson, M.A.
Beamsville ; Rev. A. Booker of Hamilton ; Rev. W. Smith
St. George : Rev. E. Clark, Ancaster ; Rev. J. Winterbotham
Scotland : Rev. James Cooper, Woodstock : Rev. J. Nesbit
Paris ; Rev. A. Slaght, Waterford : and the Rev. W. Ryerson
together with the ministers resident in the Town.

JANUARY 28TH. " * * * Whereas, there is a considerable sum of money wanted to meet the demands against the
church, * * * and whereas, an offer has been made to
loan the church the sum of $2,000 for five years, at ten
per cent. per annum—the interest to be paid half-yearly."

Resolved : " that the trustees effect such loan, by giving a mortgage on the church to the party loaning the money."

It was decided to accept an offer made to loan on a mortgage on the church $2,000 at 10 per cent. interest, half-yearly ! For obtaining this 10 per cent. loan, the writer received a formal vote of thanks, moved by Deacon McIntosh, and seconded by Deacon Winter !! Thanks for negotiating a ten per cent. loan ! " How is that for high ? "

When the chapel was built, the church numbered 157, the wealthiest of whom, with one exception, were day laboring mechanics. The writer cannot but think, that there would be far fewer appeals to the denomination for aid to build chapels, if the members of those churches used the same self-denial as did the members of the Brantford Church to build theirs.

FEBRUARY 20TH. *Died*—After a short but painful illness, Mary Elizabeth, only daughter of Deacon Thomas Huskinson. All the Sunday School scholars, led by their teachers, followed her to the grave in pensive silence. This was the fifth time in the short period of five years that this Brother and his wife had been called to follow to the grave those dear to them

MARCH 6TH. *Died*—at Brantford, aged 43 years and 7 months, Mrs. McIntosh, wife of Deacon McIntosh. The following are extracts from her published obituary notice.

" The deceased was a native of Campbleton, Argyleshire, Scotland, where she was led in the days of her youth to embrace religion, and unite with the Baptist Church, of which she has ever since continued a consistent and beloved member.

" That evening, before leaving the scene of nuptial joy, she complained that she felt unwell, and walked home with difficulty. She gradually grew worse until on the Friday following, medical aid was called, and no means left unused to conquer her disease, but all in vain.

" During her entire sickness she was calm and resigned to the will of God, prepared to die, should such prove the will of God, and willing to live if that should seem best in His sight. In the anticipation of death, she called her children—eight in number, around her bed, on two several occasions, and spoke to them as only a *dying christian mother* can speak to her children, whom she is leaving behind in a world of pain and sin."

MARCH 7TH *Resolved*, " that the Deacons be empowered to sell the old lamps at such prices as they can get for them." Was the vote unanimous ?

MARCH 30TH. *Died*—Under this date Elder Davidson
writes in the *Christian Messenger* :—"Death has once again
visited our borders. Dear old Sister Devinney is gone. She
has 'fought a good fight,' her end was triumphant. Her
reason remained to the last. She died on Sabbath evening
last, at 9 p.m."

APRIL 22ND. A letter appeared in the *Christian Messenger* from Elder Davidson, from which the following is an
extract :-

"Last Sabbath was indeed a blessed day to the Church in this place.
The work of the Lord has been steadily progressing from week to week in
our congregation ; and at this date there are about 58 persons, mostly heads
of families, who have identified themselves as inquirers after truth ; of these
about 34 have embraced Christ, of which number, 13 were 'baptized into
Christ,' last Sabbath evening, at the close of the public service. It has
seldom been my privilege to administer the ordinance of baptism to so many
happy converts, before a more solemn, and deeply interested congregation.
The chapel was densely crowded, and many who came in to witness the
administration of the Gospel rite, in its primitive simplicity, at the close of
public service in some of the other chapels in town, were unable to find
seats."

MAY 6TH. The following are extracts from a long letter
from Elder Davidson that appeared in the *Christian Messenger*
of this date :

"We met again in the evening at 6.30 p.m., when I preached before
an audience of from 900 to 1,000 persons, from Matt. xxi., 23, 'By what
authority doest thou these things, and who gave thee this authority.'
Having preached, and defended the views held by us as a denomination,
in respect to the subjects and mode of Christian baptism, I went down into
the waters of baptism, and baptized *eighteen persons*, according to the letter
and spirit of Christ's baptism, by *burying* them in 'the likeness of His
death.' Of these eighteen, *twelve* were heads of families, the other *six*
were young persons of great promise. Among these were the registrar of
this county, his wife, and deputy." (George Foster.)

MAY 16TH. The Pastor, Brethren Tisdale, Morton,
Hale and Fisher, were appointed delegates to sit in Council
with the Church at Cheltenham, to ordain Brother Hill to the
ministry.

JUNE 4TH. Brethren Winter, Moyle, Shenston, Hale.
Tisdale and Cox, were appointed delegates to the Association,
the same being held with the First Church, Brantford.

Agreeably to the wishes of the ladies, dinner and tea for
the delegates, on Friday and Saturday, were served in the
basement of the chapel. Reported membership, 242 ; baptized during the year, 101.

JUNE 12TH. The following paragraph is taken from a letter that appeared in the *Christian Messenger* of this date :

"In Brantford the ordinance of Christian baptism was administered last Sabbath morning, in the Grand River, by the Rev. T. L. Davidson to two persons, at the conclusion of the forenoon services. In the evening nine more were baptized by him in the baptistery at the close of the evening sermon, in the presence of a very large audience. It has been the happy privilege of our Brother to baptize 101 persons, into the fellowship of the Baptist Church in Brantford, since the meeting of the Grand River Association last June. Truly the Lord has greatly blessed this branch of His Zion."

"May it still continue to prosper, by the copious outpouring of the Spirit of God upon it. It is cheering to reflect, also, that during the past year three young men, two of them the sons of this church, have felt it to be their duty to devote themselves to the Gospel ministry. One of these was ordained last month, as the Pastor of the Baptist Church in Cheltenham, and the other two are pursuing their preparatory studies in one of the Universities of the United States. May the Lord send forth more labourers into His harvest, for it is truly plenteous."

The young man to whom allusion is here made I assume was Brother James Bates.

JULY 6TH. "*Resolved*, * * Our Pastor ought to have leave of absence from his duties, to enable him, by God's blessing, to recruit his health * * * without being restricted to time. * * * The Pastor gave a most affectionate and touching reply."

JULY 7TH. Brother Robert Morton elected a Deacon of the church.

JULY 19TH. On this day, died, at her father's residence, Township of Brantford, dear, mild, diffident Martha Foster, aged 21 years. From a long obituary notice published in the *Christian Messenger*, July 24th, I clip the following :

"The subject of this brief obituary was born at Sabden, in the County of Lancaster, England, September 12th, 1835, and died at her father's residence, near this town, on Saturday, July 19th, 1856, at 11 o'clock in the morning. She emigrated with her father's family in 1844 from their native land, who settled near the Town of Brantford, where she and they have lived ever since that time.

"All who *knew* Martha, will, we are sure, bear their united testimony with ours, that she was, in disposition, one of the most *lovely*, *prudent*, *meek* and *amiable* young females with whom they have been acquainted. * * * For several weeks she sought with heartfelt grief and penitential sorrow, for the pearl of great price, by the use of all the means of grace within her reach. At length, while alone with God, spiritual light dawned upon her mind, and she was enabled to rejoice in God her Saviour with 'a joy unspeakable and full of glory.'"

* * * * * * *

"On Sabbath, the 1st day of June last, she partook for the first and
last time of the Lord's Supper, after receiving 'the right hand of fellowship' as a member of the church.   Ah! how little did she or the Pastor or
any of those present think that she 'would not drink henceforth of the
fruit of the vine, until with her Divine Master she should drink it new in the
Father's Kingdom.'"

"Although her outward conduct was blameless and her moral de-
portment without a single stain, she well knew that she could not be
saved by morality or works, and that she must have a vital interest in
Christ and be regenerated in the spirit of her mind, in order to be prepared for heaven.

"In the month of March last, some ten days before the protracted
meetings were commenced at the Baptist Church, Brantford, four of the
congregation (but not of the Church,) belonging to that place, had appointed an evening for meeting together to relate their religious experience to
each other, and seek the salvation of their souls, and Martha was invited
to attend along with them.   The person who invited her to this meeting,
fully explained the object contemplated in calling it, and she seemed to
rejoice at having the opportunity, freely opening her mind to him, and
forgetting for the time her natural timidity and reservedness."

> "Sister thou wast mild and lovely,
> Gentle as the summer breeze;
> Pleasant as the air of evening,
> When it floats among the trees.
>
> "Yet again we hope to meet thee,
> When the day of life is fled;
> Then in heaven with joy to greet thee,
> Where no farewell tear is shed."

"The Fosters,"—Martha, Alice (Mrs. Wm. Buck), George,
for several years virtually sustained our church singing.   To
do which occasioned them a walk of two and a half miles each
way from their home.   Many the dark, cold and wet night
Martha, with her sister and brother, tramped this long road.

SEPTEMBER 19TH.   *Resolved*:   "That Brother Francis
Foster have a license from this church to improve his talents
as a preacher."

At the same time a similar license was granted to Brother
McIntosh, and one asked for, but not granted, to Brother
Holbrook.

OCTOBER 17TH.   A committee to which the matter had
been referred recommended the publication of Pastor Davidson's lecture on baptism.

DECEMBER 10TH. Deacon William Winter was granted license to preach.

B. H. Carryer ordained at Scotland. Pastor Davidson and R. Morton present.

1857.

JANUARY 5TH. Brother William Rockey, in compliance with the wish of the Church, preached before them, which resulted in—"We earnestly recommend Brother William Rockey to repair to Madison University, to fit himself for the solemn and responsible work of the Gospel ministry."

JANUARY 8TH. A writer in the *Christian Messenger* wrote thus respecting the Sabbath School:

"This School, we are informed, was established about 22 years since, and has continued in operation up to the present period. On entering this school we were very agreeably surprised. We expected to see a goodly number of scholars, and a respectable number of teachers; but we were not prepared to see 164 scholars, and 27 teachers—13 male and 14 female teachers. It being our first visit to a Sabbath School since we left our native land (England), we were highly delighted in witnessing a spectacle so interesting and so lovely, that of devoted and pious teachers who have so little leisure, on account of the multiplicity of their employ- ment, yet employing that little leisure in training the youth of our town in those things which are calculated to make them useful in time, and happy in eternity. The school is held in the basement of the church; the room is very commodious, and far better in every respect than we expected to find it. Mr. William Winter was Superintendent for nearly two years, but in consequence of numerous other duties, he resigned his office a short time since, and last week the teachers unanimously elected Mr. T. S. Shenston to fill the vacancy."

JANUARY 14TH. The following is an extract from a letter written by Elder Davidson, under the above date:

"Last Sabbath morning we met in it (the chapel) and worshipped with a large congregation. We returned to our homes, and in less than one hour afterward the splendid building was in flames, and the children of our Sunday School were hurrying to the school.

"Never was our heart so torn with grief as by this unlooked-for calamity. It was indeed a heart-rending scene to gaze upon, as the noble pile was enveloped in living fire, surrounded by the weeping children of our Sabbath School who had come, books in hand, to take their places as they supposed.

"Not a dollar's worth could be saved—the pulpit was burned with the bible and hymn book lying on it, bibles and books in the pews, and a new melodeon belonging to Brother T. S. Shenston which had been borrowed from him.

"The building cost about $10,000, on which was a debt of about $3,400. All is desolation, bleak and cheerless, and no one who has a heart can look on our ruined building, and think of our blighted prospects, and not feel deeply for us."

The following is an extract from a memorandum made by the writer, on the first page of the minute-book of the building committee of which he was a member.

"The writer attended the morning service of the church, January 12th, and was among the last, if not the very last, to leave the chapel, which was about fifteen minutes past one of the clock. Just before leaving, he had a conversation with two ladies by the hot-air register at which it is supposed the fire originated. *   *   * He partook of a very hasty dinner, and was on his way back to the Sabbath School before two o'clock. He met two of his clerks who informed him that the chapel was all on fire. He arrived at the chapel with all possible speed, but found it so full of smoke and flame that it was impossible to get out so much as a hymn book. All was burned up."

The four first payments made towards the erection of the church were as follows:— Erastus Benedict, $50; Ladies' Sewing Society, $100; Matthew Whitham, $57; and Hector Dickie, $37.25.

JANUARY, 17TH. "Building committee appointed :—T. S. Shenston, William Young, W. Winter, Robert Morton, James McMichael, B. G. Tisdale, James Cox and Matthew Whitham.

Arrangements were made to hold prayer-meeting and Sunday School "in the store recently occupied by Mr. Cox, on the south side of Colborne St."

Brethren Shenston and Young "were appointed a committee to wait on the County Council for the use of the Court House, in which to hold Sunday services." No minutes appear as to the result of this application. The writer, however, remembers that the Court House was used for Sunday services until the new chapel was finished.

FEBRUARY 1ST. Received this day, by letter from a Welsh Church, Sister Margaret Williams, who did not understand a word of English. Bro. William Morris acted as interpreter. Notwithstanding this ignorance of the English language she attended all our meetings regularly.

FEBRUARY 16TH. Died, in the Township of Brantford, after a protracted illness, Mrs. Mary D. Harris, the beloved

THE FIRST BAPTIST CHURCH, BRANTFORD.

BURNT DOWN, JANUARY 12, 1877. REBUILT, 1878. ENLARGED AT BACK, AND BASEMENT REBUILT FRONT, 1887

wife of Eli Harris, aged only 21 years. The following are
extracts from her obituary notice in the *Christian Messenger :*

"**The** deceased was a much beloved member of the Regular Baptist
Church in Brantford, into the fellowship of which she was received
together with her husband in the summer of 1855. Well do we remember the day of her burial with Christ in baptism. It was a lovely day, and
the sun shone brightly—every prospect pleased, for nature was clothed in
her gayest garb. At the water we sang a hymn and prayed. Her soul
was all on fire with love to Christ, and her angelic countenance was all
a-glow with joy and peace, such as the world cannot give. She waded out
into the waters of the Grand River with a firm, unflinching step, and was
immersed in the Triune name.

Her mother died when she was young. Her father, the late Benson
Jones, Esq., of the Township of Brantford, died a few years ago of pulmonary consumption—the same disease which hurried her to her home in
heaven so suddenly and unexpectedly. Not long after the death of her
father and her marriage, she passed from death to life. Her Christian
experience was clear, decided and satisfactory. Her reception of the
truth was cordial, and her welcome to the fellowship of the saints was
unanimous and hearty.

" 'When I am dead," said she, "sing at my funeral that beautiful
hymn so dear to me—

> "I would not live alway, I ask not to stay,
> Where storm after storm rises dark o'er the way."

FEBRUARY 17TH.   Building committee reported plans for
a new chapel by Mr. John Turner.

After some discussion and suggestions they were adopted,
and tenders were to be advertised for. On the invitation of
the Pastor of Waterford Church, the Pastor and Brother Mc-
Michael visited that church to solicit subscriptions.

FEBRUARY 27TH. The tenders for the erection of the
chapel were opened, and found as follows :—For the entire
chapel complete, Messrs. Broughton and Pickering, $11,992.
For the carpenter's and joiner's work alone :—Wm. Pickering,
$3,440 : Henry Ray, $3,400 ; Messrs. Strickland and Hagarty,
$3,796. The contract was awarded to William Pickering.

MARCH 12TH.

Killed at the Desjardins Canal, on the Great Western Railway, in
the deplorable and melancholy disaster which occurred there on the 12th
of March, Daniel Secord, a beloved member of the Regular Baptist
Church, in the town of Brantford, aged 37 years, nine months and six
days.

The subject of this brief memoir was born in the town of Niagara,
on the 6th of June, 1819.

" Having 'believed with the heart unto righteousness, he made confession with his mouth unto salvation,' and was received into the fellow-

ship of the Regular Baptist Church at the Cross Roads near the town of Niagara, and baptized by Brother George Wilson, who was *then*, what he would be *now*, did his shattered health permit—a whole souled laborer in the Lord's vineyard. Brother Secord remained a member of that Church for about eleven years, and ceased to be a member of it only when he removed to the town of Brantford, about one year ago.

"On the morning of that ever memorable day, March 12th, he left home early to go to Toronto to transact some important business, and was on his way home, having paid for his ticket from Toronto to Paris, when in attempting to cross the Desjardins bridge he was launched into eternity. He appears to have been in the fore end of the last car, and as no marks or scars were visible upon his body, the probability is that he was suffocated by the entire mass of people on that side falling on him. Never will the writer forget the emotions which arose in his soul as he discovered him on the evening of the 13th March, lying cold in the baggage room, among the unrecognized dead.

"His remains were followed to the grave, on Monday, March 16th, by a very large concourse of sympathizing friends, several of the ministers of the town being among the number. His funeral sermon was preached in the Court House, in the town of Brantford, on the morning of the following Sabbath, March 22nd, by his former Pastor, the Rev. Thomas L. Davidson, from Dan. vi. 5—'We shall not find any occasion against this Daniel, except we find it against him concerning the law of his God.'"

APRIL 2ND. A social was held at the residence of Brother William Young for the benefit of Pastor Davidson. $127, the proceeds, were handed to Mr. Davidson, who said:- "Much as I value the 'material aid' presented to me on that occasion, I value *far more* the kind and fraternal feeling which prompted its bestowal. No man can appreciate such tangible tokens of a people's esteem for their Pastor more than I do, however inadequate my pen or my tongue is in the expression of my gratitude and thankfulness."

APRIL 12TH.

"*Died* At the Baptist Parsonage, in the Village of Scotland, Brant County, C. W., on the afternoon of Sabbath, the 12th of April; Elizabeth Carryer, the beloved wife of Rev. Benjamin Carryer, aged 31 years and 8 months."

Mrs. Carryer was formerly a member of this church.

APRIL 16TH. The *Christian Messenger* of this date says: "The Court House is crowded to excess every Sunday. The superintendent T.S.S. is diffusing his own spirit among the teachers and scholars. He is a thorough going young man, and a punctual attendant. Twenty-three have been received into the church during the last few weeks, fourteen of whom were baptized last Sunday in the Grand River, in the presence of 2,000 spectators. Eight more will be baptized in the same place next Lord's day."

APRIL 17TH. The tenders for the brick work of the chapel were opened, and found as follows :—J. and C. Beck, $2,127 ; Charles W. Sears, $2,126. The contract was given to the last named, but the former built it.

APRIL 21ST. Purchased as per recommendation of the building committee, the north half of lot No. 3, of Mr. W. F. Chave, paying therefor $900.

MAY 7TH. D. Davidson and wife, the father and mother of Elder Davidson, were received as members, by letter from Perth.

MAY 20TH. The Pastor, Brethren McMichael, Rockey, Young and Pickering, were appointed delegates to aid in the organization of a church in the Township of Onondaga, County of Brant.

JUNE 22ND. The Rev. Samuel S. Day, the first missionary sent out by the American Union—September 20th, 1835—to the Telugoos of India, visited the Brantford Church on behalf of that society. He was the guest of the writer during his stay.

JULY 6TH. *Died*—this day, S. K. Dollar. At one time the Superintendent of the Sabbath School.

JULY 8TH. Naomi Shenston was received as a member. She is now (1889), and has been for the last ten years, treasurer of the women's department of the identical Home Mission Society of the United States, that sent Bro. Rees to Brantford, fifty years ago.

SEPTEMBER 21ST. *Died*—at Montjo Bay, Jamaica, of yellow fever, after a painful sickness of four days, Annie Hallam, the beloved wife of E. R. Phillipo, aged 19 years. She was for some time a member of the Brantford Church.

AUGUST 11TH. The church requested Pastor Davidson to have his lectures on baptism, in reply to those of Rev. John Wood, published, which was done. Church to pay any loss.

THOS. D. CRAWFORD,
DEACON.

Born October 28, 1828.   Died February 25, 1881.

OCTOBER.   Was received by letter from the United States, Thos. D. Crawford and wife.   Notwithstanding "comparisons are odious," no Deacon, I am confident, will take objection to my characterizing Deacon Crawford as a Deacon among Deacons, and one who comes nearer than any of us his colleagues to Timothy's (I. Tim. iii.-8) standard of the qualifications of a Deacon.   The following are extracts from his obituary notice:

"Thomas D. Crawford was born in the County of Brant on October 28th, 1828, and died February 20th, 1884. He was the second child in a family of six children. His father, Seth Crawford, came to Canada from the State of New York as a missionary to the Indians, and after many years of faithful service, died in the year 1848, respected and loved by all who knew him. In 1855, he settled upon the farm in Brantford Township, which his father had procured from the Indians.

"The deceased was for many years a prominent member and Deacon in the First Baptist Church in Brantford, and was universally admired for his conscientious devotion to the church which he loved.   *   *

"His work in connection with the church was always performed in a remarkably quiet, unostentatious manner, and with such fidelity and painstaking as endeared him to his brethren. 'With charity for all, and with malice toward none' he stood by his convictions of truth and right, and was recognized by all who knew him as a man of of sterling integrity. In his death the church has lost one of its very best members, and society one of its most valuable citizens.

"His funeral occurred on the 22nd of February. A very large company of neighbors and friends assembled at his late residence at two o'clock p.m , and after a brief prayer by Rev. J. B. Tuttle, the procession moved to the First Baptist Church, where the religious services were conducted by Pastor Tuttle, assisted by the Rev. James Grant of Paris. Over fifty carriages and sleighs followed the remains from the house to the church, where they were met by hundreds of the citizens of Brantford. The pulpit and furniture were handsomely draped, and in front of the desk stood a beautiful floral anchor, the gift of the children of the Mission School over which the deceased had presided for a number of years. The large audience-room was crowded, many being obliged to stand throughout the service. Deacons T. S. Shenston, Geo. Hill, E. Benedict, Geo. Chitttenden, D. Dengate and Wm. Moyle acted as pall bearers. Seldom in the history of the church has death removed one from our midst so universally mourned by the entire church and community, and none could have been more sadly missed than this dear servant of the Lord."

The following are extracts from the published funeral sermon :

"When the greatest of American statesmen died, Rufus Choate said, "Boston will be lonesome without Daniel Webster." Brethren, we shall be lonesome without Deacon Crawford. He was a valuable man to the church. Indeed, we had almost come to regard him as almost invaluable. No man has given so much time and labor to the church as he has done. Deacon Shenston, who knew him longer and more intimately than any of us, and who has always had a high appreciation of his service, has demonstrated by facts and figures that, since his connection with the church, he has travelled, in his attendance upon its services, a distance of thirty-seven thousand five hundred miles, or once and one-half times around the globe.

          *   *   ⁕   *   *

"He has done more work with less co-operation and encouragement from his brethren than any man I have ever known, and he did it without a single word of complaint. For eight years he has had charge of the Mission School on Terrace Hill, where he has conducted three services every week : and it is the testimony of one who knows, that he has not been absent but twice in five years. When we remember the distance that he had to travel, living as he did, three miles from the school, the statement seems almost incredible. Yet he did it in winter and in summer, through pelting storm and scorching heat, and no man ever heard him say that he was tired or discouraged. Surely none but a generous, self-sacrificing spirit could have done so much."

"The Christian graces were so evenly balanced as to give him strength of character. Did you ever know him to become impatient? I never did. Did you ever hear him speak an unkind word of any man, woman, or child? I never did. Did you ever see him discouraged? I never did. Did you ever know him to withhold any assistance that he could render the destitute and needy? I never did. Did you ever know him to exchange principle for policy? I never did. Did you ever see him refuse to work because some one else would not work? I never did. He was a man of such stability and strength of character that you always knew where to find him."

NOVEMBER 27TH. *Resolved*, "that the basement of the new chapel be opened for public worship on the last Sabbath of the year, and that Elder Allington of Paris be invited to preach in the morning and evening "

1858.

JANUARY 28TH. *Died* - at her late residence, Darling street, Brantford, Mrs. Mary Hammill, wife of John Hammill, after a short illness and much suffering. The following is from her obituary notice in the *Christian Messenger :*—

"Our departed sister was the eldest daughter of the late Rev. Reuben Crandell, formerly Pastor, successively, of the Baptist Churches of Ancaster, St. George, Southwold and Aylmer, C. W. She was born near Saratoga Springs, Saratoga County, N.Y., on the 24th of October, 1791 : so that at the time of her death she had attained the age of 67 years, less four days. Her father's family returned to Canada while she was quite young. The country was then for the most part a wilderness ; yet, in the Township of Townsend, the Lord appeared to her in mercy in the salvation of her soul about A. D. 1820. She there professed her faith in Christ, was 'buried with Christ in baptism,' and united with the Baptist Church in Boston. When the Baptist Church in Brantford was organized Dec. 22nd, 1833, she was one of the original constituent members, and has continued to hold her place as a member till the day of her death."

Died—at his residence, on Queen street, George Cummins, aged 43. The following is an extract from the published obituary notice : —

"About seven years ago, he removed with his family to the Town of Brantford, and with his wife and daughter united with the First Church, of which he died a member. Since the writer's acquaintance with him, he has been the subject of continued affliction. A wasting consumption had fastened its fangs upon his vitals ; and this disease at last brought him down to his grave. Throughout his long affliction, during which he wasted away to a skeleton, he never murmured, nor repined at the dealings of Providence, either with him or his family."

FEBRUARY 3RD. The church formed an Auxiliary Society to the Baptist Missionary Convention of Canada : James McMichael, President ; James Cox, Treasurer ; and George Connor, Secretary.

MARCH 1ST. The Pastor, and Brethren Broughton and Edmondson, were appointed delegates to attend a council to be held with the East Flamboro Church "for the purpose of examining an individual."

MARCH 11TH. The building committee was authorized to borrow $800 "to the best of their ability."

MARCH 22ND.

"The members of the Baptist Church and congregation in the town of Brantford, met together during the afternoon and evening of Thursday, the 22nd inst., at the house of their Pastor, the Rev. Thos. L. Davidson, for the purpose of paying him what is familiarly known as a "Donation Visit."—The house was crammed to its utmost capacity, and the hours glided away very pleasantly and profitably. Had it not been that the brethren and friends from the country had left for their homes before the friends from the town came in the evening, there would not have been anything like room for the accommodation of those who flocked in to manifest their good feeling and liberality toward their Pastor. The proceeds will amount to about $150."

MAY 13TH. Brother William Robinson received the sanction of the church to preach.

MAY 18TH. The Pastor, and Brethren J. Hale, William Winter and T. Baldwin, were appointed delegates to sit in Council with the Baptists of Ingersoll, with the view of recognizing them as a church.
Brother T. Baldwin was granted a license to preach.

JUNE 1ST. At a special meeting held in the basement of the chapel a most hearty vote of thanks was passed to Brother James McMichael, for the valuable aid he has rendered to the committee during the erection of the chapel.

JULY 4TH. The Church sent five hundred copies of the New Testament for circulation among Father Chiniquy's people.

AUGUST 11TH. *Died*—at Brantford, Lucy Winter, daughter of W. and E. Winter.

1859.

JANUARY 23RD. The following churches were requested to send their Pastors and delegates to sit with the Brantford Church, on Monday, the 31st, to examine, and if thought fit, to ordain Mr. Robert McClelland to the Gospel ministry: Brethren Morton, Pilsworth, Winter, Moyle, Jackson, Sutton, Shenston and Whitham, were delegates of the Brantford Church.

FEBRUARY 3RD. A meeting for ordaining Bro. Robert McClelland.

ORDINATION Pursuant to former notice, a Council was convened in the Baptist Chapel, Brantford, on Monday last, at eleven o'clock, to take into consideration the propriety of setting apart to the Gospel ministry the Rev. Robert McClelland, late of Cork, Ireland.

FEBRUARY 15TH. *Died*—at Mount Vernon, where she was born, Miss Sarah Anne Miles, at the time of her death the eldest daughter of William and Ellen Miles, aged 16 years and 3 months. The following are extracts from her obituary notice:

"A year ago, she was residing temporarily in the town of Brantford with her aunt, in order that she might be near the physician who was prescribing for her. A protracted meeting was then in progress in the Baptist Chapel, which she attended very regularly, evincing a deep interest in her soul's eternal welfare. When the power of the Gospel, applied to her heart, by the Holy Spirit, led her to see her lost state, she shed tears of anguish in view of the sins of her youth, and when she beheld JESUS as *her* Saviour her young heart leaped for joy. It was not until the 18th day of July that she was enabled to follow her Saviour in the ordinance of Christian Baptism, along with several others, who had been made partakers of like precious faith—among whom was her aunt, and the late MISS ELIZA M. WINTER.

"*I am young,*" she said to a friend, "*but I can live to Christ, and if I die, I can die to* HIM." When asked by her dear Christian Mother as death drew near, "Are you afraid to die?" She replied, "No, *my hope is in Jesus Christ, and Him alone.*" The day previous to her death, she

4

was as well as usual, and spent the day in knitting and making a mat of tissue paper. She was taken ill at 9 p.m., on Monday, the 14th inst., and died about 6 o'clock on the following morning.

       *   *   *   *   *   *

> "A saddening feeling seizes me,
>   As I think that thou art gone ;
> But I see thee yet by an eye of faith,
>   As thou wear'st thy dazzling crown.
>
> I will meet thee again, thou blessed one,
>   When my toils on earth are o'er—
> And grasp thy kind and gentle hand,
>   On Canaan's peaceful shore."

FEBRUARY 9TH.   The Pastor obtained the sanction of the Church for next Sabbath morning, in order that he may preach the dedication sermons of the new chapel in South Dumfries.

APRIL 14TH. *Died*—at Brantford, William D. Rockey, 28. A word or two about this Brother.   Poor Brother Rockey ! He was a stout, healthy looking young man of about twenty-eight years of age.   It was soon made manifest that he possessed more than ordinary talents for the preaching of the Gospel, and he was recommended by the church, January 5th, 1857, to devote himself to the Christian ministry, which he cheerfully consented to do : and, accordingly, went to Madison University for the purpose of qualifying himself for his life-work as a minister.

He found himself so much below his fellow students in education, that, "to catch up with them," he overworked, and thereby brought on sickness which resulted in his death.

His parents, having died when he was young, and consequently having no home, the writer invited him to his house, which, on his return, he was only too willing to accept.

When Mrs. Shenston was leading him up the stairs, which he ascended with some difficulty, he said with tears in his eyes, "Oh, Mrs. Shenston, I shall never come down these stairs again, until I am brought down in my coffin !"   And so it was.

He died the death of a Christian, April 14th, 1859.   He told the writer on his death-bed that he had preached one hundred sermons.   Poor Rockey !   A neat tombstone has been erected at his grave in the Brantford cemetery by a few friends of the Boston and Brantford Churches.

APRIL 15TH. By resolution, members were required to pay all indebtedness before receiving a church letter.

JUNE 14TH. The Pastor, and Brethren Morton, Moyle, E. Benedict, Francis Foster, W. Young and J. Hale, were appointed delegates to attend the Association. The place of meeting not named.

NOVEMBER 2ND. *Died*—at Owen Sound, Mary Winterbotham, the wife of the Rev. John Winterbotham, aged 71 years.

1860.

JANUARY 4TH. Pastor Davidson handed in his resignation. After discussion, resolution and amendment, it was moved by Bro. Shenston, and seconded by Bro. P. Buck, that the resignation be not accepted, when a very large proportion of the members voted in favor of the resolution.

JANUARY 8TH. With the exception of four who did not vote, the church was unanimous for the Pastor to withdraw his resignation.

JANUARY 16TH. The Pastor, Brethren Morton, Winter, Sutton, Smith, Young, Benedict and Crawford, were appointed delegates to meet in Council to be held in Onondaga, *Re* Brother Islip's ordination.

FEBRUARY 24TH.

Died—At his own residence in the Township of Blenheim, County of Oxford, in the 87th year of his age, the Rev. Francis Pickle, member of the Baptist Church in Blenheim. He was born in 1773, and early became the subject of deep conviction. When about eight or nine years of age, a young man came up and spoke to him about Jesus ; and this was the means of his early conversion. He removed, when quite young, to New Brunswick, and soon began to publish life and salvation through faith in Christ Jesus. He was set apart for the work of the ministry, and continued to be a zealous and successful labourer there for many years. He afterwards removed to Canada. Here he continued to preach for some years, when he again visited his old home ; and, during his stay there, he baptized about three hundred persons. Returning again to Canada, he spent the remaining years of his life in Blenheim. He was the second Pastor of that church, and the first to promote the temperance cause there. In temporal things he prospered, even as his soul prospered.

This Elder assisted in the organization of the church in 1833, and baptised some of its first members.

MARCH 5TH. After receiving the letter, it was moved by Brother Scott, and seconded by Brother Reed, that the request of Pastor Davidson be granted, and his resignation be accepted.

By a resolution of the Church, Pastor Davidson's letter of resignation was copied in the Church book, covering three pages. Extracts therefrom :—

"Two months ago, when I resigned, I was requested to continue by a sweeping vote, which carried with it the whole church, save *ten* of its members.

"With an aching heart, I again took the Pastoral charge of the church. * * * I was the more encouraged in this hope, from the fact that those who had labored to bring about my resignation, and who voted to accept it when tendered, avowed their willingness and determination to work with the Pastor, if he would continue.

"I can well afford to contend with the flesh and the Devil, without the Church ; but I have neither the will nor the heart to contend against members of the same body.

"I leave you with profound regret and sorrow ; and wherever my lot may be cast, be assured I shall never cease to love you, and think with pleasure of the years of peace and prosperity I have spent among you.

"The Church was small and distracted when I assumed the oversight in 1850, and, of the members who were then in fellowship, only twenty-eight now remain. I have baptized 340 ; members restored, 30, etc., etc.

JUNE 5TH. Edmund Foot (a colored man) was received this day by letter from the Dresden Church. Some of his addresses at our prayer meetings were both amusing and profitable. One of these I recall well. He was representing Bible promises as grapes on the vine, and holding up his hands, said : " Oh, my ! How thick and beautiful the clusters hang away up there ! They go right up out of sight ! The grapes that I eat are very poor ones compared with those out of my reach, but they keep spiritual life in me."

The writer was at his bedside a short time before he died, and made some remarks to him about "crossing the river." In a whisper he made answer :—"It is *not* a *river*. I can see it plain, it is just a *little silvery stream*, and I can easily step right over, and I will do so just as quick as the Lord tells me to."

Sometime in the month of April, and while without a Pastor, Thomas Cull, a student from Madison University, supplied the church : and continued his services for seven months with great acceptance.

This young student Brother was never Pastor of the Church, but inasmuch as he supplied several months for us and gave such general satisfaction, I felt confident that many of the old members would be pleased to be thus reminded of him, hence the portrait.

THOMAS CULL.
(STUDENT)
SUPPLIED FROM APRIL TO OCTOBER, 1881.

When leaving, the ladies of the church presented him with a well-filled purse most pleasing to both the donors and the donee. His home was with the writer.

JUNE 5TH. Brethren Winter, Morton, Moyle, Shenston, Cull, Sutton, Benedict and Whitman, were appointed delegates to attend the Association which was held in Drumbo.

JUNE 15TH. Circulars were issued appealing for subscriptions towards the payment of the church debt.

JUNE 19TH.

"*Died*—At his residence in Mt. Pleasant, County of Brant, Donald McDiarmid. He was born in Perthshire, Scotland, in 1784, and became in early life the subject of saving grace through the instrumentality of the Haldanes. He was baptized fifty years ago by the Rev. Arch. McLean, and united with a branch of the Haldane Church. He emigrated to this country in 1816, and settled in Mount Pleasant. After some time he united with the Boston Church, then under the pastoral charge of Elder John Harris, whose earnest labours did much in permanently planting Baptist sentiments in the settlement of Boston and the regions round about. When Elder Rees came to the province and commenced his labours in Brantford, it was thought advisable to secure the organization of a Baptist Church in that town. To accomplish this object, Deacon McDiarmid and wife received their letters from the Boston Church, and, with a few others, were formed into the Baptist Church of Brantford, of which he remained a Member and a Deacon until his death. Although unable of recent years regularly to attend this church, yet he regarded it as his home, and rejoiced greatly in its abundant prosperity. Soon after the organization of the Brantford Church, he procured, from Mr. Biggar, of Mount Pleasant, a site for a chapel free of charge; and through the exertions of Elder Rees and others, with himself, the old Baptist Chapel was built. This building was, but a few years since, and during the successful pastorate of Elder Davidson, supplanted by a new and costly edifice, which was destroyed by fire. Upon its ruins the present elegant and spacious Baptist Chapel stands. Our Brother's career was one of uniform consistency and devotion, and not unfrequently did his soul abound with joy as he listened to the doctrines of the Gospel. He loved to hear and converse about the cross of Christ. Frequently he was heard to say—"There is something soul-satisfying in the simple story of the Saviour's death for sinners." He loved Christ, and loved the truth for His sake. The day of our Brother's departure was not attended with any premonitions that death was so near. He attended to his usual matters of business; and after family devotion, which he was accustomed to observe, he retired to rest, and soon after called to Mrs. McDiarmid that he felt ill, and before she was able to call the inmates of the house he expired."

JULY 8TH. The Church clerk was instructed to invite the Rev. G. M. W. Carey, of St. Catharines, and Rev. E. W. Bliss, of Oswego, N.Y., to come and preach with a view to the Pastorate; "and also inform Rev. John E. Ball, who had preached for us for two Sabbaths for the same purpose, of this action on the part of the Church."

JULY 22ND. "The clerk was instructed to write to Rev. E. W. Bliss, to visit us as soon as possible— * * * to write to Rev. J. E. Ball, explaining the reason of the delay in not sending him a definite answer," etc.

JULY 31ST. "It was resolved to write to Rev. T. L. Davidson to preach and baptize for us next Sabbath." * * * "Carried unanimously, with the exception of two."

SEPTEMBER 2ND. "Moved by Brother Evans, and seconded by Brother Scott, "that Rev. John E. Ball be invited to become our Pastor until next spring."

In amendment—"Moved by Brother Moyle, and seconded by Brother Reid, that Mr. Ball be not so invited. Amendment carried."

"Moved by Brother Wm. Buck, and seconded by Brother Evans, that Mr. Ball be invited to supply for us until spring." Motion lost.

DECEMBER 16TH. "The Rev. John Alexander, Pastor of the Presbyterian Church in this town, related his change of views on baptism, and desired to be baptized and unite with the Church.

"Mrs. Isabella Alexander, his wife, made also a similar request."

1861.

JANUARY 4TH. "The following Churches were invited to send delegates to a Council to consider the propriety of ordaining Brother John Alexander to the work of the Christian ministry—namely, Beamsville, St. Catharines, Hamilton, Toronto, Ancaster, St. George, Governor's Road, Paris, Blenheim, Drumbo, Onondaga, Dundas, Boston, Woodstock and Waterford."

The delegates from Brantford Church were:—"Brethren Wm. Winter, R. Morton, T. Pilsworth, Wm. Moyle, Samuel Reid, T. S. Shenston, Wm. Buck and M. Whitham."

Such an ordination took place, but no entry whatever has been made in the Church book respecting it.

Mr. Alexander at or shortly after his ordination, became our Pastor, but no entry is made in the Church book thereof. Not very complimentary this to Mr. Alexander.

JANUARY 24TH. "The Pastor, Brethren Pilsworth, Foster, Whitman and Sutton, were appointed delegates to sit in Council with the Governor's Road Church, relating to the ordination of W. W. Moore to the work of the ministry."

APRIL 15TH   Still another effort was made to secure money to pay off the debt, and finish off the upper part of the chapel : $550 were subscribed on the spot.

APRIL 16TH.   The Pastor, and Brethren Morton, Winter, Moyle and Sutton, were appointed delegates "to attend the ordination of Brother Clerihew, of the Paris Church."

MAY 20TH.   Brethren Robert Morton, George Foster, Thomas Broughton and Chas. Jarvis, were appointed a committee "for finishing the chapel;" and it was *Resolved* that "all contracts be given out by tender."

Up to this time the church had been using only the basement of the chapel.

MAY 22ND.

" *Died*—At Villa Nova, Andrew J., beloved son of Julius and Sarah Rouse, aged 27 years and 9 months. Brother Rouse was a decided, meek, humble, and devoted follower of Christ. He was baptised into the Brantford Church by the Rev. T. L. Davidson, in the summer of 1858, and soon after united with his wife, by letter, at Boston. Consumption had marked him for its prey."

JULY 6TH.   George Tutt was this day drowned at the Homedale Dam.   Aged 20 years.

SEPTEMBER 16TH.

" *Died*—In Brantford, after a protracted illness of five weeks, Ann Collins, the beloved wife of Robert Smith, and third daughter of Deacon Winter of Brantford.   The natural amiability and quiet unobtrusive manner of the deceased, to which were added the graces of a consistent Christian character, endeared her to all her acquaintances.   She was born at Pickering, C. W., on October 2, 1838 ; and brought to a knowledge of the truth in the early part of 1855, and baptised by her Pastor and brother-in-law. the Rev. T. L. Davidson, at Brantford, on the 8th of July of that year.   Having lived from that period a life of faith upon the Son of God, she was released from her sufferings on the 16th of Sept., and fell asleep in Jesus."

SEPTEMBER 18TH.

Died—In the Town of Brantford, Harriet, relict of the late Thos. Andrews.   Our departed sister passed through a severe trial last winter in the death of her husband, an event which, we believe, was greatly blessed to her soul.   After a dreary season of spiritual declension, it pleased God to reclaim and quicken her by means of outward trials. Having been received by the Brantford Church, she was baptized on profession of her faith, on Sabbath 4th August last.   On Tuesday evening,

REV. JOHN ALEXANDER
PASTOR FROM JANUARY, 1861, TO DECEMBER, 1871.

the 17th inst., while preparing for the prayer-meeting, she was suddenly seized by the hand of death, and breathed her last at 5 o'clock next morning.

SEPTEMBER 29TH. *Died*—at Brantford, Anne Grey, the beloved wife of William Young, Esq. The following is an extract from her obituary notice :—

"The deceased was much esteemed in the community in which she resided. A well-balanced mind, richly stored with valuable knowledge— a highly cultivated intellect—a sweet and gentle disposition—a deep-toned piety were characteristics which command the respect and affection of her acquaintances. Hers was an intelligent Christianity, based upon a clear discovery, and heart-reception of Bible truth. She was born and educated in the City of Edinburgh, and in common with her country people, she was well instructed in the Scriptures. From a child, she gave evidence of love to the Saviour. At the age of seventeen she was baptized by one of the Pastors of Bristol Street Church, Edinburgh; and after coming to America was for some time a member of the Washington Street Baptist Church, Buffalo, N.Y. For the last three years she has been a much esteemed member of the Brantford Church, and till within a short time before her last illness, a valued teacher of the Sabbath-school. Not only her bereaved husband and relatives, but the whole Church feel the sad blank occasioned by her removal. This is the fifth member of the Brantford Church removed by death within a few weeks. Oh! that the loud call were laid to heart and blessed to us as a people."

OCTOBER 20TH. "On motion of Brother Foster, a special devotional meeting was appointed to be held on Wednesday next, to ask God to aid and direct us in our present financial difficulties."

NOVEMBER 24TH. "Brethren Crawford, Edmondson, and Benedict, were appointed delegates to sit in council with the Orangeville Church, to set apart Brother Allan Kitchen to the work of the ministry."

1862.

APRIL 13TH. The upper part of the new chapel was opened. In the morning a sermon was preached by Dr. Caldicott, of Toronto; in the afternoon, a sermon by Dr. Fyfe, of Woodstock; and in the evening, a sermon by Rev. G. W. M. Carey, M.A., of St. Catharines. The collections for the day amounted to $145.

On the following evening a most successful tea meeting was held, at which addresses were made by Revs. P. Clerihew and Drummond. The whole cost of the building, exclusive of the site, was $20,000; on which, at this time, there was a debt of $6,000. The amount realized from the tea meeting was $210. John Turner, of Brantford, was the architect.

APRIL 22ND. Brother Dungey (a colored Brother) was appointed sexton, at a salary of $100 per annum.

APRIL 28TH. "Moved by Brother Shenston, seconded by Brother Young, that, inasmuch as the choir has disbanded, we have none for three months, and Brother Pilsworth lead the singing for three months."

"In amendment it was moved by Brother Sutton, and seconded by Brother Minore, that Brethren Foster, Buck, Morton and Mr. A. W. Smith, be a committee to form a choir."

Second amendment, "That Deacon Pilsworth, and Brethren Foster and Buck, be a committee to form a choir." The last amendment carried.

Monday, the 26th of May, 1862, died, at the residence of her son, Erastus Benedict, Martha, widow of the late Capt. John Benedict, of Hamilton, N.Y. She was over eighty-three years of age, and for forty years had been a zealous Christian. She was baptized by Elder Haskell, of Hamilton, N.Y. Since 1851 she had made her home with her son, a few miles south of Brantford, where she died. She was the grandmother of Deacon Alonzo Benedict, and of Lewis Benedict, our church treasurer. She was often called "that dear old body" by many who knew her as the church members did. Few women possessed the same spiritual magnetism as she. She was always happy, and never spoken to but the sweetness of her Christian character made itself manifest.

JUNE 22ND. The Pastor, Brethren W. Winter, R. Morton, Wm. Moyle, E. Benedict, Wm. Young and Wm. Skelley, were appointed delegates to attend the Association.

Extracts from Church letter:—Sunday school, 200; T. S. Shenston, superintendent; George Foster, teacher of the male Bible class; Miss Jemima Shenston, teacher of the female Bible class; number baptized, 29; received by letter, 14; present number, 332. This Association was held in Brantford, June 27th.

JULY 20TH. The Pastor, Brethren Morton, and Wm. Young, were appointed delegates to sit in council with the Stratford Church, to take part in the ordination of Brother Shrimpton to the Gospel ministry, and also to aid in the formation of a new church in Wellesley.

Died, Tuesday, August 4th, in Brantford, Margaret, wife of Deacon John Jackson, and mother of the Rev. John Jackson D.D., now Pastor of a Baptist Church in Bloomington, Illinois.

She was a dear and much beloved Sister. Her loss was very much felt at the time. She was converted through the instrumentality of Elder Rees, and baptized by him.

AUGUST 29TH. The auditors reported that they had examined the accounts of T. S. Shenston, treasurer of the building fund, and that "they are found all correct," showing the amount owing by the church, interest added up to September, to be (exclusive of the sum borrowed from the Trust and Loan Company) $2,430.69, as shown by the following: Due Wm. Young, $734.66 ; Erastus Benedict, $223.28 : T. S. Shenston, $853.31 ; Wm. Mitchell, $62.50 ; Wm. Winter, $516.94 : I. Cockshutt, $40 ; total, $2,430.69.

Sunday, September 6th, died, at Brantford, David Davidson, aged 81 years, and father of the Rev. T. L. Davidson. He was born in the town of Brechin, in Scotland, in the year 1782. He was early the subject of religious impressions, but took no decided step in religious matters until after his marriage.

He was twelve years in the British Army ; subsequent to which, he travelled with the Earl of Panmure as confidential attendant. In the year 1832, he came to Canada, and his family in the year following. His funeral sermon was preached by Rev. A. Caldwell, of Dundas, from Psalm xxxvii : 37.

DECEMBER 4TH. Pastor Alexander tendered his resignation in a long letter, of which the following are extracts :—

" Having received, unsought and unexpected by me, a unanimous call from the First Baptist Church, of Montreal, I beg to inform you that, after mature and prayerful deliberation, and taking all the past circumstances into account * * * I feel it my duty to accept of that call ; and, in consequence, to tender my resignation of the Pastorate of this church, to take effect at the close of my financial year in the end of January.

        * * * The peculiar inviting field of usefulness presented in Montreal * * * I can heartily say that my heart's wish is, that the richest blessings of a Covenant God may rest on you all. I can never forget the many proofs of affection and esteem that I have received, etc."

On reading this letter, it was moved by T. S. Shenston, and duly seconded and carried:—"Whereas our much beloved Pastor, Rev. John Alexander, has resigned the Pastoral charge

of this church in order to accept that of the Baptist Church in
Montreal city :—*Resolved*, that, while with great reluctance we
accept the resignation of a Pastor whom we all love, and under
whose brief ministry we have all been so much profited, we
desire to place on record that, in our opinion, the causes assigned by him for such an important step are not of such a
character as to justify the severance of the relationship of
Pastor and people ; while, at the same time, we are fully
satisfied as to the purity of motives which have led our Pastor
to this decision."

Died—Sabbath Morning, December 7th, at the residence
of her son, Henry Moyle, Mrs. Anne Moyle, aged 71 years.
This much beloved sister was born in Dorsetshire, England,
in the year 1790. At the early age of fifteen, she became
seriously impressed with the importance of eternal things.
These impressions resulted in her conversion to God. Of her
the *Canadian Baptist* of January 8th, 1863, says :—

"Her earnest love to Christ soon gave her pleasing work. Finding
many of the young around her ignorant of God and the way of Salvation,
she exercised her mind in teaching a Sabbath school, and using her spare
time in behalf of the destitute, and for those who knew not God. It was
her meat and her drink to work for Christ and His glory. The sick and
the poor found in her a warm-hearted friend, and one that delighted to
lead them to the treasures of Divine truth. In the village in which Sister
Moyle resided, the Sabbath school, commenced by her, grew by degrees
to an evening meeting, there being no place of worship nearer than two
miles."

1863.

JANUARY 25TH. "On motion of Brother George Foster,
Friday evening next was appointed for a social meeting, in
view of Pastor Alexander's leaving us."

JANUARY 29TH. Was held a farewell social, and bidding
good-bye to our then ex-Pastor, Rev. John Alexander : Deacon Moyle, chairman. He expressed his entire satisfaction
with Mr. Alexander's past ministry, and the kindest wishes for
his future prosperity and usefulness.

Bro. George Foster was called, on behalf of the committee
to present an address to the retiring Pastor, and a purse containing $102. Miss Jemima Shenston, in behalf of the Bible
class ; and Naomi Shenston, in behalf of her class, presented
testimonials.

Mr. Alexander regretted that he was called to part with a people he so much loved, but, having made his removal a subject of earnest prayer that he might be led aright, he could not doubt, from the indications he had received, that the step he was taking was in the path of duty, and, therefore, it became him to follow the good hand of God in this painful separation.

Expressions of sympathy and good-will were *spoken* by many, and *felt* by all.

Died—on Wednesday, February 4th, at Brantford, after a brief illness of only thirty-two hours, the wife of the Rev. John Alexander. On the Sabbath previous to her death she attended church in her usual health and cheerfulness, and commemorated with her fellow church members the death of her Redeemer. She informed several of her more intimate friends that she had more than usually enjoyed the presence of her Lord at His table that day.

On the previous Tuesday Mr. Alexander left for Montreal. Mrs. Alexander retired to rest the night of her decease at the usual hour, without any warning of approaching death.

The writer, his wife with other members were present when she died, and will never forget the scene. She was indeed a dear, good woman, and one whom no one could help loving.

In alluding to her death, the *Canadian Baptist* says :

"Mr. Alexander spent an hour or two with us on Wednesday evening, and showed us the photographs of his dear family, whom he hoped soon to bring down to his new home in Montreal. * * * At the very time Brother Alexander was seated in our parlor conversing socially with us, death deprived his dear ones of their mother, and removed his earthly comforter."

The following are extracts from her published obituary notice :

"It is seldom, indeed, that we are called upon to chronicle a providence more striking, or a death more unexpected, than that contained in the above announcement.

"On Tuesday, Mr. Alexander left her for Montreal, bidding her for a time farewell; but expecting in a very few months to be joined by his beloved wife and family. After his departure she seemed happy and cheerful, attending with her usual activity to domestic duties, and occasionally singing some verses of her favorite hymn. She retired to rest at her usual hour, with no symptoms of disease, but shortly after midnight was seized with what proved to be the last enemy; and after a short period of painful suffering, lapsed into unconsciousness, and thus gently passed away from earth to the spirit world.

"That it was a *sudden death* leaves no room for regret, so far as our departed sister was concerned. To her sudden death, most assuredly was sudden glory. The fragmentary expressions that fell from her dying lips, in her conscious moments, 'How sweet,' 'How precious,' indicated to those around that death was swallowed up in victory. But in her conflict with the King of Terrors, she missed the sympathising look and tender voice of her nearest and dearest friend on earth. She was taken also at a time when we would have judged it most desirable she should live, when she had gained much experience of the past, when her character had become consolidated, when her gifts and graces were becoming more manifest, and more than ever serviceable in the household of faith, and when along with her partner in life, she was looking forward to a new and important sphere of labor in the Church of Christ."

"Mrs. Alexander has left behind her, wherever she was known, a fragrant memory. Born of a godly family—four of them connected with the ministerial office—she early in life gave herself to the Saviour, and ever since was a most consistent and devoted follower of the Lamb. As a wife, she was in the largest sense a helpmeet to her husband. Her piety was of that happy, cheerful character so befitting the companion of a servant of the Lord, and so well adapted to cheer him in the arduous labors of his calling. As a mother she was devoted to her family, training them up in the nurture and admonition of the Lord, and leading the little ones to the Saviour.

"Occupying in the Church of Christ a prominent position, she ever conducted herself with a rare prudence and wisdom that became her station. She was active in the practise of every good work, her ears were ever open to the cry of distress. Her public life of over eight years in Brantford is well known to the members of the different Churches, and such a record, blameless before the eyes of the Church and the world, is more than sufficient to show the sterling qualities she possessed." etc.

Died—February 8th, at Brantford, the wife of David Davidson, and mother of Rev. T. L. Davidson.

FEBRUARY 15TH.—At the suggestion of Brother George Foster, Brethren F. Ellis, Charles Jarvis, George Foster, Thomas Pilsworth and William Moyle, were appointed to visit Pastor Alexander, with a view to retaining him as our Pastor.

FEBRUARY 17TH. The committee reported that Pastor Alexander "could not entertain the thought of remaining."

Died—in Brantford, Wednesday, February 25th, dear Deacon William Winter, in the 60th year of his age. He was born at Soham, in Cambridge, England, October 3rd, 1803. In early life he was left an orphan : was brought to the knowledge of the truth "as it is in Jesus," and was baptized into the fellowship of the Baptist Church, of which the Rev. Dr. Thos. Price was Pastor. While in London he was married to Miss

Elizabeth Stokes, and shortly after emigrated to Canada. He started in Brantford the *Christian Messenger*, October, 1st, 1854, about the first real live denominational paper in Ontario, and from which sprang the *Canadian Baptist*, our present organ.

All were pleased to see Deacon Winter enter our prayer meetings; and there were no dull, lifeless prayer meetings when he was present. It seems as though I can hear his encouraging voice even now. I was present at his peaceful death. What a loss he was to the church.

The following is an extract from his published obituary notice:—

He emigrated to Canada in 1844, and settled in the township of Pickering. He was there first elected to the office of Deacon; an office which he has since filled with honor and advantage to the cause of the Regular Baptist churches of Woodstock and Brantford. He held a prominent position in the body to which he belonged, and yielded an importance in the management of its affairs. The name of Deacon Winter has become a household word in the Baptist Churches of Canada, and his praise has long been in them all. For five years he has held the position of Treasurer of the Baptist Missionary Convention of Canada West, and has given great satisfaction to his brethren by the faithful manner in which he discharged the duties of his office. His decease created a profound sensation in the town, and men of all parties and classes unite in their lamentations in view of his death. His death will be deeply felt in the church in Brantford, of which he was an officer, and his loss will be deeply deplored throughout the whole denomination."

MARCH 8TH. The pulpit supply committee (Brethren Robert Morton, T. S. Shenston and John P. Sutton) reported, "that we have written to Rev. Dr. Boyd, of Chicago, and Rev. Mr. Cathcart, of Philadelphia, inviting each to visit us with a view to the Pastorate, but neither of them felt inclined to leave their present fields of labor. * * * We recommend the church to extend a call to Rev. Professor Stewart, of Woodstock," etc., etc.

The matter was deferred for two weeks. T. S. Shenston was appointed a Deacon in the place of William Winter, deceased.

MARCH 29TH. By a unanimous standing vote Professor Stewart was invited to become our Pastor.

APRIL 19TH. William Stewart, by letter, accepted the Pastorate. "Moved by Brother Shenston, seconded by Bro.

Crawford, that Pastor Stewart's salary be $800 per annum. In amendment, it was moved that it be $700. The original motion carried."

MAY 3RD. "Brethren Moyle, E. Benedict, M. Whitham and W. C. Scott, were appointed delegates to meet with the St. George Church, to set apart Brother Robert Dunlop to the work of the Christian ministry."

JUNE 7TH. The Pastor and Brethren Morton, Moyle, Sutton, Benedict, Crawford and Whitham, were appointed delegates to attend the Association. This Association was held in St. George, June 9th. The number of members reported were 325, and the number baptized 8. It was announced that the young ladies' Bazaar had realized $150.

AUGUST 2ND. Rev. John Alexander gave the right hand of fellowship to Rev. Wm. Stewart and wife. Pastor Stewart was delegated to attend a council with the Elora Church to aid in ordaining Brother——— to the work of the ministry.

AUGUST 6TH. *Resolved*, that the recognition and installation services of the Rev. W. Stewart take place on the evening of August 18th, and that we have a public tea-meeting on that occasion. No minute has been made respecting this tea-meeting.

Died—on Thursday, August 13th, at Brantford, Emma Bosworth Winter, sixth daughter of the late Deacon Winter and our Sister Elizabeth Winter, and sister of George Winter. One alluding to her death in the *Canadian Baptist*, says :

"From her childhood she was meek, loving, and lovable. Of her it may be safely said, that she never had or made an enemy.
Emma was a true Christian, and nothing in her whole life cast a shade of doubt in regard to her religious character."

The writer can bear his testimony as to the remarkable loveliness of her Christian character. Both he and his wife were with her when she died. She was naturally very modest and timid, and consequently disinclined to say much as to her own religious experiences. On one occasion, however, when her mother, with the writer and his wife were standing around her bed, she raised both her arms together, and brought them down on the bed with some force, at the same time saying with

5

energy, "O, how happy I am!" I close with another extract
from the obituary notice.

"Since her father's death she has cheered the desolate heart of her
dear widowed mother, who stands like a venerable tree, stripped of half
its branches, to brave the rude storms of life. A sad trial for the aching-
hearted and fond mother to part with such a darling and affectionate
daughter; yet the rainbow of promise was painted on the dark cloud, that
at last hid her from mortal eyes; as in her dying hours she gave the clear-
est and most satisfactory evidence that all was well. 'I am going home to
see Jesus, and meet my dear father and sisters. I have no fear of death—
I love Jesus, and know He died for me.' These, and such like utterances
fell from her lips. When she drew near her end, she called her brothers
and sisters round, and begged each to live, so as to meet her in heaven.
Thus passed from earth the fifth daughter of our dear departed Brother
Winter, and 'these all died in faith.'"

Rev. William Stewart preached her funeral sermon on
the 16th from Isaiah lxiv., 6 : "We all do fade as a leaf."

OCTOBER 25TH. The Pastor, Brethren R. Morton, E.
Benedict and S. Reed, were appointed delegates to attend a
council to be held in the Dundas Church, "to set apart Brother
———————to the work of the ministry."

NOVEMBER 11TH. Another attempt made to reduce the
debt on the chapel.

1864.

JANUARY 24TH. The Pastor asked for, and obtained permission, to preach at the opening of the Elora Chapel on the
first Sabbath in February, Rev. Mr. Kitchen to supply for him
in his absence.

It was reported to the Church that $145 was the deficiency
to be made up to the publishers for publishing Mr. Davidson's
book on baptism. The sum was paid by Brethren Buck,
Young and Shenston. Still another effort was made towards
reducing the Church debt.

JANUARY 31ST. The Deacons reported : "We cannot
regard baptism by any other than a properly ordained Baptist
minister as regular ; and, while we believe that the administration of the ordinance should be confined to ordained ministers, yet, inasmuch as we cannot take the ground that the

REV. WILLIAM STEWART, (D.D.)

PASTOR FROM MARCH 1861 TO MAY 1869.

validity of baptism depends upon the administrator, we cannot conceive it to be our duty to take upon ourselves the responsibility of refusing membership to those whose baptism, although irregular, because administered by unordained or unbaptized Christians, has been the answer of a good conscience, and whose Christian character, then and since, has been such as to commend the religion of Jesus."

In amendment : "This Church can receive none to its
fellowship except such as have been baptized by an ordained
Baptist minister."

In further amendment, *resolved*, "that the words 'unordained or unbaptized Christian' be struck out of the original
motion, and the words 'ordained ministers of other denominations' added in their stead."

The second amendment carried by 28 to 18.

The first amendment was then put, under protest, and lost.
The original resolution of the Deacons was then carried by a
majority of one—27 to 26.

Brother Shenston, who had hitherto declined to vote, offered the following resolution :   "That all the proceedings of the
day, whether regular or irregular, be confirmed," which was
carried.

MARCH 8TH.   Brother Buck reported that Brother Van
B———— had deserted from the American army, bringing his
soldier's clothes with him, and moved that he be excluded, and
he was accordingly excluded.

MARCH 24TH.   The Pastor, Brethren Crawford and Reed
were appointed delegates to attend a council with the Simcoe
Church to ordain Brother J. E. Vining.

JUNE 5TH.   The Pastor, and Brethren Morton, Moyle,
Pilsworth, Benedict, Crawford, Whitham, Sutton, Young and
Foster, were appointed delegates to the Association.   This
Association was held in Drumbo June 17.   The number of
members reported was 329.   The number baptized, 6.

JUNE 12TH.   The Treasurer was directed to pay the
amount due to the estate of the late Deacon Winter.

JULY 24TH.   Another attempt made to reduce the Church
debt, $700 had been raised.   The collectors were requested to
ask those who had subscribed already towards the $700, to add
to their subscription so as to make it up to $1,000.

JULY 31ST.   The Pastor and Brethren Morton, Moyle,
Foster and H. Jarvis, were appointed delegates to meet with the
Scotland Church, to ordain Brother Robert B. Montgomery (?)
to the work of the Christian ministry.

SEPTEMBER 7TH. "Thanks are hereby tendered to Deacon Shenston for his liberality in enclosing the chapel grounds with an excellent fence, laying a brick pavement from that to the chapel, and ornamenting the grounds ; also to Brother Wm. Buck for painting the fence, and to Brother Tisdale for valuable aid."

"That our best thanks are gratefully tendered to Brother Wm. Young for his magnificent donation of $367.60."

SEPTEMBER 25TH. The Pastor and Brethren Morton, Crawford and Ormerod were appointed delegates to meet with the Governor's Road Church, to ordain Brother John W. Clark to the work of the ministry.

The Pastor was appointed a delegate to meet with the Orangeville Church to ordain Brother——— to the work of the ministry, and also to attend a council with the Seaforth Church.

NOVEMBER 27TH. The Pastor was permitted to attend an ordination at Mount Forest on the last Sabbath of this month.

1865.

DECEMBER 14TH. *Died*—Elizabeth M., wife of Rev. T. L. Davidson, and daughter of William and Elizabeth Winter.

FEBRUARY 4TH. Brethren Crawford, Benedict, George Foster, Scott, Sutton, Wm. Buck, Hunter, Morris, Draper and Whitham, were nominated for Deacons. Brethren Buck, Whitham, Benedict and Sutton declined to stand.

MARCH 5TH. Brethren Crawford and George Foster were declared duly elected Deacons.

MARCH 19TH. Brother Alonzo Benedict and William Pearce were elected Deacons, they each receiving the majority of the votes.

APRIL 4TH. Another attempt made to raise money to meet the interest on mortgage then due.

APRIL 19TH. Brother Foster refused to accept the office of Deacon.

JUNE 7TH. *Resolved*, that A. W. Smith be requested to preside at the melodeon, and invite whom he pleases to form a choir : and that our best thanks are tendered to him for his past services.

JUNE 12TH. The Pastor and Brethren Benedict, Moyle, Morton, Crawford, Reed, C. Jarvis, William Miles, William Buck, Sutton, E. Benedict and J. Hale were appointed delegates to attend the Association. The place of meeting not named.

AUGUST 20TH. Another attempt made to raise more money. Five brethren appointed to secure funds.

SEPTEMBER 10TH. Brother Joseph Smith was baptized in the Grand River in the presence of a large assembly. Preferring the river to the baptistry.

SEPTEMBER 18TH. Brother Shenston proposed that, if the Church would raise three-fourths of the entire debt by the 1st of April, he would pay the remaining fourth.

1866.

MARCH 23RD. On this day was baptized a dear young Sister, a notice of whose death, which took place March 3rd, 1885, we insert here : *Died*—at the residence of her sister, in Toronto, Miss Susan Dimmock. The following is an extract from her obituary notice :

" The deceased was a member of the First Baptist Church, Brantford, for about twenty years, and while in Toronto seeking medical advice and aid, the Lord called her home. Now she rests within the everlasting arms on the bosom of unchanging love, and her life is hid with Christ in God. As a professing christian her conduct was exemplary. She loved to do what she could for the glory of the Master and the extension of His Kingdom. Her protracted sufferings were borne with patience and becoming resignation to the will of God.

APRIL 29TH. "This has been a most interesting day to the Baptist Church, Brantford, in view of the entire liquidation of the debt, for so many years injuriously resting upon the chapel. The Pastor preached from Psalm cxxix, 3 : "The Lord hath done great things for us whereof we are glad." * * *
The entire debt was $5,600. No one dreamed, a year ago, that the great burden of debt would be removed. Liberal offers were made, provided the whole $5,600 were paid off. So far as known not more than one or two names of those who should, at least, have given something, are conspicuous by reason of their absence from the list of subscribers. Of the whole sum not $5 has been obtained outside of the Church and congregation. The Ladies' Aid Society, during the past two

years, paid about \$700 towards the debts. Hearty thanks to that Brother who so generously contributed one-fourth of the whole amount, and to the Pastor for his labors in connection with it. * * * During the past thirteen years the Church has raised \$21,242 for chapel building. of which sum \$2,006.85 was raised by the ladies.

"The average annual sum raised for all purposes, during the said thirteen years, has been \$3,056.85."

JUNE 4TH.—Pastor Stewart was requested to allow his morning sermon to be printed.

The Pastor, Brethren Sutton, Shenston, Morton, Benedict, Dickie, Crawford, C. Jarvis, Wm. Buck, Scott, McIntyre, Whitham, Mordue and Foster were appointed delegates to the association. Where held is not stated.

JULY 24TH. *Died*—at Brantford, Robert Tutt, aged 22 years,

JULY 15TH. Moved by Robert Morton, Sen., seconded by William Buck, that the salary of the Pastor for the ensuing year, commencing August 1st, be \$1,000. Carried unanimously.

AUGUST 5TH. A. W. Smith, the leader of the choir, urged for the purchase of a \$1,000 organ. A committee was appointed to carry out the same.

AUGUST 21ST. To authorize an additional outlay of \$50 on the organ, in order to render the instrument more effective.

NOVEMBER 16TH. Sergeants A. Drake and Charles Britt, and Private Cole, were received by letter from the Quebec Church —soldiers in the 7th Fusileers. This regiment, at this time, was stationed in Brantford.

1867.

JANUARY 1. The following is a copy of our Sunday School programme for Wednesday evening, January 2nd, 1867:

1. Opening Address, (original)..................Geo. McDonald.
2. Music—"Happy New Year,"..........................Choir.
3. Recitation—"Sir John Moore," (original,)..........Fred Jenkins.
4. Recitation—"The Master has come over Jordan." Mary A. Minore.

5. Music—"Forbid them not," ....Choir.
6. Recitation—"The Lord is my Shepherd," ....Annie Stewart.
7. "The Heathen Mother," ....Jennie Morton.
8. " Poor Lilly Moore," ....Grace Pierce.
9. "The Boy's Enquiry," ....Frank Howard.
10. Music—"Shall we sing in Heaven?" ....Choir.
11. Recitation—"The Life Boat at Cheltenham," ......Warwick Pierce.
12. Dialogue—"Temperance," Mary Pickering, Chas. Dimmock, Joseph
      Shenston.
13. Music—" Little Pilgrim," ....Willie Turner.
14. Simultaneous Recitation—"The Ten Commandments," ...... Alice
      Dalrymple, Annie Jarvis, Polly Clough, Louisa Diamond,
      Christina Harrison, Agnes Jackson, Bertha Hale, Ida Turner,
      Ruth Shenston, John Minore, Benj. Clough, Albert Ormerod,
      Homer Johnson, Robert Robson, Fred Chalcraft, Samuel
      Diamond, James Large.
15. Recitation—"The Mother's Day Dream," ....Eliza Mintern.
16. Music—"The Land beyond the River," ....Mary Schultz.
17. Recitation—"Canada," (original) ....Orlond Benedict.
18. Recitation—" Soldier's Farewell," ....Eugenia Excell.
19. Music—"Do what you can," Eliza Mintern, Jane Tanton, Mary A.
      Holt, Mary Robson.
20. Music—"Ring the bells softly," ....The Dimmock Family.
21. Recitation—"The hut on the vacant lot," ....Mary Robson.
22. Music—"In olden times," ....Choir.
23. Recitation—"A Beautiful Illustration," ....John Butterworth.
24. Recitation—"The Union Jack," ....George Dimmock.
25. Music—"The Bugle Calls," ..Willie Strike and Walter Monson, 7th
      Reg't R. F.
26. Simultaneous Recitation—"The Lord's Prayer," Maggie Stewart,
      Minnie Winter, Wm. Chalcraft, Frank Whitham, Ada Stubbs,
      Maggie Morris, C. Butterworth, Ester Cowley, Wm. Turner,
      F. Foster.
27. Dialogue—"Bible Puzzle," ....Mary Cawley, Bessie Woods, Mary
      Diamond, Christina Harrison, Jane Tanton.
28. Music—"Little Brown Cot," Albert Ormerod, Christina Harrison,
      Mary Harrison, Mary Schultz, Samuel Diamond.
29. Recitation—"Dissatisfaction," ....Alice Jex.
30. Address to the Sunday School, ...Ed. Vanderlip.
31. Music—"Chime on," ....Mary Pickering, Chas. Dimmock.
32. Recitation—"Business Maxims," ....Robert Pierce.
33. Recitation—"God Bless the Sunday School," (original), Mary Lake.
34. Music—"Little Eyes," Jennie Morton, Nelly Foster, Minnie Winter,
      Annie Weinaugh, Willie Bax, Amelia Weinaugh, Adelaide Todd,
      Frank Witham, Ada Back, Frank Foster, Maggie Stewart,
      Willie Turner, Annie Bax, Melinda Lund, Frank Bishop, Mary
      Hazleton, Alfred Jex, Alice Morris.
35. Recitation—"A Reverie," ....Sarah Dimmock.
36. Dialogue—"Guardian Angels," .....Jennie Blaylock, Emily Knox.
37. Music—"Gentle Shepherd," ..Mary A. Minore, Lydia Poole, Willie
      Strike.
38. Recitation—" Meekness," ....James Ormerod.
39. Recitation—"The Graves of the Household," ....Eliza Foster.
40. Music—"Twenty years ago," ....Horace Hale.

41. Recitation—"Not in vain,"............ ....Mary Diamond
42. Recitation—"Dies Irae,"......................James Peachie.
43. Music –"Have courage to do right," Berthx Hale, Jennie Blaylock,
    Christina Harrison, Joseph Shenston, Fred Jenkins, Willie
    Aikman.
44. Recitation—"Old things,"......................Horace Hale.
45. Recitation—"A day at a time,"...... ....Alfred Fenton.
46. Music—"Christmas Carol,"...........................Choir.
47. Recitation—"Little Lights,"...................Harry Smith.
48. Recitation—"The Fenian Scare at Kingston,"...... J. N. Jackson.
49. Dialogue—"Canada our Home," original,.... Walter Hawkins, and
    Albert Green.
50. Music—"Always speak the truth." Jennie Millard, Grace Harrison,
    Bessie Woods, Albert Ormerod, Edward Vanderlip, Wm. Schultz.
51. Recitation—"Trust in God and do right,".........Chas. Sanderson.
52. Music—"Never forget the dear ones,"...................Choir.
53. Recitation—"The tree is known by its fruits,"...... John Robsor.
54. Music—"A Home in Heaven," Mary J. Broughton, Mary Diamond,
    Lizzie McAdam, Walter Munson, James Ormerod.
55. Music—"Beautiful River,"..............................Choir.

Sabbath School officers and teachers for 1867 :—

T. S. SHENSTON, Superintendent.
A. W. SMITH,   Secretary.
WM. BUCK,   Librarian.

TEACHERS.

Edwin Chalcraft,	Andrew Edy.
John Minore,	John Hext,
James N. Edy,	J. C. Yule,
James Aldred,	S. K. Passmore,
Angus Murray,	Thos. Morris,
Robt. Mathison,	Wm. C. Holt,
Thos. Pickering,	S. Tapscott,
N. Diamond,	Ann Whitham,
E. Walker,	Helen Walker,
Lizzie Reynolds,	Augusta Stewart,
Elizabeth Maxwell,	Ellen Ormerod,
Isabella Hall.	Pamelia S. V. Yule.
Jennie Dalrymple,	Albina L. West,
Annie J. Rice,	Mrs. Chas. Pouley,
Margaret Fletcher,	Sarah Cox.

JULY 3RD.

"SECORD. Died at her residence, in St. Catharines, Mrs. Secord,
widow of the late Major Secord. The deceased was over 70 years of age.
For many years she was a professing Christian, and a member of the Bap-

tist denomination. She was pre-eminently a meek, quiet and gentle Christian. Her faith and hope were strong and bright during her last illness, and in the hour of death."

She was, for several years, a member of the Brantford Church. She was the mother of Daniel Secord who was killed at the Desjardin canal accident.

JUNE 16TH. The Pastor, and Brethren Reed, Broughton and McIntyre, were appointed delegates to the Association. Where held is not stated.

JULY 11TH. *Resolved*, to circulate a subscription list to meet our liabilities.

JULY 16TH "Mrs. Yule, Mrs. Buck, Mrs. Shenston, Mrs. Benedict, Mrs. Tisdale, Mrs. Broughton and Mrs. Stewart, were appointed to aid in purchasing and preparing an outfit for Miss Jane Bates, who, as the wife of Brother Timpany, is soon to go out with her husband as a missionary to the Telugoos of British India."

SEPTEMBER 3RD. Brother Shenston, as executor of the late Wm. Jackson, (colored) informed the Church, that by his will, his lot had been left to the Church.

OCTOBER 20TH. *Resolved*, "to ask the following churches to send delegates to attend the ordination of Brother A. V. Timpany, missionary elect to the Telugoos :— Paris, Governor's Road, St. George, Jerseyville, Dundas, Hamilton, 1st Onondaga, Boston, Scotland and Waterford."

Brother Timpany, being not only a member with us, but the first missionary sent out to India by our own Foreign Missionary Society, it will not be out of place just here to narrate a few facts in connection with him :

Brother Timpany was born in the Township of Bayham, County of Elgin, Ontario, on the 21st of December, 1840. He graduated from Woodstock College in the spring of 1867. On the 15th of October, in the same year he was married to Miss Jane Bates, eldest daughter of the Rev. John Bates. On the 24th of the same month they left Canada for India, and arrived at Nellore, May, 1868, the Suez canal not being yet opened. In July, 1876, he and Mrs. Timpany returned to Canada to recruit their health, and left Canada again for India, September, 1878.

REV. AMERICUS VESPUCIUS TIMPANY.

BORN DECEMBER 21st, 1840.
DIED IN INDIA, FEBRUARY 19th, 1885.
Our first missionary to India.

"Mr. Timpany died, February 19th, 1885, from a severe attack of cholera, at about 2.30 p m., and was buried the same day, at 9.30 p.m., in Coconada, India. On Wednesday, the day previous to his death, he had conducted a prayer meeting, and spoke most earnestly and lovingly of heaven. There was a look of weariness on his face, and the mere recounting of the joys of heaven appeared to refresh him."

The following is an extract from a private letter to the
writer from Mr. Timpany's widow :—"Mr. Timpany died in
the Coconada Mission House. We occupied the right hand
half as you look at the cut on the 177th page of your Scrap
Book. Down the centre of the building was a large room, and
on the right side of this room was our bedroom. In that room
his loving, faithful soul passed away to enjoy the glorious rest
of a blessed immortality.

"When he came in after attending to the early duties of the
morning, instead of coming to breakfast, as usual, he lay down
on a sofa in his study, from which he never arose, getting ill so
rapidly that it was impossible to move him to another room.
We managed to lift him into a single bed of Miss Faith's, which
we brought in a short time before he left us. He was only ill
from 7 a.m till 3 p.m."

Three weeks before he died he wrote as follows :—"The
day of salvation of this people draws near at length. Where five
years ago there were about 300 Christians, now there are 1,500 :
and I fully expect to see in another five years this 1,500 reach
as many thousands. 'The living God is on our side.'"

The following are extracts from a letter written to Rev.
John Craig, then in Ontario, by Mr. Geo. H. White :—"I forgot to mention that poor Mary was in school, and when sent
for came home too late to see her father alive. Owing to the
nature of the disease Dr. Beech hurried on the funeral arrangements, and we buried him at 9 30 p.m. At a little past 8 p.m.
we put him in his coffin, and he was borne to the chapel in the
Mission compound. There Jonathan had a short service, as
Dr. Beech was averse to exposing the body long. * * *
The night was dark, we had eight torches to illuminate the
long procession which followed him to the grave."

*   *   *   *   *   *   *   *

"Our sorrows were his sorrows, and our joys his joys ;
the smallest affairs of each one of us interested him as if they
were his own. We, the members of the Church of England,
are overwhelmed with our great loss. We have lost a loving,
large-hearted, humble Pastor and we feel that we shall never
look upon his like again."

"On Sunday, the 15th, he preached one of the most
eloquent sermons I ever heard him deliver. His theme was
'Jesus,' and oh! how lovingly he spoke! What glorious
pictures he drew of the bliss of heaven! During the sermon,

COCONADA MISSION HOUSE
IN WHICH MISSIONARY COMPANY DIED.

in a state of rapture, he exclaimed, 'Sun of my Soul!' He
little thought then that before five days had gone by he would
be basking in the light and warmth of that 'Sun.'"

NOVEMBER 26TH. The Pastor and Brother Broughton
were appointed delegates to attend the ordination of Bro. ——
at Seaforth.

1868.

MARCH 5TH. An extra effort made to raise money.

APRIL 19TH. The Deacons reported that they had
borrowed $100 to meet present liabilities. Brother Tapscott
was appointed to the office of seating strangers, instead of Bro.
Shenston who had filled that position for six years.

MAY 26TH. The Pastor was appointed a delegate to attend the organization of a church at Goble's Corners.

JUNE 21ST. The Pastor and Brethren Benedict, McIntyre,
Jarvis and Broughton, were appointed delegates to the Association. The place of meeting not named.

OCTOBER 6TH. A special collection recommended to
raise $600.

1869.

FEBRUARY 2ND. *Resolved*, " to hold special meetings and
invite Mr. Carroll and Mr. Needham to make us a visit.
Dancing pronounced a vain and worldly amusement, unworthy
a professed follower of the Lord Jesus Christ."

The Pastor informed the Church that he had been appointed Superintendent of Schools for the town, and asked if any
objection would be made to his acceptance of the position.
No objection offered.

Resolved, " that room be appropriated in the gallery for the
orphans from Deacon Shenston's Home."

APRIL 23RD. "The Pastor then stated that as the Church
seemed unwilling to grapple with the question of finance, and
as the repeated efforts of the last two years had all failed to
effect a remedy, he had no other resource than to tender his
resignation, which he now respectfully did. He explained that
the management of the finances had been a source of great
discomfort to him," etc., etc.

REV. CHARLES CARROLL,
"SUPPLIED" FROM AUGUST, 1869, TO FEBRUARY, 1870.

MAY 18TH. The Pastor explained at some length his reasons for resigning the pastoral charge of the Church was for the purpose of accepting the pastorate of the Bond Street Church, Toronto, and asked the Church to grant it.

The answer, "That while we, as a Church, regret that our Pastor, Rev. Wm. Stewart, deems it his duty to resign the pastoral charge of the Church, we cannot but think the reasons assigned by him are not of sufficient moment to account for such a separation, nevertheless we accept his resignation, and earnestly pray that God's richest blessings may attend him in his new field of labor."   Carried.

MAY 30TH.   The Pastor and Brethren Moyle and Brough-ton, were appointed delegates to attend the Association, held June 18th, at Hillsburgh.   Number of members reported 387, baptized 31.

JULY 25TH.   The Ministerial Committee reported that they recommend that Bro. Carroll be invited to become our Pastor.   In amendment, that Brother Carroll be invited to supply us for six months.   After long and free discussion, the amendment carried.

AUGUST 1ST.   On behalf of the supply committee, Bro. Foster stated that Bro. Carroll declined the invitation.   The committee had received a numerously signed requisition for them to call a special meeting to reconsider the former vote.

AUGUST 3RD.   Refusing to take a straight vote, a want of confidence in them was manifested by the Church, and the com-mittee thought it best to resign.   The resignation was not ac-cepted.

OCTOBER 27TH.   Supply committee stated that, under the circumstances, they would recommend that Bro. Carroll be engaged to supply for six months, and, in the event of his declin-ing, that Rev. John Alexander be invited to become our Pastor.

The vote was as follows :— For Bro. Carroll for six months, yeas, 42 ; nays, 32.   For Bro. Alexander as Pastor, yeas, 34 : nays, 22.   It was resolved that Bro. Thos. Cull, of Albany, N. Y., be invited to become our Pastor.   Ballot :— Yeas, 34 ; nays, 32.

NOVEMBER 10TH.   *Resolved*, that $50 be appropriated for the purpose of extending the gallery in front to accommodate the organ.

That the pew-holders be requested to advance the annual rental of their pews, in order to make up the deficiency in the income of the Church.

1870.

FEBRUARY 15TH.   The Clerk read a letter from Brother Carroll tendering his resignation as pulpit supply.   Resigna-tion accepted.

MARCH 15TH. "A communication was sent by Brother George Foster and twenty-eight others, intimating that they thought it best to leave and form another Church. The matter was postponed."

MARCH 22ND. The letter of Brother George Foster and twenty-eight others was referred to a committee who reported·

"*Whereas*, twenty-eight members, in our judgment, have too hastily withdrawn from the membership of this Church, and have sent in a requisition for letters of dismission, in order that they may form a Church of *baptized believers*.   *   *   * Notwithstanding that this Church fails to see the necessity for the formation of a second Regular Baptist Church in the Town of Brantford : and, notwithstanding that there is a lack of friendliness in the requisition, we grant the twenty-eight members *certificates of Christian character* up to the 22nd March. Report unanimously adopted.

APRIL 3RD. *Resolved*, "that a committee be authorized to send a delegate to St. John, New Brunswick, to convey the Church's call to——————————, the said delegate not being able to induce Brother Carey to accept, he be authorized to confer with Brethren D. M. Walton, W. H. Porter or any other minister he might consider suitable to visit us with a view to a call.

APRIL 7TH. On behalf of the Church, Brother Broughton started this day for Nova Scotia, for the purpose of securing as Pastor a minister then residing there.

Failing in this, on his way homeward by way of Boston, he met with Dr. Hurd, of whom all he saw spoke highly. An interview with him resulted in Dr. Hurd's visiting Brantford, with a view to a call, and in his becoming our Pastor in May.

APRIL 13TH. *Resolved* :—"Whereas twenty-eight members of this Church recently made application for letters of dismission, to enable them to form a new Church of *baptized believers*, whereby doubt was honestly entertained as to the character of the Church they proposed to form ; and, in consequence of which *certificates of Christian character* only were granted.   *   *   * And, whereas, the Secretary *pro tem*, of the contemplated Church has made application on behalf of those members, for letters to form a *Regular Baptist Church*, in substitution for the certificate of Christian character already

6

granted them. * * * Yet as these brethren think otherwise and have removed the only objection that previously existed to their receiving such letters." So letters granted.

APRIL 14TH. List of members dismissed by letter.

Robert Morton,
Helen Morton,
Charles Jarvis,
Mrs. Charles Jarvis,
Joseph Cawley,
Esther Cawley,
Mary Cawley,
Martha Cawley,
Edwin Chalcraft,
Margaret Chalcraft,
George Foster,
Helen Selina Foster,
Mary Dalrymple,
Jessie Walker,
Betsy Walker,
Helen Walker,
George McDonald,
Mrs. George McDonald,
Mrs. Isabella Hall,
Miss Helen Langmire,
Elenor Henry,
Thomas Birkett,
Lucy Birkett,
Henry E. Cawley.

Mrs. John Turner,
Samuel Passmore,
Mrs. Francis Foster,
APRIL 20TH.
Miss Isabella Christie,
Alfred Cox,
Mrs. Alfred Cox,
MAY 12TH.
William Buck.
Mrs. Wm. Buck,
John Whitham,
Mrs. John Whitham.
Daniel Osborne,
W. C. Holt,
Mrs. Daniel Osborne,
Mrs. Francis Ellis,
Miss Kate Foster,
Mrs. Fletcher,
MAY 14TH.
Mrs. Andrew Morton,
MAY 17TH.
Francis Ellis,
MAY 24TH.
Mrs. William Young,

I well recollect reading in one of our Sunday School books an address of Father Knapp's, of Nova Scotia, in which, among other things, he said :—"It often happens that when large churches were too selfish to branch out as they ought, of their own accord, that God sent the Devil among them and forced them to separate." With deep sorrow and humiliation I am obliged to confess that to a limited extent this was true in this case. Personally I can conscientiously say, that in the part I acted therein, I would rather be judged by the "not seen," by God, than by the "seen," by man. All has, however, been mysteriously over-ruled for good. The final result of the separation is the erection of the prettiest Church building in the city, and beyond all question in the best locality. It corners on "Victoria Park," and is, in consequence, called the "Park Church."

The following are extracts from a published report of the ("Second" "Tabernacle") "Park" Church, prepared evidently by one of its members:

PARK BAPTIST CHURCH, BRANTFORD.

"The Park is a healthy off-shoot from the First Baptist Church, one of the pioneer Churches of Brantford. Shortly prior to the year 1870 the parent Church had grown to rather unwieldy strength, and early in that year a number of prominent members met at the residence of Mr. Charles Jarvis to consider the organization of another church. Those present at that meeting were Mr. George Foster, Mr. Edwin Chalcraft, Mr. S. K. Passmore, Deacon Robert Morton and Mrs. Morton, Mr. and Mrs. Geo. McDonald, Mr. Alfred Cox, Mr. Thomas Draper, Mr. Wm. Foster, and Mr. and Mrs. Jarvis. These were the first members of the new church. They were sheep without a shepherd, but Mr. George Foster ably conducted the services and the little band of thirteen soon grew to such a number that Mr. Jarvis' house was too small to hold those who desired to unite with them and more commodious premises were sought and obtained in Palmer's Hall. The next list of members on record shows the church to have grown considerably in a very few weeks, the membership including at the time of organization, February 24th, 1870."

" At the meeting for organization held February 24th, 1870, the following officers were elected, viz :—Deacons, Robert Morton and Thos. Draper ; Treasurer, Charles Jarvis ; Church Clerk, Edwin Chalcraft. Rev. John Alexander, Pastor of a Baptist Church in Montreal, was invited to take Pastoral charge, and accepted. On April 29th, 1870, the Church was formally recognized by the Baptist denomination, the services on the occasion being presided over by the Rev. Dr. Fyfe, of Woodstock."

" The Sunday School was organized on April 3rd, 1870, with these officers :—William Foster, Superintendent ; George McDonald, Secretary-Treasurer ; Alfred Cox, Librarian."

The Rev. Rob. Cameron, M. A., became their Pastor in October, 1875. On the 23rd of August, 1881 a commencement was made to erect the present beautiful edifice, Mrs. Wm. Buck being privileged to turn the first sod, August 22nd.

Rev. David Hutchison, the present Pastor, has been such since April, 1886. All future rivalry, will, I trust, be the " provoking each other to good works."

APRIL 27TH. Brethren Crawford, Moyle, Tapscott, Beemer, Broughton, Shenston and Smith were appointed delegates to attend the organization of the Brantford 2nd Church.

MAY 9TH. Brethren Shenston, Crawford, Benedict, Broughton, Tapscott and Beemer were elected Deacons.

MAY 17TH. The Church declined to change the day of prayer-meeting from Tuesday to Wednesday, as requested by the Ministerial conference.

MAY 22ND. Sunday, after the morning meeting, the Church gave a standing unanimous vote—119 members present—to extend a call to Rev. J. C. Hurd, M.D., his salary to be $1,000 per annum.

Brethren Broughton, Crawford, Shenston, Pearce, Sutton and Smith were appointed a committee to inform Dr. Hurd the result of the vote and receive his reply.

In the evening it was announced that Dr. Hurd had accepted the call, and would move to Brantford at an early day.

REV. J. C. HURD, M.D.,

PASTOR FROM MAY, 1870, TO JULY, 1875.

MAY 28TH. Brethren Shenston, Crawford, Moyle, Diamond, Benedict, Peace and Beemer, were appointed delegates to attend the Association at Richwood.

MAY———Another committee appointed to collect money for Church debt.

SEPTEMBER 13TH.   Brethren Shenston, Crawford, Beemer and Benedict, were appointed delegates to a council to be held in the Onondaga Church, for the ordination of —————.

1871.

JANUARY 31ST.   Pastor, and Brethren Moyle, Grant and Crawford, were appointed delegates to assist at the organization of a new Church at Wolverton.

Brother T. S. Shenston and Brother Crawford appointed trustees of the Church property.

MAY 9TH.   Brethren George Chittenden, T. D. Crawford, D. McIntyre, B. G. Tisdale, Wm. Moyle, A. Benedict, S. Tapscott, Beemer, Brown and Shenston, were appointed delegates to the Association, held in Brantford, June 2nd.   The number of members reported, 225 : baptized, 7.

NOVEMBER 19TH.   *Resolved*, that 20 per cent. be added to price of the inside pews, and 15 per cent. to the outside ones.

NOVEMBER 29TH.   " A donation " was held in the basement for the benefit of Pastor, Dr. Hurd.

DECEMBER 17TH.   Pastor, and Brethren Chittenden, Benedict, McIntyre and Crawford, were appointed delegates to aid in the organization of the " Burtch Corners' " Church.

1872.

JANUARY 28TH.   Brethren Chittenden and Tapscott were appointed, as delegates, to aid in organizing the Yorkville Church.

FEBRUARY 25TH.   *Died*, in West Street, City of Brantford, Marion Hurd, wife of Rev. J. C. Hurd.

MAY 21ST.   " The Pastor, and Brethren L. Benedict, A. Benedict, George Chittenden, T. D Crawford, B. G. Tisdale, L. J. Breemer, Samuel Tapscott, John Brown and T. S. Shenston, were appointed delegates to attend the Association." Place of meeting not named.

DEACON JOHN HARRIS.

BORN, JULY 21ST, 1811; DIED, AUG. 25TH, 1887.

" *Resolved*, that $100 be allowed to Mr. Lockwood, organ-
ist for the year."

AUGUST 6TH.   " Church was asked, by the St. Catharines
Church, to associate with them and the Hamilton and Toronto
Churches in inviting and defraying the expenses of Rev. Hugh

Stowell Brown, who was expected soon to visit the United States.

The Church declined.

AUGUST 11TH. The committee reported "that in consequence of so few of the members agreeing to entertain delegates in the event of the Convention being held in Brantford, it was resolved not to invite it."

OCTOBER 20TH. The Pastor, and Brethren Shenston, Beemer, Chittenden, McIntyre, and A. Benedict, were appointed delegates to sit in council with the Boston Church, with the view of ordaining Brother J. B. Huff.

DECEMBER 1ST. "Dr. Hurd tendered his resignation, stating that he had done so thus early in order that the Church might have plenty of time to secure another Pastor before he left."

On this day was received into the Church, by letter from Beamsville, John Harris, Esq , who died on the 25th of August, 1887, at his residence, Lorne Avenue, Brantford.

It was the writer's intention to give in this work the likenesses of the ministers only who have been Pastors of the Church. But, inasmuch as Brother Harris was so pre-eminently conspicuous in connection with all that appertained to the Church and the Sunday School, both spiritually and financially, none, I am sure, will deem it out of place, my making an exception in this case.

John Harris was born in the Township of Townsend, in the County of Norfolk, July 21st, 1841, and was, consequently, forty-six years of age at the time of his death.

Of him the Brantford *Expositor* says :—

"Few men pass away amid such general regret in the community, as that attending the death of John Harris, 'President of A. Harris, Son & Co.' The feeling of a personal bereavement passes far beyond the limit of tie and kindred, and the general sentiment is that Brantford could ill spare such a man as he who has now gone over to the majority.

In the home, in the business world, in the Church, in the Sunday School, in the community, John Harris was a man among a thousand ; and he has gone in the prime of his manhood, in the flush of business success, and just when his friends were hoping that his marvellous tact and experience might be increasingly utilized to the benefit and advantage of the community of which he was such a prominent and honored citizen.

"Approachable at all times, the soul of honor, with genial greeting and utter absence of dissimulation, he was honored and respected by all with whom he came in contact, even to the humblest of his three hundred employees.

"His christianity had no prudish tinge about it. It was common, every-day christianity, which was reflected in the example and the life."

The Toronto *Globe* gave an extended notice of him, from which the following is an extract :—

"Mr. Harris' activities were not confined to business and public life alone. In religious matters he was a devoted and efficient worker, and an earnest christian.

"He was a very successful Bible class teacher, having, probably, the largest class in the city, and also was often engaged in evangelistic work. His liberality to Church objects is a matter of repute outside his own denomination, although without any ostentation, or display or disport."

The *Canadian Baptist*, over the signature "G.M.W.C.", speaks of him as follows :—

"It is a very mysterious providence, but He who makes no mistakes has so appointed, and it must be right. The loving husband, the tender father, the dutiful son, the prominent business man, the exemplary Church member, the active and eminent Christian worker, has fallen asleep in Jesus ; his "sun has gone down while it was yet day." He has ceased from his labors, he is now among the blessed dead, and his life is hid with Christ in God. When Christ, who was and is his life, shall appear, then shall our departed brother appear with his beloved Lord in glory. On the 27th the funeral took place, the services being conducted by his Pastor, Rev. G. M. W. Carey, M.A., assisted by Rev. Dr. Cochran and Rev. W. H. Porter, M.A. A large number of citizens with subdued hearts followed his body to the city of the dead, where it awaits a glorious resurrection. May the Lord graciously comfort the bereaved wife and her family, the aged parents, relatives and mourning friends in their heavy loss and sore bereavement."

The City Council, the Board of Trade, and his employees each sent letters of condolence to his widow and family.

1873.

JANUARY 19TH. The Pastor wrote from Buffalo, stating that he had accepted a call from the Cedar St. Church of that city and desiring to be relieved from the Brantford Church at once. His request was granted.

FEBRUARY 12TH. Brother B. G. Tisdale was appointed Church Treasurer, and Brother Joseph Hamlyn, Church Auditor. Reports : received during the quarter, $616.80 ; paid out, $547.22. Balance in hand, $69.58 ; Poor fund, balance in hand, $24.11.

Resolved, "that the poor-fund be disbursed by the Deacons."

FEBRUARY 23RD. The Deacons brought the names of Rev. J. L. Campbell of Chatham, and Rev. Wm. Stewart of Woodstock, before the Church as most suitable parties for the pastorate. By an unanimous standing vote, it was decided to extend a call to Brother Campbell, and that his salary be $1,000 per annum.

Brethren Crawford, Chittenden and McIntyre, were appointed delegates to the Scotland (Co. Brant) Church, for the purpose of ordaining Rev. H. L. Griffin, late of England.

MARCH 9TH. "A letter from Rev. J. L. Campbell was read, bearing the assurance that as soon as he was able to recognize the path of duty he would answer our letter."

A letter was read from Deacon Robert Morton (formerly a member of this Church) full of christian sympathy and kind exhortation, saying that as to human view his days seemed numbered, he wished to send a farewell greeting to the Church with which he had spent so many happy seasons. An answer was sent from the Church in reply.

MARCH 23RD. A letter was read from Rev. J. L. Campbell, declining to accept the Church's invitation to become their Pastor.

It having been made known that the Rev. Mr. Welton was about to visit Ontario, Brother Shenston was delegated to invite him when he came, to supply for the Brantford Church.

MARCH 27TH. *Died*—at Chatham, Ontario, in the 78th year of his age, dear Deacon Robert Morton: respected and loved by all who knew him. The following are brief extracts from his published obituary notice:

"He was born in Perthshire, Scotland. At the age of twenty-two he emigrated to this country, arriving in June, 1817, and settled in Montreal, where he resided for thirty-seven years. Shortly after reaching that city, a good Providence placed him under the influence of the preaching of that esteemed servant of Jesus Christ, the late John Gilmour, and he became a member of the Baptist Church in Montreal during the time Brother Gilmour was Pastor. He was, shortly after joining the Church, chosen to the Diaconate, an office he filled until his removal to Port Hope in 1864. Here he spent a year and a half, and was largely instrumental in the formation of the Baptist Church now in that town. From Port Hope he removed to Brantford, in 1856, connected himself with the Baptist Church there, and was appointed a Deacon therein, a position he filled until the formation of the Tabernacle Church. With this new Church, he from the first was identified, filling, as in all his former Church connection, the office of Deacon. For some months past, his health has been failing, and in the hope that a change of scene and air might be beneficial, he visited his sons, who are established in business in Chatham. A Gracious and Wise Father had, however, otherwise determined, and instead of any improvement, a gradual sinking occurred, which resulted in his death. His remains, in accordance with his own request, were brought to Brantford for interment. Our dear Brother was one of those in whom the work of grace was most marked. Added to a genial and kindly disposition, was that love which is of God. A spirit of love was the atmosphere in which he lived and moved. From the time of his conversion he possessed perfect confidence in his dear Lord, and he lived in the perpetual sunshine of His conscious favor. He seemed never to have a doubt of his acceptance ; and as might be expected, he died in 'the peace of God which passeth all understanding.' He was greatly esteemed and most tenderly beloved, and his death will be lamented by a large circle of friends.'

Rev. John Alexander preached his funeral sermon from Acts xi., 24 : " For he was a good man and full of the Holy Ghost."

Among the last, if not the very last, letters written by Deacon Morton, was a long one to the writer, breathing the very atmosphere of Beulah, by which my heart was touched. Assuming that others would be equally profited by its perusal it was my intention to insert copious extracts therefrom, but most unfortunately it cannot be found.

APRIL 6TH. A letter was granted to Ex pastor Dr. Hurd, to the Cedar Street Baptist Church, Buffalo City, of which he had become Pastor.

A private letter informs me that, " Dr. Hurd died suddenly in Burlington, Iowa, U.S. Having preached in the morning and evening, he was going upstairs to his study, when he fell in a faint at the foot of the stairs, and died about 9 that Sunday evening." Date not given.

APRIL 20TH. A letter was read from Rev. D. M. Welton, signifying his willingness to supply for us on Sabbath, May 25th, and June 1st.

MAY 18TH. The Church letter to the Association gave the following statistics : Baptized, 9 ; present number, 229. Total amount paid out, $1,874.66 : scholars in the Sunday-school, 350. Delegates to the Association,—Brethren E. Benedict, Geo. Chittenden, Thos. Crawford, J. Harris, A.

Benedict and J. Hamlyn. Where held, not stated. The Church letter to the Association among various other things said :—

"The members of the Church are thoroughly united, and earnest in their efforts that the cause of Christ may not suffer in the absence of pastoral oversight, and fervent prayers are continually being offered to the great Head of the Church, that He may send us a Pastor whose labors may be abundantly blessed among us."

JUNE 8TH. Rev. Mr. Welton, having preached for us, it was decided to take a vote by ballot, with the understanding that if two-thirds of the members present did not vote in favor of extending to him a call, one would not be given.

It was found that two-thirds had not voted for him, consequently the call was not given.

JULY 27TH. The Supply Committee recommended that the Church extend a call to Rev. W. H. Porter, A.M., of Yarmouth, Nova Scotia. This recommendation was immediately acted upon, and resulted in an unanimous ballot vote in favor of extending a call to Mr. Porter ; and, by a subsequent resolution, his salary was to be $1,200 per annum.

OCTOBER 2ND. Died at Brantford, Grace Harrison, aged 20 years. This dear young Sister was received by the Church, May 26th, 1868, and baptized by the Rev. William Stewart with four others, two of whom (Jane Tanton and Mrs. E. S. Webster) preceded her to the " Happy, happy land, far, far away." She was connected with the Sabbath School as scholar and teacher for sixteen years, and declared only an hour or two before she died, that it was the truth she had learnt therein that had led her to give her heart to the Saviour. Death did not alarm her, for the blessed doctrine of salvation through the merits of her Redeemer which she had learnt in the Sabbath School, and for three years taught therein, she found to be more than adequate for the dread emergency. At one time she said to her father, " I would not change my position to be Queen of England." Only two hours before her death while surrounded by a cluster of friends, the writer asked her, among other questions, whether she had enjoyed and profited by our meetings in the basement, she replied "very much." " I should like to sing ' Shall we gather at the river '—I would like to hear it sung now—will some one please

REV. W. H. PORTER,

PASTOR FROM JULY, 1875, TO JANUARY, 1880.

start it?" Agreeable to her request a few verses of that beautiful hymn were sung and sobbed by the few friends clustered around her dying bed, *Poor Grace joining with the most distinct voice of them all.* Pages would be required to record all the triumphant expressions which passed her lips during the last twenty-four hours of her life, and which can never be forgotten by those who heard them. Suffice it to add that during the delightful, though awfully affecting scene, she had full possession of her mental faculties, and in the assured persuasion of her approaching dissolution, her faith was firm, her patience unexhausted, and her hopes bright—gloriously bright. During the awfully affecting scene, the expression of her smiling countenance was animating in the extreme and gave the most positive assurance to all around that her hope was "full of immortality." So silent and easy was her departure that as if asleep, without the least motion she breathed, and—ceased to breathe.

OCTOBER 21ST. It was *resolved* to allow Mr. Porter $100 for the expenses of moving.

1874.

FEBRUARY 11TH. Annual meeting. Brother Tisdale resigned the Treasurership, and Brother T. S. Shenston was appointed in his stead. Balance in Poor Fund, $64.03. A quarterly statement only of Church finance given.

FEBRUARY 15TH. Brethren Tapscott and J. Harris were appointed Deacons by ballot.

MARCH 24TH. On this day there was received by baptism, a dear young Sister, an account of whose death is inserted here.

Died—September 1st, at the residence of H. J. Arnold, Esq., city of Rochester, of typhoid fever, Hattie D. Porter, eldest daughter of Rev. W. H. Porter, aged 18 years.

Extracts from "In Memoriam":—

"Everything that love or skill could do for her was done, but still the fever raged till the living fuel was consumed.

"On Thursday evening, at 10 o'clock, the weary feet of the unconscious sufferer touched the river brink—a shuddering seemed to pass over her, as deeper and deeper in the cold waves she sank, till the waters reached her neck, when, all at once, the shivering ceased ; as though the voice of Him she had learned to lean upon from childhood spoke to her— 'when thou passeth through the waters, I will be with thee,' etc., etc.

"At a very early age she exhibited womanly ways and religious tendencies. At the age of 11 she was baptized, and united with the First Baptist Church, Brantford, and was ever a willing witness and active worker for Christ. 'She won the love of all' said a friend near Paris, in writing to us of her visit there.

"Brother Shenston telegraphed :—'I weep with you for the loss of that dear, dear girl'; and in writing, said :—I always loved that dear, dear girl ! Indeed, everything about her was lovable !

" A very dear friend, in writing from Rochester, says :—'This great sorrow has taken hold of us as no other sorrow ever did ; and, strange to say, though I think you will understand it, if no one else does—it has softened our hearts, so that I think we shall always be happier for it.'

" Several friends, as they viewed the corpse, lovingly lingered, and tearfully kissed the pallid face of the sleeper. Her remains were taken to St. Catharines, thence to Brantford, where they were laid to rest beside her mother's.

APRIL 5TH. Brethren McIntyre, Whitham, Grant, Tisdale, Broughton, Large, Sutton, Harris and Hamlyn were appointed a committee "on chapel repairs."

APRIL 17TH. *Died*—this day, Mrs. Helen Morton, aged 74, about one year after the death of her beloved husband.

"She was one of those women whom to know, as to her spiritual character, required more than a casual acquaintance with her personal and domestic life. With less of Mary's quiet contemplativeness, and more of Martha's matter-of-fact activity, it may have been the case that being 'careful and troubled about many things' may at times have concealed the depth and spirituality of her piety. You could scarcely know the woman without intrusion into the privacy and sanctity of the home. She was one who felt that woman's truest and noblest sphere of action was that of her own family, the claims of which she could not sacrifice to the outside calls of duty. She ever felt, as every wife and mother should feel, that a careful attention to the secular duties of domestic life was one effective way of glorifying God. Had Mrs. Morton not been the home wife she was, Deacon Morton might not have been the pillar in the Church he was. But under a practical exterior there was a deep undercurrent of religious life. If her family and household had a first they had not an exclusive claim.

Nothing could interest our Sister more than tidings of the welfare of Zion. While confined to the house by sickness she always eagerly enquired when I called as to any indications of spiritual prosperity in the Church. I often noticed that when her mind was engaged with worldly cares that demanded attention, she seemed ever ready at once to enter heartily into conversation on religious subjects, and in these gave evidence of deep spiritual experience. Her faith in the Redeemer's merits was strong and unclouded, and her consciousness of a personal interest in these was seldom clouded by doubts. Her longing to depart and be with Christ was intensified as she neared the close of the journey. Amid the severe sufferings that preceded the day of her death she often repeated, with a sense of personal appropriation, the precious promises of the Gospel spoken in her hearing.

"During the night that preceded her death, her mind was evidently reverting to those early days, when she and her dear husband received so much good under the ministry of the late Rev. John Gilmour of Montreal, and to those mental conflicts and enquiries which led to her separation from the Church of her fathers, and her solemn consecration to God in baptism. 'Christian baptism!' and 'Bruce's schoolhouse!' doubtless referred to the time and events of 1830, when in the old schoolhouse on McGill Street, Montreal, the first Baptist Church of Montreal was formed.

Take it all in all, our Sister's character was a well-balanced, robust Christian development that commanded respect and confidence, and was well fitted for grappling with the stern realities of everyday Christian life. The memory she has left behind is a precious legacy to her children and to the Church."

The foregoing has been kindly furnished me by Rev. John Alexander.

This Sister was received, together with her husband the late Deacon Morton, by letter from Port Hope Church, July 6, 1856.   She is the mother of Mrs. George Foster, and Andrew and James Y. Morton.

APRIL 19TH.   Building committee reported :—"that it would require $900 to do the necessary chapel repairs"; and a committee was appointed to canvass the members of the Church for this amount.

MAY 5TH.   The Chairman of the Church repairs committee reported favorably as to finances.   Brethren Broughton, Chittenden and J. Harris were appointed to superintend the work "at once."

MAY 31ST.   The following Brethren were appointed delegates to attend the Association to be held "at Burtch," namely; Dickie, Chittenden, Crawford, Benedict, Tisdale, Hatcher, Harris, Putnam Sen., Beemer, Roy and Passmore. The number of members reported was 291.   Baptisms during the year, 48; amount paid for Church and denominational purposes, $2,459.44; Scholars in Sabbath School, 393.   In the Church letter, allusion is made to the blessing of a good Pastor, (Rev. W. H. Porter,) and that 91 boys and 116 girls in the Sunday School had signed the Temperance pledge.

AUGUST 2ND.   The Rev. L. Jewett, the well-known Missionary to the Telugoos was remaining at the house of the writer for several days.

The Pastor suggested that some suitable acknowledgement be made him.   The same was done but the writer does not remember what was given.

SEPTEMBER 15TH.   A committee of ladies was appointed to make preparation for the entertainment of a portion of the delegates who would be in attendance at the Provincial Sabbath School convention, to be held at Brantford.

OCTOBER 18TH. It was agreed to substitute the " Baptist Hymn Book " for the " Psalmist."

NOVEMBER 1ST. On this day was received into the membership of the Brantford Church, and died at the residence of her husband, Geo. W. Brown, some years later, Sarah E. Brown, in the 31st year of her age. The following is a short extract from her obituary notice :—

"She did not suffer long, for when the pale messenger called, she soon entered into the presence of the Master. Her death was like her life, calm, quiet and peaceful. Resigned and submissive to God's will, she gave up all her earthly care, husband, children, parents, friends, and trusting in her Saviour, passed away from earth to be with the redeemed in Paradise. At Belvidere, Ill., when quite young, she was born again, and shortly afterwards she professed her faith in Christ, was baptized,and became a member of the South Baptist Church. About twelve years ago she was married, moved to Brantford, and joined the First Church.

NOVEMBER 17TH. The Church was asked by the ministerial conference of the city if they would be willing to change their night of prayer-meeting from Tuesday. In answer, it was *resolved*, "that, if all the Churches of the city agree to use Wednesday evening for prayer-meeting, we would adopt the same."

NOVEMBER 22ND. It was *resolved* to accept the proposition of the various Churches of the city, and agree to change our night of prayer-meeting from Tuesday to Wednesday for the sake of union.

1875.

JANUARY 2ND. *Died*—this day, aged 73 years, Mrs. Rachel Foster.

"Her funeral sermon was preached on Sunday evening, the 10th of the same month by the writer, who can best say what he would like to say by giving the reader the following extract from that sermon. The text was Rev. xiv., 13: 'Blessed are the dead that die in the Lord.'

"Never were words more appropriate than these, as applied to the venerable saint whose mortal remains were last Monday consigned to their resting place to await the resurrection of the just; and never has this text received a more forcible illustration than in her peaceful and triumphant death. Hers had been the Christian's life, and hers was the Christian's death. Although only baptized some considerable time after her marriage, she had been recognized and respected as a Christian young woman for a long time previous. Nature had done much for her, but grace refined and ennobled nature's work. Hers was one of the sweetest, gentlest and most beautiful natures we ever knew. Her piety was deep, sincere, un-

7

affected, the result of profound views of her personal unworthiness and sinfulness, and of the all-sufficiency of the righteousness of Christ, to which she ever clung as her only, but her all-prevailing plea. If ever there was a human being who had a minimum of those failings incident to fallen humanity, that being was Rachel Foster. If ever there was one who could claim the possession of those virtues which commend their possessor to the confidence and affection of others, our departed Sister and mother in Israel might assert pre-eminence in that direction. Yet she seemed profoundly unconscious of such excellencies, and often oppressed with a sense of her great sinfulness, and of the degree in which her actions and motives were tainted by sin. Without a doubt of her pardon and acceptance, she felt even to the close of life that the prayer of the publican was one that she must use.

"Her piety, developed on the basis of natural disposition, while sincere, unaffected, beautiful, was unobtrusive and undemonstrative. She was made, not to lead in some great crusade, or to control and guide the activities of social life, but to shine in her own sphere, where her genial and Christ-like influence was always felt, stamping its own impress on those around her, and imparting noble Christian impulses which, through the loved ones who survive her, may be felt for generations to come.

Her children can never know how much they owe to that sainted mother, nor society so far as reached through these children. Seasons can be recalled by some of them, possibly by all of them, when she led them by the hand to the seclusion of her closet and there knelt in earnest prayer with them. Nor was it only her prayers with them, but her constant pleadings for them for which they have cause to be thankful. Many of these prayers for children's children remain yet to be answered; but they are recorded in heaven, and she died in expectation of their being answered in God's own time. * * * Our departed Sister exhibited a most unselfish and self-sacrificing spirit. She was always thinking of and planning for the comfort and welfare of others, and that often when her own ailments might have pardonably absorbed all her attention. Of these she had little to say; so little, that, combined with her habitual cheerfulness, few would suspect how much at times she suffered. Her appreciation of any little attention shewn her was really remarkable. Her last words to me the evening before she died, as she clasped my hand in hers, were: "I thank you for all your kindness, my dear, dear Pastor." Her sympathy with the cause of Christ was deep and constant. Even in seasons of discouragement, she always had a cheering word, and a wonderful knack of giving prominence to the bright side. She never had a harsh word to say of anyone, and if one aspect of some questionable act or conduct were more favorable than another, to that she gave prominence; and if any excuse were possible, she never forgot to urge it. There is much more that I could say, but I must close with this summary: our Sister, Mrs. Foster, came as near the ideal of a perfect Christian character as any one I ever knew."

The foregoing was kindly furnished me by Rev. John Alexander.

This Sister was the mother of George and Thomas Foster, Mrs. I. Cockshutt, Mrs. William Buck, Mrs. F. Ellis and Mrs. William Young, all of Brantford. Was a member of the First Church prior to 1850.

MARCH 21ST. The recommendation of a committee to extend the chapel at the back, and slate the roof, was passed.

MARCH 28TH It was *resolved* that Brother Shenston be relieved from any subscription to the fund for the enlargement of the Church, in order that the proposed Mission Church in the East Ward may be proceeded with at once with his aid.

APRIL 18TH. "The Deacons presented the following report:—Brother S—— ——, a member of this Church, having long felt the great desirableness of commencing a new interest in the East Ward of this town : and being convinced that it would be hazardous to delay the matter any longer : and feeling that the cause of Christ equally required that this chapel should be immediately enlarged : and believing that the Church would be unable to grapple with both these undertakings this year, offers himself to erect a neat brick chapel (38 x 58), capable of holding 300 persons, contributing $500 towards it himself, and advancing the balance by way of a loan, at a low rate of interest, he holding the deed of the property in his own hands until he was refunded the amount of the loan. This offer, however, was conditional on the remaining members of the Church making large improvements on *this* chapel."

After a somewhat lengthy discussion it was *resolved* : "That the land be held by the Church, and the chapel and all matters connected with its erection, and management after its erection, be under the entire control of the Church, as the same may, from time to time, be expressed by resolution passed at any Sabbath morning meeting of the Church."

Resolved : "That Brethren A. Harris, J. Harris, and T. S. Shenston, be a committee to carry out the wishes of the Church, as expressed in the foregoing resolution."

Resolved : "That, inasmuch as the aforesaid committee have agreed to contribute $1.00 to every $2.00 contributed by the remaining 340 members of the Church, it is, therefore, recommended, that they be allowed to expend the whole amount of their subscription on the East Ward Chapel, and, in the event of their united subscriptions, and any further sum furnished by the Church, being insufficient to finish the said chapel, that the Church borrow, by mortgage on the said premises, a sum sufficient to cover such deficiency."

The Church appointed a committee to consider the best means of meeting the proposal of the said three Brethren.

MAY 2ND. It was *resolved* "that the East Ward Chapel
be 5 feet longer, and 3 feet wider than the original plan."

MAY 9TH. The committee reported "that it would cost
$4,000 to enlarge the West Street Chapel, slate the roof, and
make other requisite repairs ; and, in view of the contemplated
addition being made, it will be necessary to purchase sufficient
land for the removal of the sheds, and if the said land can be
at once secured, let the erection of the addition be commenced
immediately. If otherwise, let the addition be dispensed with
for the present with the understanding that the land be secured
as soon as possible, and the addition be proceeded with—that
if the whole work is done let $3,000 be raised by mortgage on
the chapel, and $1,000 by subscriptions extending over four
years."
If the addition is not made, let $2,000 be borrowed by
mortgage and $2,000 be raised by subscription extending over
three years ; in either case the mortgage to be paid by annual
instalments of $1,000 each."
The report unanimously adopted.

MAY 16TH. A. Benedict and Geo. Chittenden elected
Deacons by ballot.

MAY 30TH. The Pastor, and Brethren Chittenden,
Benedict, Crawford, Tisdale, McIntyre, Yule, File, Roy,
A. Harris, Geo. Chittenden, J. Harris and A. McMichael
be appointed delegates to attend the Association to be held
at Paris. The Church letter to the Association reported 435
members ; baptized during the year, 128 ; pupils in Sunday
School, 343. Total amount paid for Church purposes,
$2,531.57.
Among other things said in the Church letter is the following :—"As Pastor and people, we are still happily united.
Our Sabbath services are well attended, and the labors of our
Pastor appreciated. Some of our Brethren, feeling the importance of establishing a Baptist interest in the East ward of
our city, have nobly contributed of their means and labor to
the undertaking."

JULY 15TH. Brethren A. Benedict, Geo. Chittenden and
Roy were appointed delegates to attend a council —for
what purpose is not named.

JULY 18TH. The Deacons reported that the East ward interest was assuming an important aspect ; and they therefore moved the following resolution :—"That the Deacons, the East ward Building Committee, and fifteen Brethren be now appointed a Committee, to whom, for the time being, shall be intrusted the East ward interests : and, as soon as they are prepared to recommend a definite policy with regard to the same, to report to the Church for their approval :—Brethren of the East ward, Burr, Howie, Westover, Gunston, Yule and Baldwin ; of the First Church, Murray, Grant, Broughton, Brown, Wm. Pearce, McIntyre, Dengate, Winter and Hamlyn. Report adopted.

EAST WARD CHURCH.

ERECTED IN 1871.

AUGUST 20TH. *Resolved*, "that the proper steps be immediately taken, to ascertain whether there is a sufficient number residing in the neighborhood of the East Ward Chapel who desire to be formed into a distinct Church." Carried, and such a meeting when called to be held in the East Ward Chapel on Friday evening next, of which notice was to be given.

AUGUST 22ND. Leave was granted to Pastor Porter "to lengthen out his stay in England so long as he may see fit."

SEPTEMBER 5TH. The East Ward Committee reported, "that the parties who were most interested in the new undertaking, were perfectly unanimous for the formation of a new Church in connection with the chapel, and that your committee have no hesitation in recommending that a Church be formed there at once; and that this Church give prayers, sympathy and aid to the new Church when formed." The report adopted.

SEPTEMBER 12TH. Under date, August 27th, 1875, the following parties, in a pointed letter, ask to be dismissed for the purpose of forming the East Ward Baptist Church:

Samuel Tapscott,	Wm. Bishop,
Mrs. Samuel Tapscott,	Mrs. Harriet Bishop,
John Yule,	Edwin Gunston,
Mrs. John Yule,	Mrs. Jane Gunston,
Thos. Webster.	A. W. Hazelton,
Mrs. Thomas Webster,	Mrs. E. Hazelton,
Wm. Batchelor,	Miss Amelia Hazelton,
Mrs. Wm. Batchelor,	S. W. Hazelton,
Benj. Batchelor,	W. G. Burr,
Miss Lizzie Batchelor,	Mrs. W. G. Burr,
Miss A. Cunningham,	A. E. Westover.
F. S. Field,	

The foregoing applicants were all dismissed and in one letter.

The Pastor and Brethren Benedict, Crawford, J. Harris, A. Harris, Grant, McIntyre and Barber, were appointed delegates to attend the recognition service in connection with the East Ward Baptist Church on Monday, the 20th inst., at 3 p.m.

The Pastor asked for a preaching license for Brother George Chittenden. Granted.

SEPTEMBER 19TH. Inasmuch as the pew-rents are not meeting the expenditure of the Church —*Resolved*, "to adopt the weekly offering system." (*Weakly* enough.)

OCTOBER 1ST. It was *Resolved* "to exonerate the members, dismissed from the East Ward Church, from their subscriptions towards the repair-fund of the Church."

1876.

JANUARY 26TH. Brother Hamlyn was presented with a purse of money and an address by the Church, and an album by his Bible Class, on the eve of his departure for England

The Pastor was requested to publish his sermon on " Baptism " in book form.

JANUARY 28TH. *Died*—at his own home, in Woodstock, of pulmonary consumption, James Colton Yule, M.A., late Professor of New Testament Interpretation and Evidences, in the Canadian Literary Institute—now Woodstock College.

Brother Yule was a worthy member of this Church for over two years ; and many who were then his pupils here, still hold his name in loving remembrance. The following are some extracts from his memorial—" Records of a Vanished Life"—published by Mrs. Yule, his widow, in this year :—

" From the *Canadian Baptist*, Feb. 3rd, 1876 : 'On Friday last, about half-past two in the morning, without a fear or doubt, Prof. J. C. Yule calmly fell asleep in Jesus. Of cultured intellect, exact scholarship, and fine taste ; possessing a singular combination of quietness and power, with a heart deeply imbued with the love of Christ, and burning with a desire to serve Him in the salvation of souls, he seemed to be indeed a chosen vessel, sanctified and meet for the Master's use. Seldom has the process of committing ' ashes to ashes, and dust to dust,' been performed with more of the sure and certain hope of a blessed resurrection. Seldom has any young man in his prime left the record of a purer spirit or a nobler life.' "

" From the funeral sermon by Dr. Fyfe, we take the following :—
'What more perplexing event than the one which has occasioned the remarks I have thus far made, can we consider? A man who, by great self-denial and patient exertions, fitted himself for an important department of service in the Church of Christ—a department which needed his services, and for which he was well prepared—is cut down, almost as soon as he entered upon his work.
' The life and labors of Mr. Yule stand out as an example to students for the ministry. He did ' covet earnestly the best gifts.' ' This one thing, he did.' Few men more eagerly or persistently sought to discipline their powers and store their minds with useful knowledge. He had a cultivated taste as a writer, and a nice appreciation even of those delicate shades of meaning which (in the original) enrich and adorn the sacred Scriptures.
' In a word, he laid a broad and solid foundation on which to build for others a grand structure of Scripture knowledge. This great object stood before him, namely, to make known to his fellowmen the unsearchable riches of Christ.' "

" A resolution passed at a meeting of the Y.M.C.A., of University College, Toronto, reads as follows :—

'That we, the members of the Y.M.C.A., of University College, Toronto, place upon record our deep regret at the loss of one, who, as one of the founders, and the first President of the Association, and as an earnest worker and sympathetic Christian Brother, endeared himself to this Association.'"

"Of him another has sung :—

'Thou hast entered the land without shadows,
Thou who, 'neath the shadow, so long
Hast sat with thy white hands close folded,
And lips that could utter no song :—
Through a rift in the cloud, for an instant,
Thine eyes caught a glimpse of that shore,
And earth with its gloom was forgotten,
And Heaven is thine own evermore !

'Oh joy for thee, glorified spirit !
With Jesus forever to be,
And with sinless and Sainted companions
The bliss of His paradise see !—
Joy, joy !—for the warfare is ended,
Thy perilous journey is o'er,
And, above the deep gloom of earth's shadows,
Thou art dwelling in light evermore.'"

MARCH 5TH.   It was *Resolved* "to borrow $600, for six months, to meet present demands."

MAY 21ST.   The Pastor, and Brethren Crawford, G. Chittenden, A. Benedict, J. Harris, J. Barber, Broughton, A. Harris, McIntyre, Hatcher, Putnam and Potts, were appointed delegates to attend the Association to be held in the Tabernacle Church, in Brantford, on the first Friday in June.   The Church reported :—Membership, 448 : Sunday School pupils, 310 ; total amount paid during the year, $2,519.53.

JULY 9TH.   Rev. Dr. L. Jewett and wife were present at our services, they being guests of Bro. Shenston.

JULY 30TH.   *Died*—At Brantford, after a lingering illness of consumption, Eliza Jane, wife of Rev. W. H. Porter, aged 35 years.   The following is from her "Obituary" published in *The Advocate*:

"She died as she had lived, beloved by all, but most by those who knew her best, and in calm and perfect reliance upon her Saviour.   Her Christian life was too beautiful to be recorded.   It will rather live in memory where by many it will be long and fondly cherished."

"Her nature, though retiring, was courageous ; and to her heart and conscience, her loved ones and her sorrow—though with sweet unconsciousness—she knew not but to be a martyr.

"To have seen her, and heard the heavenly expressions of her last hours, was a rare privilege."

"We cannot dismiss this sketch without expressing our sincere gratitude to the many kind friends who have so generously sought to alleviate Mrs. Porter's sufferings, and our sorrow the Sisters who have so tenderly watched, and the Brethren who have so ardently prayed for and sympathized; the friend who so generously sued the favor of furnishing so elegant a casket; and the other Brother who, to alleviate the burden, quietly dropped a cheque of $50 into our letter box; and last, but not least, our highly esteemed family physician, Dr. James Digby."

SEPTEMBER 7TH. Brethren G. Chittenden, Crawford, Barber and A. Harris, were appointed delegates to meet with the Onondaga Church on the 14th of the month, to consider the advisability of ordaining Brother N. Wolverton to the work of the ministry.

DECEMBER, 31ST. On this day was received as a candidate for baptism, dear, dear young Sister Florence Large, and was baptized.

This dear girl had attended our Sabbath School from childhood till she removed to England, in 1880. She was gifted with more spiritual magnetism than any young person with whom I have ever been acquainted. Having one of her photographs by me, and she being a foreign missionary, I thought it would be appropriate to have her likeness in this book. She was born in Brantford, July 3rd, 1857, educated at the Brantford Ladies' College and at Toronto. In April, 1880, she left Ontario to visit her relations in England, hoping that such a change of climate would improve her poor health. While in England at the earnest solicitations of friends, who readily recognized her talents, she addressed several large meetings with much acceptance. In 1881 she was united in marriage to Mr. F. Nicholson, an earnest Christian and successful Evangelist. In the fall of 1885, she, with her husband and two children, went to India at their own expense "to live and labor for Christ in that land of idolatry." They located at Lahore, where, through her instrumentality, several were brought to a knowledge of the "truth as it is in Jesus." From Lahore they removed to Derah, where, in addition to other missionary work, she paid a weekly visit to the Leper Asylum in which there were more than seventy lepers. A friend writes me:

"The poor creatures loved to hear her play and sing to them of a 'Saviour's love and a home above, a joy they all might know.' When the master heard she was dead he hurried over to her bungalow and threw himself on the ground in front of the veranda and cried most bitterly, and said to Mr. Nicholson, 'She was too good to stay down here with us, so God has taken her to live with Him.' The sorrow of the poor lepers was most touching. One of them said, ' he loved her as the flowers do the earth, and when she spoke to us of the place where pain and death never enter we forgot our own troubles.'"

She died of cholera on the 1st July, 1887. Her mother closes a letter to me thus :

> "Sleep on, beloved, sleep and take thy rest,
> Lay down thy head upon thy Saviour's breast ;
> We loved thee well, but Jesus loves thee best.
>   Good night,
> 'Till the resurrection morning."

With this dear Sister the writer corresponded while she was residing in Embro, Toronto and England. I give an extract or two from her letters :

"DECEMBER 23RD., 1879, EMBRO. Dear Mr. Shenston I often pray for you, especially on the Lord's day. I have such sweet season with Jesus asking Him to aid and bless you and all His dear servants who are engaged in the large harvest field. I tell Him of your work in the Sabbath School, and ask Him to help and bless you."

"AUGUST 24TH, 1879. Since I had the privilege of walking and talking with you last September I have been so blessed with many experiences of His abundant, abiding and never failing forgiveness. I here want to tell you I love to think and pray for the work of the Lord to prosper in the dear First Baptist Church of Brantford."

"Again:—"Another sweet little work He has given me to do is the visiting from house to house with my Bible. I find some care-worn mothers who are strengthened and refreshed by a little portion of the word and a season of prayer, which affords a good opportunity of praying for the poor husbands who are out of Christ. I had the privilege of visiting eleven families and realized the power of God's presence in speaking, reading and prayers."

Again :—"Mr. and Mrs. Needham could not remain with us any longer. It did seem so good to me to see some one who had just come from Brantford, and ask after dear friends there ; and then your short letter, though short, it was so very welcome, and brought such longing to be with and see you all again."

Again :—" *   *   * The Lord has used Florence as His instrument and she wants Him to have all the glory. So often when I have enjoyed a happy season in witnessing for Jesus in my way, I think of how I wish I could tell Mr. Shenston I shall never forget the first Sabbath School Superintendent I ever knew and loved."

"ABERDEENSHIRE, SCOTLAND,
                    "November 8th, 1880.

"You have always been such a dear friend to me, that I like to tell you from time to time of our dear Lord's dealings with me. I do wish the broad Atlantic Ocean did not separate me from my dear Canada.

MISS FLORENCE LARGE.

I have felt nothing so hard as giving up Canada, my own native land, with all its happy associations and the many loved ones there. God only knows what it is costing me in the flesh, my heart is so selfish. I have offered myself to the Lord for India, and went forth from my home, feeling that if He should send me forth into that field, I could say, by His grace— 'Here am I, Lord, send me.' I think the Lord is shewing me that He has work for me first in England. Oh! Mr. Shenston, how wonderfully the Lord has been dealing with me since I last saw you. My dear Mr. Shenston, I cannot tell you the feelings and memories awakening in my heart as I write to you. I hear the sweet echo of God's living voice as it has and doth move me above the things of the world, and how that gentle Spirit has been working in me for His glory; how you have often been the messenger of God to my soul, when your loving words of counsel and exhortation to the children of the Sunday School have fallen upon my heart and left deep impressions there, and I can look back to those loving bright greetings; the long, warm shake of the hand, and kind words.

How God has blessed to me many lessons learned in the dear old First Baptist Church of Brantford!

"Now let me say here, my very dear friend, go on 'sowing beside all waters,' and I must just tell you that *every* Saturday and Sunday I pray for you, and have done so for a long time, and I *expect* blessings *for you.*"

1877.

FEBRUARY 22ND. A house on the south side of Chatham street was leased for a term of years for a parsonage.

FEBRUARY 25TH. Brethren J. Harris and J. T. Barber were re-elected Deacons.

MAY 6TH. Brethren G. Chittenden, T. D. Crawford, J. T. Barber, A. Harris, R. Grant, J. B. Moore and W. J. Beal, were appointed delegates to attend the Association to be held this year at Dundas, June 1st.

The Church letter this year reported the membership 455 : baptized during the year, 23 ; pupils in Sunday School, 250 : total amount paid for all purposes, $1,694.71 : value of Church property, $18,000, with a debt of $2,850 thereon.

JULY 26TH. The Pastor and Brethren Chittenden, Barber, Beal, Grobb and Geo. Chittenden, jun., were appointed delegates to meet in council with the Dundas Church, on July 31st, "for the purpose of ordaining Brother Ira Smith to the work of the Christian ministry."

AUGUST 30TH. Brother L. Benedict was appointed Treasurer of the Church Debt Fund.

SEPTEMBER 29TH. Thursday, Missionary Rev. John Craig, was present and gave an address.

Resolved, "that a Council be called, Oct. 12th, to consider the propriety of setting apart Brother Deacon George Chittenden to the work of an Evangelist."

OCTOBER 7TH. This was the 4th Anniversary of Pastor Porter's pastorate of the Church, and an Anniversary Sermon was preached.

OCTOBER 12TH. The Council for the ordination of Bro. Chittenden passed the following resolution :—"That the Council express their great satisfaction with the statement of Brother Chittenden, and encouraging his gifts for Evangelistic work, would recommend the First Baptist Church, of Brantford, of which he is a member, to give expression to this recognition by licensing our Brother to preach the Gospel."

DECEMBER 30TH. A Committee was appointed to consider the financial condition of the Church with a view to arrange a settlement of outstanding debts.

1878.

JANUARY 6TH. "Moved by Brother Winter, and seconded by Brother Large, that the sum of $1,400 be raised by way of mortgage on the Chapel, to discharge some of the outstanding debt." Carried.

MARCH 3RD. The following letter was received from the East Ward Baptist Church :

"At a meeting of the Trustees and Managing Committee of the East Ward Baptist Church, at which your Church was also represented by your Pastor and Brother A. Harris, the following recommendation to the East Ward Baptist Church was unanimously agreed to, namely :—'That the Church be carried on as an independent Church, under the supervision of the First Baptist Church, of Brantford, with Pastor Porter as Moderator, until such time as it may be able to secure a Pastor of its own : and that the Board of Deacons of the First Baptist Church be represented at its business meetings ; and that Brethren Barwell, Westover and Tapscott, be a committee to present this proposition to the First Church, requesting their assent thereto.' Passed unanimously by the East Ward Baptist Church, January 28th. The above was passed unanimously on the understanding that the First Church should be released from all financial responsibility."

MARCH 10TH.   Brethren George Winter, Benedict and Beal, were, by ballot, elected Deacons.

MARCH 21ST.   On this day was received as a member of this Church, by letter from the East Ward Church, Alfred Popplewell, who died at his residence, Brant Avenue, Brantford, on the 6th of July, 1886, aged 29 years.

"The deceased was the only descendant of the late F. Popplewell, and son-in-law of A. Harris, Esq.   On Tuesday the 22nd ult., he attended the funeral of his sister-in-law, Mrs. F. Chalcraft ; on the 29th he was a pallbearer at the burial of Mrs. George Brown, and on the same day the next week he passed into the silent land.   The command, 'Set thine house in order, for thou shalt die and not live,' applies to the young as well as the old.   His remains were borne to the grave on the 8th inst., and followed by a multitude of friends, for he was widely known and greatly beloved.   Our departed Brother was an esteemed member of the First Church for about eight years.   He was a cheerful, Christian worker, interested in the Sunday School, and always ready to do what he could for the happiness and spiritual profit of the young.   ' Not slothful in business, fervent in spirit, serving the Lord ;' a devoted husband, a kind father, a dutiful son ; he will be much missed ; his death has made a sad vacancy."

MAY 23RD.   The Pastor and Brethren Chittenden, File, A. Benedict and James Cox, were appointed delegates to attend the ordination of Brother George B. Davis, at Onondaga.

JUNE 2ND   The Pastor and Brethren Chittenden, Benedict, Crawford, A. Harris, Tisdale, James Cox and J. B. Moore, were appointed delegates to attend the Association to be held with the Beverley Church.   Reported :— Members, 460 ; baptized during the year, 21.

It was resolved to change the Sunday evening services from 6.30 to 7 o'clock.

JULY 31ST.   *Died*—Erastus Benedict, aged 71, for many years a useful and valued member.

AUGUST 19TH.   A Committee was appointed to make arrangements for the coming Convention, which was to be held in Brantford.

OCTOBER 3RD.   The Pastor and Brethren Chittenden, Cox and Brown, were appointed to meet with the Galt Church, to ordain Brother Clark.

1879.

JANUARY 30TH. It was *resolved*, "that Mr. Hammond, an Evangelist, be invited to labor amongst us, and the Pastor and Brethren T. S. Shenston and J. Harris, appointed a Committee to make arrangements therefor."

APRIL 3RD. *Died*—This day, Francis Foster, aged 74 years.

"This Brother was in many respects a remarkable man, sprung from a family of more than ordinary intelligence and energy. His brother, George Foster, was well known, not only throughout their native Lancashire, as one of the grandest of self-made men, but throughout England as the friend and business partner of the late Richard Cobden. With less of the *suaviter in modo* than his brother, he possessed all the robustness of character, and sturdy independence that distinguished George. With a mind less broadened by liberal culture and contact with some of the most scholarly and thorough business men of his day, his tendency was to take a narrower and more-exclusive view of men and things. But, notwithstanding the disadvantage of early training and associations, he was a broad minded and uncompromising Christian man. The strong convictions he felt in certain theological and ecclesiastical questions, at times inclined him to be intolerant towards those who differed from him. But what he believed to be God's truth he believed with all his soul; and what he felt to be his duty he followed, even if it left him to walk alone. One thing about him was certain, he exalted Christ above all human system in opinions, and magnified the sovereign grace of God in the salvation of the sinner. His labors for Christ in his early years were abundant and greatly blessed. Souls were converted under his preaching, who long years afterwards told us of the blessing he had been to them; and the little Church he formed at the 'Landing' was for a considerable time the centre of Gospel influences. To his early connections and that of his family with the First Church of Brantford, that Church owes obligations beyond what it can estimate. All of us who knew him had confidence in him as a thorough Christian man, who loved and studied his Bible, and sought to honor Christ, but whose idiosyncrasies and strong self-will, sometimes hindered his usefulness, and at times partially concealed the best features of his character. His trust in Christ was simple and child-like, and back of a brusque exterior there was a gentleness and warmth of heart which they who knew him best could best appreciate. We shall ever thank God that we knew Francis Foster, for though we had many a tilt with him, we always respected him for his sterling adherence to what he believed to be truth and duty."

The foregoing notice was kindly furnished by Rev. John Alexander, who knew the deceased well for several years. Mr. Foster was the father of George and Thomas Foster, Mrs. Cockshutt, Mrs. Wm. Buck, Mrs. F. Ellis and Mrs. Young, all of the city of Brantford. He became a member of the First Church some time prior to 1850.

APRIL 20TH. Sabbath. On this day the right hand of fellowship was given to fifty-three recently baptized members, among whom was gentle, unassuming Willie Winter, the oldest son of Deacon George Winter, and grandson of the late Deacon William Winter, aged 24 years. This dear young Brother died at Woodstock, July 27th, 1890, while this book was in the hands of the printer, of whom the published "Obituary" notice says :

"The young man whose death we now record was converted to Christ when a mere boy through the agency of E. P. Hammond, Evangelist, and baptized into the fellowship of the First Baptist Church, Brantford, by the Rev. W. H. Porter, the then Pastor. For some years he entertained thoughts of the Gospel ministry, but not until about two years ago, did he fully decide to give himself to the work. About that time the Lord opened his way to a course of preparation in Woodstock College. Although his course in the College was short, yet he had won by the Godly life and earnest work the love and confidence of both professors and students. As an evidence of the confidence placed in him by the Baptists of Woodstock, he was chosen as the most suitable man to take charge of the missions under the supervision of the Woodstock Church. Our young Brother longed to enter upon the work for which he had been willing to give up all, but the Master ordered otherwise. After a brief illness, and without any thought of a serious issue, he was suddenly and unsuspectedly called home. The report of our young Brother's death was to his people and to his Church like a thunder clap out of a clear sky. The confidence on the part of those who knew him best, that he was one of the Lord's richly endowed servants, and that the Master has called him to a higher service, removes from this otherwise sad dispensation much of its bitterness. Our heart-felt sympathies go out to the bereaved home, and our only word of cheer is, 'The Lord cometh.'"

While this book was in the hands of the printers, was issued the fifth number of *The Woodstock College Monthly*, of which our young Brother was one of its editors. It contained the following touching notice :—

"It is as fitting, as it is the natural thing to the members of the Editorial staff, in this their first number after vacation to express in as tender words as possible their deep regret at the loss of their associate and treasurer, Mr. Winter. There is something almost inexpressible sad in the death of a student, especially of one intending to devote his life as a Minister of the Gospel to the welfare of his fellowmen. All the old boys, all the masters, all that were acquainted with Mr. Winter feel deeply thus grieved. What student can ever forget that address of his at the debate with the Collegiate Institute boys last winter! And then his whole student life—his modesty, kindness, ability and piety—almost perfect."

APRIL 23RD. Brother Joseph N. Shenston was appointed Church clerk. The Deacons were appointed to revise the Church Constitution.

MAY 4TH. Brother J. Harris and T. D. Crawford re-elected Deacons by ballot.

MAY 15TH. A number of alterations were recommended to be made in the Church Constitution. * * * Inasmuch as the alterations made were adopted, and are embodied in the present Constitution, it is thought useless to note them here.

MAY 29TH. The Pastor, and Brethren T. S. Shenston, Chittenden, Winter, A. Harris, J. Harris, Dengate, Cox, Henderson, Tisdale and Pearce, were appointed delegates to the Association to be held at Drumbo. Statistics given—number of members, 570, baptised during the year, 110.

AUGUST 25TH. The Pastor, and Brethren Geo. Chittenden and James Cox, were appointed delegates to attend the ordination of J. D. McCall, at Drumbo.

NOVEMBER 14TH. A dear member of our Church writing me from Camberwell, London, under this date says :—

"It does me good to see that I am not forgotten, and I can assure you that I will never forget the dear friends of the First Baptist Church of Brantford. They are uppermost in my thoughts, even in foggy, noisy, dirty London.

"In talking with Mr. Spurgeon the first day I came to London, he asked me very particular after you, especially about your book the 'Berean', and when I told him you had printed it yourself on a little press of your own, he laughed boisterously.

"About taking my letter from the First Church, I do not think I will do it, as I will only be two years here. Another reason is that before I came here I was somewhat inclined towards 'open-communion', but now, after looking into the subject I do not think so much of it. In the Tabernacle the invitation was extended to members of other Christian Churches, but each one, before they could stop, had to go down to a room below and give their names and the name of the Church of which they were members, to the Deacons, then they received a ticket which admitted them."

1880

JANUARY 8TH. The Rev. W. H. Porter handed in his resignation as Pastor of the Church.

On recommendation of the Deacons, action was deferred until the following Sabbath.

8

Just previous to ex-Pastor Porter leaving, one of the largest meetings ever held in the Church assembled to bid him good-bye.

JANUARY 11TH. The following resolution was duly placed before the Church : " That it is with sorrow and deep regret that we have listened to our esteemed Pastor's letter proposing to sever his relations with this Church ; and, in view of the happy and successful labors of Brother Porter as our Pastor during the last six years, his resignation be not accepted ; and, as some evidence of our appreciation of his abilities, and sympathy for his personal comfort, we hereby increase his salary to $1,500, from the 1st January."

In amendment it was resolved that the resignation be accepted—the latter part of the original motion relating to salary having been dropped.

The amendment was carried by a considerable majority.

The Deacons, with Brethren Truss, J. N. Shenston, Benedict and Broughton were appointed a pulpit committee.

JANUARY 25TH. The Pulpit Committee reported : " We recommend that the Church extend a call to Rev. Geo. M. W. Carey, of St. John, New Brunswick, to become their Pastor, at a salary of $1,300 per annum ; and that his travelling expenses from St. Johns, N.B., be paid." Carried unanimously.

FEBRUARY 12TH. Brethren Chittenden and William Grant, were appointed delegates to Plattsville, "to consider the propriety of organizing a Church at Drumbo."

" A letter was received from W. L. Moore, of Brockville, proposing himself as a candidate for the Pastorate. Referred to the Pulpit committe."

MARCH 21ST. A communication was read from the ladies of the Church, saying that they would raise $500 to pay off the debt on the Church, if the rest of the members would raise the balance, $1,700.

APRIL 3RD. The Pulpit Committee reported :—"We recommend that a call be extended to Rev. Wm. Brookman to become our Pastor, at a salary of $1,200 a year ; and that his moving expenses be paid." Report, on motion of Brother Thomas Large, seconded by Brother D. Dengate, was adopted.

APRIL 17TH. The clerk read a letter from Brother Brookman accepting the call to the Pastorate.

REV. WM. BROOKMAN

PASTOR, APRIL 17, 1890. FOR A SHORT TIME ONLY.

MAY 6TH. Was read a letter from Pastor Brookman, asking to be permitted to withdraw his acceptance of the call recently extended to him, and enclosing a letter from his medical adviser, Dr. Adams, of Toronto.

The resignation was accepted.

MAY 21ST. *Died*—Peter Buck, aged 87, who was among the very first members of the Church.

MAY 30TH. Brethren Crawford, Benedict, A. Harris Chittenden, File, Tisdale, Chamberlain, Moore, Dengate, Brown, Grant and McIntyre, were appointed delegates to attend the Association which was held with the Onondaga Church. The Church letter reported:—Members, 526; Baptized during the year, 6.

JULY 8TH. The Sabbath evening services was changed from 6.30 to 7 o'clock.

JULY 18TH. The Supply Committee recommended "that a call be extended to Rev. J. B. Tuttle, of Springfield, Ohio, at a salary of $1,300; and his travelling expenses from there paid." The recommendation of the Committee was adopted.

AUGUST 1ST. Brethren T. S. Shenston, J. Harris, A. Harris, D. Dengate and L. Benedict, were appointed to meet with the East Ward Church, "to take into consideration the desirableness of continuing the said Church, or of forming it into a Mission Church."

AUGUST 5TH. A letter was read from Rev. J. B. Tuttle, accepting the call extended to him. Brother J. N. Shenston resigned the office of Church clerk, and Brother Lewis Benedict appointed in his place.

OCTOBER 3RD. The Committee reported that it was necessary, in order to meet all expenses, that 15 per cent. be added to the present offerings. Brethren George Chittenden, sen., T. S. Shenston, John Harris, D. Dengate, T. D. Crawford and A. Harris, be appointed to attend the Baptist Union to be held in Toronto.

OCTOBER 14TH. A Committee appointed to canvass the Church to secure larger contributions.

NOVEMBER 7TH. Brother Dengate reported on behalf of the Committee in regard to the forthcoming Anniversary, that, instead of a tea-meeting as usually held, recommended a union social to be held in the afternoon and evening of New Year's Day. The recommendation adopted.

1881.

JANUARY 2ND. Was read a letter from ex-Pastor Porter, Rochester, "urging upon the Church the necessity of the Church increasing the salary of their Pastor.

On motion of Brother John Harris, the Pastors salary was increased to $1,500, per annum.

MARCH 17TH. Brother George Winter, Treasurer, handed in a financial report for the year.

Total receipt $2,124.31 : disbursements, $2,115.51. Poor fund, $125.28 : disbursements, $108.10.

The amended Constitution for the Church, read, discussed, and adopted. This is yet the Constitution of the Church.

MARCH 25TH The Nominating Committee reported as follows :—Recommending Deacons, T. D. Crawford, A. Benedict, John Harris, T. S. Shenston, D. Dengate and George Hill.

Treasurer, W. T. Wickham : Clerk, Lewis Benedict ; Auditors, Brethren Chalcraft and Harris.

Managing Committee, George Winter, A. Harris, Thomas Large, J. McMichael and J. N. Shenston.

Report unanimously adopted.

APRIL 23RD. On this day was formed by the young ladies of the Church, a missionary organization called "The Gleaners," its sole object being to raise funds to aid in supporting the Missionaries sent to India by our own Foreign Missionary Society.

The following were appointed the officers for the first year :

President,   MRS. CAMERON.
Vice-President, CLARA TUTTLE.
Secretary,   A. M. BELL.
Ass't-Secretary, T. CRAWFORD.
Treasurer,   LIZZIE TANTON.

Present, aiding its formation, Mrs. Tuttle, Mrs. Needham and Mrs Crawford.

Amount raised by October 15th, the end of the financial year of the Foreign Mission Society, $99.12 ; amount paid, over $75.

For the first few years of its infancy the President contributed $50 a year.

MAY 26TH. The Deacons, and Brethren Cox and Roberts, were appointed delegates to attend the Association—place of meeting not named.

The Church letter reported membership, 549 : baptized during the year, 19.

The Deacons were appointed delegates to attend an ordination at Goble's Corners. The name of the party to be ordained, not given.

SEPTEMBER 22ND. The Pastor, and Brethren John Harris and J. D. Crawford, were appointed delegates to meet with the St. George Church in connection with the ordination of Brother David M. Mihell.

OCTOBER 13TH. The Pastor, and Brethren T. S. Shenston and John Harris, were appointed delegates to the Baptist Union, to be held in Montreal, October 26th.

1882.

FEBRUARY 21ST. *Died*—Margaret A. Harrison, aged 60 years.

MARCH 2ND. Annual meeting. Received from all sources, $3,749.27 ; expended, $3,765.95. Poor fund, received, $110.45 : paid out, $90.00

Officers appointed. Treasurer, W. F. Wickham ; Clerk, L. Benedict ; Auditors, F. Chalcraft and A. Murray ; Finance Committee, Geo. Winter, J. N. Shenston, A. Harris, Clayton Slater and H. Howie.

A Committee appointed in connection with suggestions respecting the constitution.

MARCH 3RD. Brother J—— was refused a letter of dismission to another Church, until he had paid the pew rent due by him.

MARCH 17TH. Some alterations made in the Constitution ; but what the alterations were, is not stated.

APRIL 23RD. At this the first annual meeting of the "Gleaners" the following officers were elected :—

President,   MRS. CAMERON.
Vice-President,   MISS JENNY LINDSAY.
Secretary,   A. M. BELL.
Ass't-Secretary, BELLA WILSON.
Treasurer,   LIZZIE TAXTON.

Amount raised, $81.78 . amount donated, $25.00.

MAY 4TH. The Pastor, and Brethren George Chittenden and Alfred Roberts, were appointed delegates to an ordination service at Drumbo, on May 10th. The name of the party not given.

MAY 28TH. The Pastor, and Brethren L. Benedict, Wickham, Tisdale, Grant, Beal, Cox and Passmore, were appointed delegates to attend the Association to be held at Brantford.

Church letter reported membership 493 : baptized during the year, 12.

JUNE 24TH. *Died* This day at her husband's residence, in the city of Brantford, M. A., wife of Nicholas Dymond, aged 61 years. She was born in Devonshire, England, emigrated with her husband to Canada in 1845, and became a member of the Church May 1st, 1856. Her loss was much felt by her family, Church and neighborhood.

JUNE 29TH. The Pastor spoke of certain changes in the basement proposed by the Sisters in the Church, namely, carpeting, changing the platform to the opposite end, etc. The Church approving of the suggestion, Sisters Powley, T. S. Shenston, Whitham, George Winter, John Harris, Crawford and Tuttle, were appointed a committee to carry out the proposed alterations.

AUGUST 27TH. A young Brother made application for a "license to preach, in order that he might, in the near future, devote himself wholly to the work of the ministry." Moved by T. S. Shenston, seconded by John Harris, and *resolved*, "That while the Church have no hesitation in acknowledging the gifts of the Brother to be such as will qualify him to preach as he has been doing for some time past with considerable acceptance . they feel that they ought not to assume the grave

responsibility of recommending him to abandon his present
secular employment for the purpose of devoting his whole
time to the ministry, thereby earning his livelihood, especially
as there is a wide field of usefulness open for him among the
class not now reached by the ordained ministers.   Therefore
they do not see their way clear to recommend the granting of
a license unless the Brother accepts the recommendation above
named."

SEPTEMBER 14TH.   The Pastor and Brethren Chittenden
and Crawford were appointed delegates " to an ordination service to be held with the Jerseyville Church on Tuesday, September 26th."   The party to be ordained not mentioned.

OCTOBER 1ST.   *Resolved*, " That a license to preach be
granted to Brother George Chittenden, Jr., now attending the
Woodstock Institute."

OCTOBER 15TH.   Pastor Tuttle was requested to have
published in the *Canadian Baptist* the sermons preached by
him this morning.   The request was complied with.

1883.

FEBRUARY 21ST.   Annual Church meeting.   Reported
membership, 504 ; baptisms during the year, 12 ; total amount
raised by the Church during the year for Church purposes,
$3,252.70 ; Church debt, $2,050.89 ; Poor Fund receipts,
$99.30 : paid out, $55.02   Church officers :   Lewis Benedict,
Treasurer : Frederick Chalcraft, Clerk : Geo. Winter, James
Cox, Auditors.   Finance Committee :   A.   Harris,   Clayton
Slater, J. N. Shenston, W. T. Wickham and A. Murray.

APRIL 23RD.   At this the second annual meeting of the
" Gleaners," the following officers were elected :—

President,	LIZZIE TAXTON.
Vice-President,	MISS T. CRAWFORD
Secretary,	BELLA WILSON.
Ass't-Secretary,	CLARA TUTTLE.
Treasurer,	A. M. BELL.

Amount raised, $308.37 : amount donated, $275.00.

Inasmuch as the jubilee year closes January 1st, 1884, it
would be out of place to record the minutes of any subsequent meeting.   Suffice it to say that the " Gleaners " are
still carrying on their good work.

REV. J. B. TUTTLE

PASTOR FROM AUGUST, 1889, TO SEPTEMBER, 1889.

The following are the amounts raised and denoted up to date.

1884-5	Raised	$119	60	Donated	$233	88
1885-6	"	133	84	"	136	18
1886-7	"	64	47	"	63	98
1887-8	"	109	79	"	111	78
1888-9	"	79	71	"	75	00

APRIL 29TH. The Pastor and Brethren Geo. Chittenden, sen., were appointed delegates to "The Baptist Union," to be held in Toronto, with a request that Brother Needham, from the Indian Reserve would accompany them.

MAY 1ST. During the last years that the Orphan's Home was in my hands I had employed therein as teacher a young woman who often told me with tearful eye that she was alone in the world, not having a relation therein. She faithfully attended all the services of the Church, including the Sabbath morning prayer meeting. Subsequently she gave such satisfactory evidence before the Church of a change of heart that she was received as a member and baptized by Pastor Porter. Her name, however, does not appear in the Church book. Under these circumstances I have it on my heart to preserve her name from oblivion by inserting the following letter, which in all probability was the last one she ever wrote :

SOUTH SAGINAW,
April 26th, 1883.

DEAR BRO,—

Just a line to tell you that I am really dying, no false report as you heard before when I saw you last. The doctors say I cannot live long. Dropsy is setting in so that the end cannot be far off. I still have dyspepsia. I am, however, quite prepared to go whenever the Master shall call for me, and the fear of death has been removed. I suffer considerably, but Jesus gives me grace to bear it. Mr. Frazer will send you the book you lent me two year's ago.   *   *   *   *   *   *

I am too weak to write any more, except to ask your constant prayers that God will sustain me until the end.

Rev. Mr. Frazer will send you a paper with the notice of my death. I should much like to hear from you, but you will have to write soon for I feel that my time here is short. I feel that I am growing weaker every day.

Your dying Sister in Christ,
MARIA MOSS.

JUNE 3RD. The Pastor, Brethren G. Chittenden, B. G. Tisdale, T. D. Crawford, A. Howell, A. Benedict and D. Dengate, were appointed delegates to attend the Association to be held at St. George. The Church letter reported : Membership, 518 ; baptisms, 8 ; pupils in Sunday School, 157 : total amount raised for all purposes, Church and denominational, $6,904.59. An extract from the official Church letter :—" Our financial condition has been materially improved within the past year ; besides meeting our current expenses, we have paid off over two thousand dollars of our indebtedness, which

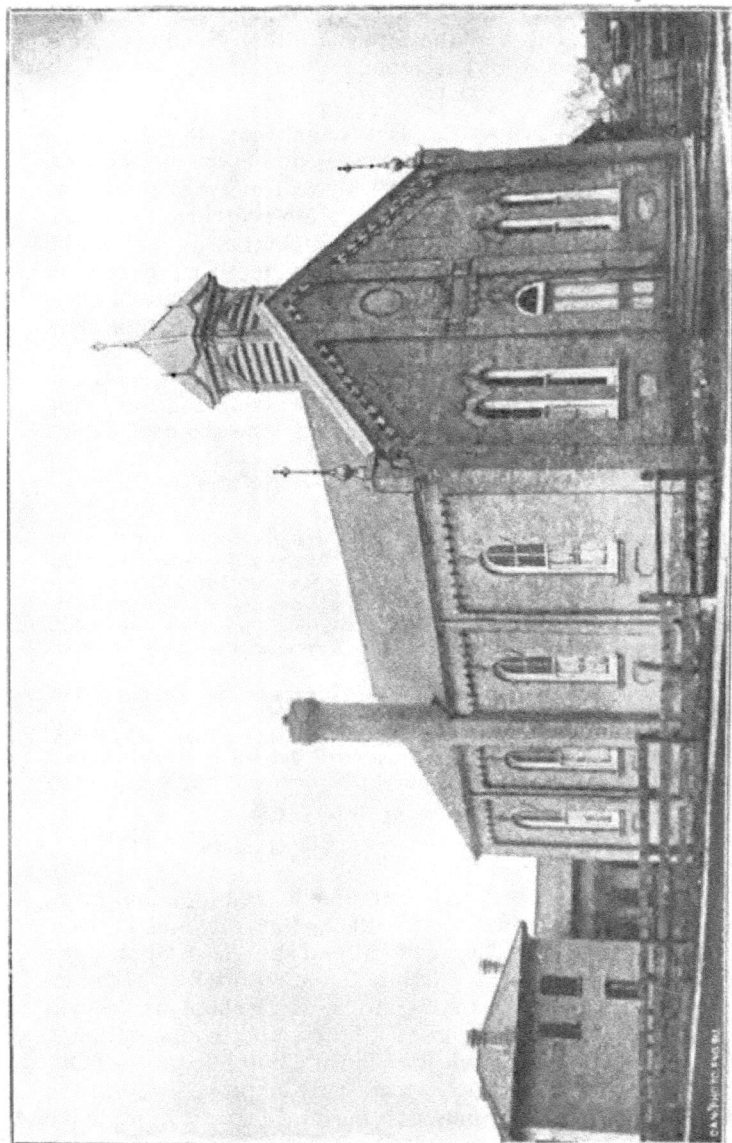

NORTH STAR MISSION CHAPEL.

rested on the Church, and our contributions to other denominational objects have been larger than any previous year. *   *
We can once more say that we owe no man anything but love."

"In addition to our Home School, the Church has the
'North Star' Mission School under the Superintendency of
Deacon T. D. Crawford, which is doing a good work for the
Master in the northern end of the city. They have a neat
comfortable building, worth, with lot, $3,000, provided by
Brother S————, and furnished by Brother John Harris.
Besides the Sabbath School work, public services are held every
Sabbath and Thursday evenings."

NOVEMBER 4TH. A letter was received from Rev. John
Stewart, Beamsville, recommending the services of Brother
Chubbuck in holding Evangelistic meetings.

NOVEMBER 10TH. *Resolved*, "to extend a cordial invitation
to Brother Chubbuck, to hold some special Evangelistic
meetings."

DECEMBER 16TH. It was decided to hold special Jubilee
services on the 1st January, 1884.

DECEMBER 26TH. *Resolved*, "that the ladies of the
Church be a committee to provide for the Jubilee tea, and that
tickets of admittance be placed in the hands of the Deacons
and the Sisters of the Church for distribution in the Park and
East Ward Baptist Churches and among our own congregation."
No entry is made of this most interesting Jubilee Meeting.
The Rev. Wm. Rees, the Church's first Pastor, was present,
and the writer read a paper relating to the Church's progress.

The following are extracts from the *Brantford Expositor's*
report of the Jubilee Meeting.

"Monday afternoon William Moyle, Esq., of Paris, formerly a
Deacon of this Church for 28 years, was asked to address the meeting.
He alluded to the Church when a lad in company with his mother, and
had often heard her speak of the trials and joys which they expressed
in that early day. He became a member under Elder Winterbotham's
Ministry, its second Pastor. *   *   * Very few of those who were then
members when he came in were left. *   *   * He spoke with much
feeling and his reminiscences were exceedingly interesting to the audience.

"George Foster, Esq., of the Park Church, then addressed the meeting. * * * He alluded to the cordial welcome which had been given him. He spoke of the long experience which he had in connection with the Church, and referred most feelingly to the circumstances which led to his separation from it. He solemnly believed that there were things said and done that would not bear the light of the judgment day ; but God had over-ruled it all for His glory, and the furtherance of the Baptist cause in Brantford. With all honesty, and sincerity of heart, he could say, so far as he was concerned, the old wound was healed, and more than that, the scar itself was effaced. The entire address was characterized by a beautiful Christian spirit and made a deep and lasting impression upon the hearts of those who heard it.

"Rev. Wm. Rees, the Minister who first organized the Church, was the next speaker. He spoke of the beginning of the Baptist cause in Brantford, of the opposition he met with in the fields, of the trials and hardships throughout which he had passed, and the ultimate triumph of the cause which he had planted. It was an occasion of great joy to him to witness the unparalleled progress of the Baptist Denomination in this city. For all the labor and sacrifice he felt that the Master had repaid him fourfold for it all. He cherished something of the spirit of Simeon, ' Now Lord let thy servant depart in peace, for mine eyes have seen thy salvation.'

"In the evening a very large audience assembled in the Church to hear the history of the Church, which had been most carefully prepared by Mr. T. S. Shenston. The history was very complete, and was much interesting ; its length alone prevents us from publishing it. It gave evidence of much re-search and labor.

"Addresses were also delivered by Rev. James Grant, of Paris, Rev. Wm. Rees and Rev. Rob. Cameron. Mr. Charles Dimmeck gave a pleasing solo."

"Thou shalt number seven sabbaths of years unto thee ; seven times seven shall be unto thee forty nine, and ye shall hallow the fiftieth year, it shall be a jubilee unto you. Then shalt thou cause the trumpet of the jubilee to sound." *Levit.* xxv, 10-11.

THE AUTHOR

Feels that it is due to himself to state, that notwithstanding the appearance of his name so often, it has been omitted whenever it could be done without detracting from the his tory the book purports to give.

BRETHREN AND SISTERS

ALLOW me to have with you a parting word respecting the doctrine of Baptism, which distinguishes us from all our Pedo-Baptist fellow-Christians. We view Baptism as a distinct command, made to intelligent beings, to do a certain act, in a certain manner, at a certain time, to symbolize a certain important truth. We believe that this Christ-appointed ordinance and the Lord's supper were instituted solely for the observance of those comprising the membership of His visible Church on the earth, and no others. The last command of our Saviour was (Mark xvi., 15), "Go into all the world, and preach the Gospel to EVERY CREATURE. He that BELIEVETH and is baptized shall be saved : but he that believeth NOT shall be condemned." This class which the Apostles were here commanded to *baptize*, are elsewhere called (Rom. viii, 17) " *children.*" " *heirs of God and joint heirs with Christ,*" (1 Peter. ii, 9) "*a peculiar people,*" who have been " *born again,*" (1 Peter, ii, 9) "*called out of darkness into his marvellous light,*" to whom (2 Cor., v., 17) " *all things are become new,*" and who therefore (John iii., 36) have "*everlasting life,*" and to whom "the Son of man" shall say, (Matt. xxv., 34), " *Come, ye blessed of my Father, inherit the kingdom prepared for you from the foundation of the world.*" On the other hand those who were " *to be condemned*" and NOT baptized, are elsewhere represented as (Ephes. ii., 12) " *aliens from the commonwealth of Israel * * * having no hope and without God in the world,*" as possessing (Rom. viii, 7) " *the carnal mind,*" which is "*enmity against God,*" and therefore (John iii., 18) "*condemned already,*" and to whom it will be said " *Depart from me, ye cursed, into everlasting fire, prepared for the devil and his*

9

Angels." Surely, surely it could not have been persons of this
latter class, who were commanded to *" keep the ordinances as
they were delivered."*

The Baptists believe that those, who indiscriminately
baptize (sprinkle) children without any qualification whatever
and admit to the Lord's Table only a small portion of those
thus baptized, "put asunder" what Christ has "joined together," while Baptists are "open" enough to admit to the
Lord's Table ALL whom they baptize, and thus keep "together"
what they believe God has "joined."

The Freemasons, Odd-fellows, etc., all require certain
qualifications of their members previous to reception ; but as
soon as they are received—and not before—they become
obliged to conform to certain laws and rules, peculiar to such
organizations, with which they had nothing previously to do,
and with which their children have nothing whatever to do
In like manner there are certain qualifications requisite in
order to become members of Christ's Church ; but, having
become such—and not before—all are immediately obligated
to conform to such laws as the Head of the Church has seen
fit to appoint for its government, and more especially "to
keep the ordinances as they were delivered," but with which
their children have nothing whatever to do. As a rule, the
Baptists have *" shunned"* in the pulpit, in the prayer meeting
and sabbath school *" to declare   *   *   all the counsel of God"*
by not giving this most important and significant doctrine a
prominence equal to that given to it in God's word. If from
these places it had been oftener proclaimed, that none were
baptized but those, who, they believed, had *"passed from death
to life"* by *"believing on Jesus as the scripture hath said,'* they
would not be so often bantered about "making too much" of
baptism. It would have been readily seen what the position they
held as Baptists was. If no mistakes were made so that none
were baptized but those who had scripturally believed on the
Lord Jesus Christ, there would not be found in hell any one
who had been baptized. Whereas if infant baptism were

universally adopted (and all Christians must admit that the
more universally any command of Christ is obeyed the better),
there would not be an unbaptized soul in hell :

If the Lord should come at this moment, in what position
would He find the vast majority of those who had been the
recipients of one of His ordinances? Would they not com-
prise the majority of those in the prisons, gambling dens,
saloons, theatres, horse races, and such like places?

The following is an extract from one of John Wesley's
sermons, which I find on page 324 of *Hibbard's Christian
Baptism*, a book much valued by the Methodists : "How
many are the baptized gluttons and drunkards, the baptized
liars and common swearers, the baptized rioters, evil speakers,
the baptized whoremongers, thieves, extortioners : What think
you? Are these men children of God? Verily, I say unto
you.   *   *   *   Ye serpents, ye generation of vipers, how can
ye escape the damnation of hell ! "

The total population of Ontario, by the last census, was
1,923,228.   Subtract from this the four leading denominations
(Roman Catholic 320,839, Church of England 367,528,
Presbyterian 417,749, and Methodist 567,777) leaves 350,335
to cover the remaining as follows :—

Baptists	94,222	
Congregationalists	16,340	
Universalists	1,333	
Adherents	696	
Brethren	7,714	
Jews	1,193	
Unitarians	1,213	
Lutherans	37,901	
Pagans	1,499	
No Religion	15,945	
Tunkers	13,458	
Disciples	16,051	
Bible Christians	23,726	
Others	12,965	

In the criminal statistical report all but the four leading
denominations above named are classed together as "other
denominations."   It is a most singular fact the *greater the
virtues attributed to infant sprinkling, the greater the proportion-
ate amount of crime committed by the sprinkled.*

Attentively note the following from the published official
report of 1888.

Denomination	Population (official.)	Criminal (official.)	One in Every
Roman Catholics	320,839	4,499	71
Church of England	367,528	3,925	94
Presbyterians	417,749	1,519	275
Methodists	567,777	1,646	345
Other Denominations	250,335	794	315

Now please note attentively what the four leading Pedo-
Baptist denominations say themselves respecting their mode of
baptism, the subjects to be baptized, and the spiritual advantages
to be derived therefrom.

FIRST.—ROMAN CATHOLIC.—"Baptism is a sacrament
which cleanses us from original sin, makes us Christians and
the children of God, and heirs of the Kingdom of Heaven, it
remits actual sins committed before it and all punishment due
to them, and without it one cannot enter the Kingdom of
God, and conveys grace to the soul in the way of a new
birth."—*R. Catholic Catechism.*

Of all the Pedo-Baptists the Roman Catholics are, beyond
question, the most consistent. *First.* In their Catechism they
frankly say :—"The Holy Scriptures speak only of baptism by
immersion. The dogma of the Church is to sprinkle, and we
should in this, and in everything else, follow the Church."
Secondly. They make it *imperative* on all their members to
have their children baptized. But notwithstanding this pre-
caution, and the blessed privileges said to be conferred by the
ordinance, no less than 4,499 found themselves in the
common gaols, and 239 in the Central Prison, in 1888.

SECOND.—THE CHURCH OF ENGLAND.— "Concerning the
baptism of this child * * * being born in original sin
and in the wrath of God, is now by the laver of regeneration

in baptism received into the number of the children of God, and heirs to everlasting life."

"Seeing now, dearly beloved brethren, that this child is by baptism regenerated, and grafted into the body of Christ's Church."

"Question. Who gave you that name? Answer. My godfathers and godmothers, wherein I was made a member of Christ, a child of God, and an inheritor of the Kingdom of Heaven."

Burial of the dead : "Here be it noted that the office ensuing is not used for any that die unbaptized   or have laid violent hands upon themselves."— *Church of England Prayer Book.*

Next to the R. Catholics, the Church of England keeps the strictest serveillance over its members, in order that their children may become "heirs of God, and inheritors of the Kingdom of Heaven." But alas! alas! we find no fewer than 3,925 were in our common gaols, and 259 in the Central Prison, in 1888.

THIRD.—THE PRESBYTERIANS. "Baptism is a sacrament of the New Testament, ordered by Jesus Christ, not only for the solemn admission of the party baptized into the visible Church, but also to be unto him a sign and seal of the covenant of grace, of his engrafting into Christ, or regeneration and remission of sins."

"Although it is a great sin to condemn or neglect this ordinance, yet grace and salvation are not so inseparably annexed unto it that no person can be regenerated or saved without it.— *Presbyterian Confession of Faith.*

What a pity that 1,590 of this class should have been in the common gaols, and 76 in the Central Prison during the year 1888.

FOURTH. THE METHODISTS.—"Baptism is not only a sign of profession and mark of difference, whereby Christians are distinguished from others that are not baptized : but is also a sign of regeneration, or the new birth."—*Methodist Book of Discipline.*

How sad to learn that no less than 1,646 thus baptized should have been incarcerated in our common gaols and 86 in the Central Prison during the year 1888 !

FIFTH.—THE BAPTIST.—"We believe that Christian Baptism is the immersion in water of a BELIEVER ; into the name of the Father, and Son, and Holy Ghost, to show forth in a solemn and beautiful emblem, our faith in the crucified, buried and risen Saviour, with its effect, in our death to sin and resurrection to a new life ; that it is pre-requisite to the privileges of a Church relation, and to the Lord's Supper in which the members of the Church by the sacred use of bread and wine, are to commemorate together the dying love of Christ : preceded always by solemn self-examination."-*Baptist Manual.*

The Baptists, with eleven other classes of religionists, send only 794 to the common gaols, and 39 to the Central Prison. While there is one in every 94 of those sprinkled by the Church of England in the common gaols, the Baptist, (mixed with the "*Universalist,*" "*Pagans,*" "*Jews,*" "*Adherents*" and "other") have only one in every 315. When the census is taken it is the invariable—indeed only—rule to include each family—children and adults—as belonging to the same church. For example. The enumerator calls on a family the united heads of which are Methodists and have four children. The whole six are, of course, classed as Methodists, and it must be assumed that *all the children have been baptized.* The next family called on is a family of the same size, but the parents are Baptists, all of whom on the same principle, would be classed as Baptists, notwithstanding none of the four children would have been baptized. Consequently when a prisoner reports himself as belonging to some one of the Pedo-Baptist Churches there are at least ten chances to one that he had been baptized in his infancy, but when a prisoner reports himself a Baptist it is ten chances to one that he never was baptized by immersion on a profession of faith in Christ. Only such are Baptists.

To illustrate still another phase of infant baptism. Suppose the Methodists, in order to distinguish themselves from other denominations, should at some Conference make it obligatory on all its members to wear a breast-pin on which was the head of Wesley. Suppose further that this breast-pin being very cheap and pretty it was being worn not only by "Tom, Dick and Harry" but by the drunken blasphemers as they stagger along the street, by the inmates in the *gaols*, and the culprits on the gallows. This would not only most signally defeat the purpose intended, but would bring the whole Methodist body into ridicule and disgrace, and one of the first acts of the next Conference would be to repeal the order. Christ instituted the ordinance of baptism, as before stated, for the members of His Church only, but inasmuch as this ordinance has not been confined to those only who "believe," consequently a result somewhat similar to the above follows. Man's laws bring those of Christs into contempt and ridicule.

Suppose a Pedo Baptist is asked: "Did Christ or did He not institute the ordinance and command that it be observed?" The answer doubtless would be in every case "Yes." Now suppose the same party is asked: "How is this positive command to be obeyed" The answer, I assume, would be the same as that given by Pedo-Baptist Webster: "Pedo-Baptist, one that holds to infant baptism; one that practises the baptism of infants." If this definition is accepted as correct, to have been merely baptized in infancy, cannot of itself constitute the recipient a true Pedo-Baptist, until they "*practise* the baptism of infants." All such are really nothing more than Pedo-Baptists in embryo, and by no possibility can they become anything else without they become parents !

Let us now see how the three leading Protestant Pedo-

Baptists in the United States obey the *command of Christ as they say they understand it*. The following baptismal statistics I copy from the official published reports in my possession :

YEARS	METHODISTS		PRESBYTERIANS		CONGRE- GATIONALISTS	
	CHILDREN	ADULT	CHILDREN	ADULT	CHILDREN	ADULT
1885	*58,221	59,138	21,012	15,191	7,139	9,509
1886	67,410	98,723	21,616	18,474	7,364	13,075
1887	74,338	101,409	23,469	20,114	11,966	20,123
1888	72,400	90,947	23,869	18,799	8,328	12,039
1889	73,104	100,701	24,566	19,547	8,889	13,786
1890	†43,718	42,511	25,187	17,471	Nonepu	blished
	389,191	493,429	113,719	109,596	43,686	68,532

* 1889. † Spring Conference only.

RECAPITULATION.

	CHILDREN	ADULTS
Methodist	389,191	493,429
Presbyterians	113,719	109,596
Congregationalists	43,686	68,532
Totals................	546,596	671,557
Total Children.........		546,596
More Adults than Children		124,961

From the foregoing some most useful lessons may be readily learned. Let them be learned :

1. By "Adult" is evidently meant those who have not been baptized until their formal admission as Church members.

2. If, within the year 1889, no less than 134,034 "Adults"

were baptized by the three Churches named, there must be at least three times that number of unbaptized children awaiting their " Adult " admission into the Church in the near future.

3.   Each of these 134,034 fathers and 134,034 mothers positively ignore baptism as understood by their respective Churches, and yet they are allowed to retain their membership. The three Churches named above maintain that to obey Christ's command, their members must have their children baptized. The Presbyterian creed says, " that it is a *great sin* to condemn or neglect it," yet notwithstanding this, it is seen that *hundreds of thousands* of the members of the Churches systematically ignore their creeds with impunity, and yet none are disciplined. How inconsistent ! None can become a member with us until baptized by immersion on profession of faith in Christ, consequently there is *uniformity* on this doctrine with us.

4.   We learn that within the last five years, in these three leading Churches, there have been 124,961 more "Adults " baptized than children.

5.   From these facts it is self-evident, that, within a few years, infant baptism will be abandoned altogether.

6.   How often, with solemn face, have Pedo Baptists chided the Baptists with neglecting "to dedicate their children to the Lord in Baptism." They cannot consistently do so any longer, inasmuch as so many of themselves ignore the baptism of children.

7.   It is not at all likely that these " Adult " children of Pedo Baptists parents will themselves practise infant baptism.

8.   All the children (40 in all) but one of our eight Deacons, and three ex-Deacons, over ten years of age, have been baptized by immersion on a profession of their faith in Christ. This does not look like "neglecting" the children.

9.   The *mode* of baptism by immersion is important, but very little compared with the *subject* baptized.

In spite of all that can be said some will contend that, inasmuch as baptism is not a saving ordinance, it is of little im-

portance how it is performed.   Had this class lived in the days
of Saul they would doubtless have commended his sagacity and
fore-thought in sparing "the best of oxen and sheep to sacrifice
unto the Lord."   For this disobedience he was rebuked and
punished.   Samuel asks, "Has the Lord as great delight in
burnt offerings and sacrifices as in obeying the voice of the
Lord ?"

Had any Jew sacrificed a *black* or *spotted* heifer instead of
a *red* one, as commanded, he would have been turned out of
the synagogue.

"If ye love me keep my commandments.   JOHN xiv., 14."
"If ye know these things, happy are ye if ye do them.   JOHN xiii., 17."

T. S. SHENSTON.

INDEX TO ILLUSTRATIONS.

INDEX TO OBITUARIES.

The following is a list of all those who have been connected with the Church during the first fifty years of its existence, whose names appear on record in the Church's books ; but inasmuch as the books have been kept in a very perfunctory manner, I have every reason to believe that the names of many a score have never been entered on the books. The date of each member's *reception*, and not that of their *baptism*, is given. The members who have left without receiving regular Church letters, have been classed as "dropped out." "First mention," these names first appearing in connection with some church business.

A.

When Received	How Received	Names	Date of Leaving	Reason for Leaving
1853—June 26	Baptism	Martha Adams	1860 June 19	Dropped out
1855—March 8	First Mention	Sister Aldison		Unknown
" July 5	Baptism	Joseph M. Aikman		
" July 5	Baptism	Ennice Aikman		
1857 May 20	Baptism	James Anderson	1860 June 19	Dropped out
1860 December 16	Baptism	Rev. John Alexander	1862 December 4	Montreal Church.
" December 16	Baptism	Mrs. Isabella Alexander	1863 February 4	Died, aged 33
1861—February 18	Baptism	Samuel Anderson	1867 March 3	Waterford Church (?)
" July 22	Baptism	Harriet Andrews		Died, September 18, 1851
1867 March 3	First Mention	Samuel Anderson		Unknown
" October 10	First Mention	James A. Aldred	1868 October 4	Woodstock Church
" October 10	Baptism	A. Aldred	1868 April 19	Woodstock Church
" October 22	Baptism	Mrs. Aldred	1868 April 19	Woodstock Church
" October 4	First Mention	Sarah Aldred	1868 October 4	Woodstock Church
1874—June 7	Beamsville Church	James Armstrong	1870 May 4	East Ward Church
" June 7	Beamsville Church	Mrs. James Armstrong	1870 May 4	East Ward Church
1875 February 11	Baptism	Wm. Aikman	1880 November 11	United States
" February 18	Baptism	Naomi Aikman		
1878 June 6	Baptism	Kate Ashly		

LIST OF MEMBERS—FIRST BAPTIST CHURCH, BRANTFORD.

B.

WHEN RECEIVED	HOW RECEIVED	NAMES	DATE OF LEAVING	REASON FOR LEAVING
1835—December 4	First Mention	John Bryning	1835—December 4	Townsend Church
" December 4	First Mention	Mrs. Bryning	1835—December 4	Townsend Church
1836—March 4	First Mention	Sister Burtch		
" March 4	First Mention	Sister Brown	1842—April 3	Oakland Church
" March 4	First Mention	Mary Benedict	1885—November 21	Died, aged 81 years
" March 4	First Mention	Peter Buck	1880—May 21	Died, aged 87 years
" September 2	First Mention	Brother Bust	1836—November 7	Dropped out
1840—June 13	First Mention	Erastus Benedict	1878—January 31	Died, aged 71 years
1841—October 17	First Mention	Brother Buchan	1842—November 19	Paris Church
1842—July 3	First Mention	Brother Barrett		
" July 16	First Mention	Mrs. Baker	1845—June 15	Dropped out
" November 19	First Mention	Mrs. Bates	1848—February 5	Dundas Church
" November 19	First Mention	Mrs. Buchan	1842—November 19	Paris Church
" November 19	First Mention	Mrs. Buchan, Sr.	1842—November 19	Paris Church
" December 17	Letter	Thomas Broughton	1852—June 18	Letter
" December 17	Letter	Mrs. Martha Broughton	1852—June 18	Letter
" December 25	First Mention	Brother Barrett	1842—December 25	Brantford T'ship Church.
" December 25	First Mention	Sister Barrett	1842—December 25	Brantford T'ship Church.
1843—April 1	Baptism	Alonzo Benedict	1848—March 4	
1844—May 18	First Mention	Mrs. Burtch	1844—May 18	West Oxford Church
1845—April 5	Baptism	Theodore Brown	1846—September 5	Dropped out
" April 5	Baptism	Jane Buck		
" April 5	Baptism	Maria Bates	1848—February 5	Dundas Church
" June 15	First Mention	Mr. Baker	1845—June 15	Dropped out
" June 17	Letter	Mr. Brown	1845—June 15	Dropped out
1846—Sep'ember 5	First Mention	Theodore Brown	1846—September 5	Droppd out.
1851—February 11	First Mention	Jimima Bickerdite	1851—May 3	Dropped out

Date	Event	Name	Date	Disposition
1851—February 11	First Mention	Mary Brown	1851—May 3	Dropped out
" May 23	Baptism	Rachael Brooks		Died
" May 23	Baptism	Wm. Brooks		Died
" May 23	First Mention	Joseph Bates	1851—May 23	Dropped out
" July 6	First Mention	Jane Baptie	1853 March 27	St. George Church
" September 21	Baptism	Elizabeth Bond		Dundas Church.
" October 5	Woodstock Church	George Barnes		
1852—January 4	New York	Martha Benedict	1862—May 26	Died, aged 83 years
" June 18	Experience	Brother Burton		
" June 18	Experience	Sister Burton		
" July 4	Experience	Lucinda Bird	1856 June 4	Dropped out
1853—March 13	Baptism	Mary Bates	1853—June 5	Dropped out
" April 17	Baptism	Thomas Burtch		
1854—October 6	Woodstock Church	Charles Baguley		
1855—May 20	First Mention	Ilosy Baker		
" May 20	First Mention	Sister Baker		
" May 27	Baptism	Mrs. Josephine Beaupre	1855 September 27	2nd Charlotteville Church
" June 20	Baptism	Harriet Bristol	1857—July 28	A letter
" June 20	Baptism	Edward P. Broughton	1856—March 7	Simcoe Church
" June 20	Baptism	Sarah A. Beaupre	1855—September 27	2nd Charlotteville Church
" July 1	Returned	Mrs. T. Broughton	1871—January 31	Tabernacle Church
" September 21	Baptism	Martha Burgess	1860—June 19	Dropped out
1856—April 17	Baptism	Wm. Buck	1870 May 11	Tabernacle Church
" May 3	Charlotteville Church	Sarah A. Beaupre	1860—June 5	St. George Church
" May 16	Baptism	James Butterworth		
" May 16	Baptism	Margaret Butterworth		
" November 12	Baptism	Henry Reves		
1857—March 3	Baptism	Miss E. Bell	1857 November 3	Chatham Church
" April 10	Baptism	Henry Bond	1860 April 24	Dropped out
" May 7	Letter	Julia Benedict		
" May 20	Baptism	Judson Buck		

LIST OF MEMBERS—FIRST BAPTIST CHURCH, BRANTFORD.

When Received	How Received	Names	Date of Leaving	Reason for Leaving
1857—May 20	Baptism	James Buckrell	1866—March 6	A letter
" May 20	Experience	Alonzo Benedict		
1858—January 26	First Mention	Susan Barnes		
" March 11	Baptism	Elizabeth Barnes	1861—July 22	Dropped out
" April 8	Baptism	George Buckrell		
" April 22	Baptism	Rebecca Birkett		
" May 13	Baptism	Rev. Thomas Baldwin	1858—May 16	Letter
" May 16	Baptism	Mrs. Thomas Baldwin	1858—May 16	Letter
" June 6	England	Wm. Bowers		Died
" September 10	Baptism	Mary J. Buckrell		
1859—February 9	Baptism	Rachel Rawtinhemer		
" December 25	Letter	Judson Buck		
" December 25	Baptism	Thomas Birkett		
1860—January 5	Baptism	Emeline E. Blackburn		
" January 5	Baptism	Alfred Blackburn		
" January 16	Baptism	Mrs. Alfred Brown		
" January 16	First Mention	Mary Ann Brown		
" March 5	First Mention	Mary P. Bradley	1860—March 5	United States
" November 4	Letter	John Butterworth	1850—November 27	Cohoes Church, U. S.
" November 27	Experience	Stepney Brown	1864 March 22	St. Catharines Church
" November 27	England	James Bellhouse		
1861—July 22	Woodstock Church	Samantha Burtch		
1862—June 17	Baptism	Elizabeth Barton		
1863—January 30	Baptism	Charlotte Brown		
" May 3	First Mention	Mary Butterworth	1863—May 3	Cohoes Church, U. S.
1865—January 8	Experience	Mrs. Batty	1870—July 15	A letter
" January 22	Baptism	Mr. Brown		
1866—April 27	Baptism	John Batty		
" April 27	Baptism	Nancy Batty	1870—July 15	A letter

1866—May 29	First Mention	Mrs. Bailey	1866—May 29	England
" November 16	Quebec Church	Sergeant Charles Britt	1867—July 23	A letter
" November 30	Returned	Thomas Broughton		
1868—April 9	Baptism	John Butterworth	1875—May 27	Dropped out
1868—May 26	Baptism	Matilda Bond	1875—December 30	Dundas Church
1869—February 2	First Mention	Keemer	1869—February 2	Dropped out
" April 2	New Brunswick	John Brown		
" April 4	Baptism	Mary Blackwell	1875—May 27	Dropped out
" April 4	St. George Church	Sarah Batchelor	1875—August 27	East Ward Church
1870—February 15	First Mention	Sarah A. Batty	1870—February 15	Dropped out
" May 26	First Mention	Miss M. A. Brown		
" June 29	Experience	Edward P. Broughton	1871—April 11	Tabernacle Church
" November 15	Baptism	Elizabeth Batchelor	1875—August 27	East Ward Ch rch
" December 4	England	John Barber		
1871—January 31	Baptism	Mrs. Boyd	1878—December 19	Governors Road Church
" February 14	Baptism	Amelia Barwell		
" April 11	Letter	Edward P. Broughton		
" August 6	Baptism	Mrs. L. Benedict		
" November 5	Letter	Mr. Basler		
" November 5	Letter	Mrs. Basler		
" December 17	Selkirk Church	William Blackman	1873—January 19	Selkirk Church
" December 17	Selkirk Church	Jane Blackman	1873—January 19	Selkirk Church
1872—January 14	Burtch's Corners Church	Lucy Bagueley	1875—April 1	Ancaster Church
" February 4	Baptism	Mrs. Baguely		
" April 5	Baptism	Newton Burtch		
1873—August 3	Hartford Church	Rev. H. Boulton		Died
" August 3	Hartford Church	Mrs. H. Boulton	1878—August 22	Ormond Church
" November 2	Tabernacle Church	Mrs. Thomas Broughton		
" November 2	Tabernacle Church	Minnie Broughton		
" November 11	Experience	Elizabeth Barber	1883—June 27	England
" December 5	Baptism	Mrs. Ira Burtch		

LIST OF MEMBERS—FIRST BAPTIST CHURCH, BRANTFORD.

When Received	How Received	Names	Date of Leaving	Reason for Leaving
1873—December 7	Hartford Church	Mr. Bishop	1875—August 27	East Ward Church
" December 7	Hartford Church	Mrs. Hattie Bishop	1875—August 27	East Ward Church
1874—February 10	Baptism	Hannah Bowers		
" June 7	Beverley Church	Lizena Burr	1875—August 27	East Ward Church
1874—June 16	Baptism	Mary Jane Batters	1883—May 2	Galt Church
" November 1	Illinois	Mrs. Sarah Brown	1886—June 21	Died
" November 22	Baptism	Orlo J. Benedict		
" November 22	Baptism	Mary J. Benedict		
" November 22	Baptism	R. W. Benedict		
1875—January 7	Baptism	Fanny Bellhouse		
" January 28	Baptism	Katie Baird		
" January 28	Baptism	Benjamin Batchelor	1875—August 27	East Ward Church
" February 4	Baptism	Elizabeth Baird		
" February 4	Baptism	Henry Butterworth	1877—April 5	Dropped out
" February 25	Baptism	Charles Butterworth		
" March 11	Baptism	Mrs. James Barker	1877—September 13	Dropped out
" March 11	Baptism	James Brown		
" March 25	Baptism	William G. Burr	1875—August 27	East Ward Church
" May 27	First Mention	Brother Batchelor	1875—May 27	Dropped out
" August 27	First Mention	Mrs. William Batchelor	1875—August 27	East Ward Church
" November 7	New Brunswick	Sarah E. Brown		
1876—February 4	Baptism	Bessie Burns		
" February 20	Baptism	W. J. Beal		
" February 20	Baptism	Mrs. W. J. Beal		
" April 8	Baptism	Henry Burton		
" April 16	Baptism	H. Barlatt	1883—May 30	Dropped out
" August 3	Baptism	Miss Barlatt		
" December 3	First Mention	Mr. Beemer	1876—December 3	Dropped out.
" December 3	First Mention	Mrs. Beemer	1876—December 3	A Letter

1877	July 1		St. Catharines Church	F. W. Banton		
"	September 13		Frederickburgh Church	Mrs. George Brittain		
"	November 29		Hamilton Church	Emma Bingham		
1878	January 10	First Mention	Woodstock Church	John T. Barber	1878—December 19	Governors Road Church
"	February 3		Woodstock Church	John Bauslaugh		
"	February 3	First Mention	Woodstock Church	Mrs. John Bauslaugh	1883—December 26	Burtch's Corners Church
"	March 21	First Mention		Eusley Barber	1878—March 21	Harford Church
"	March 21	First Mention		Louise Barber	1878—March 21	Harford Church
"	April 7	United States		Hester Burkill		
1879	June 6	First Mention		Sister Brown	1878—June 6	London Church
"	March 30	Baptism		Grace Barnfather		
"	April 1	Baptism		Sarah Beal		
"	April 1	Baptism		Lizzie Brown		
"	April 1	Baptism		Alice Batty		
"	April 1	Baptism		Lena Barker	1879—August 25	Stratford Church
"	April 1	Baptism		Edith Bauslaugh	1883—December 26	Burtch's Corners Church
"	April 1	Baptism		Emily Balne		
"	April 1	Bap ism		Lewis Benedict		
"	April 6	Baptism		William Batters		
"	April 6	Baptism		John Beal		
"	April 11	Baptism		Henry Barnett	1883—May 30	Dropped out
"	April 11	Baptism		Lizzie Barnfather		
"	April 11	Baptism		Nancy Brown		
"	April 11	Baptism		Mary Bromwich		
"	April 15	Baptism		Alfred Balne		
"	April 15	Experience		Judson Buck		
"	April 20	Baptism		Jennie Beal		
"	April 20	Baptism		Truman Benedict		
"	May 8	Baptism		Mrs. Judson Buck		
"	May 8	Baptism		Minnie Barker	1879—August 25	Stratford Church.
"	May 29	Baptism		Mr. Bates		

When Received	How Received	Names	Date of Leaving	Reason for Leaving.
1879—June 1	Tabernacle Church	James Banton	1881—November 10	London Church.
" June 1	Tabernacle Church	Mrs. J. Banton	1881—November 10	London Church.
" July 10	Baptism	Mrs. Barnett	1882—June 29	United States.
1880—October 2	Wolverton Church	Mrs. Bell		
1880—October 2	Wolverton Church	Miss Bell		
" October 2	Wolverton Church	Miss A. Bell		
" October 2	Beamsville Church	Jessie Bell		
1881—January 13	East Ward Church	W. G. Burr		
" January 13	East Ward Church	Mrs. W. G. Burr		
" January 13	St. Georges' Church	Emma Barber	1881—November 3	Manitoulin Island.
" February 3	Baptism	Grace Bell		
" February 3	Baptism	Minnie Brown		
" March 10	First Mention	Sister Bromwich	1881—March 10	London Church.
" March 24	Baptism	Maggie Bell		
1882—March 3	Paris Church	Mrs. Wm. Batty		
" August 31	England	Ann Berry		
1883—January 4	Baptism	Lilly Blackburn		
" December 19	Baptism	Hannah Boughner		
" December 26	Baptism	Thos. A. Blackburn		
" December 26	Baptism	Charles Brown		

C.

1837—July 21	First Mention	Sister Collar		
1841—December 19	First Mention	Charles Chapin		
1843—April 15	First Mention	Sarah Crandall		
1844—June 24	Baptism	Wm. Cannon	1846—July 4	To form a new Church.
" June 24	Baptism	James Cowherd	1846—July 4	To form a new Church.
" June 24	Baptism	Mrs. James Cowherd	1846—July 4	To form a new Church.
" October 20	First Mention	Mrs. Collins	1844—October 20	Simcoe Church.

Year	Date	Event	Name	Date	Notes
1845	—December 17	Experience	Charles Chapin		
1846	—February 20	First Mention	Betsey Clements		
"	July 4	First Mention	Mrs. Cannon	1846—July 4	To form a new Church.
1847	—March 4	New York	Bro. Cyrus		
"	March 4	New York	Sister Clark		
"	October 2	First Mention	Elizabeth Carryer	1855—March 25	Onondaga Church.
"	November 6	United States	Thomas Chase	1855—March 25	Onondaga Church.
"	November 6	United States	Mrs. E. Chase	1855—March 24	Onondaga Church.
1849	June 25	Baptism	Wm. Crawford		
1848	—February 5	?	Mr. Chave		
"	February 5	?	Mrs. Chave		
1850	September 15	Baptism	Elizabeth Cox		
"	September 15	Letter	Mrs. Cockshutt		
"	November 2	First Mention	Bro. Canfield		
1851	January 3	Baptism	Harriet Crawford	1860—June 19	Dropped out.
"	February 1	First Mention	Dorah Chamberlain		
"	June 1	Blenheim Church	Wm. H. Cochrane		
1852	January 4	Baptism	Wm. Cole	1856—October 25	A letter.
"	January 4	Baptism	Letitia Campbell		
"	February 22	Baptism	Ann Christie		
"	April 4	Second Brantford Church	George Cummings	1855—January 29	Died—aged 43 years.
"	April 4	Second Brantford Church	Mrs. Cummings		
"	April 4	Second Brantford Church	Miss Cummings	1861—October 29	Paris Church.
"	April 4	Second Brantford Church	Netta Cummings		
"	July 4	Baptism	Anna Cameron		
"	December 5	Beverley Church	Richard Cudney	1855—November 4	Beverley Church.
"	December 5	Baptism	John M. Colver	1861—July 22	Dropped out.
"	December 5	Baptism	Huldah Colver	1862—May 27	United States.
1853	April 17	Baptism	Nathan Cummings	1856—October 17	Letter.
"	April 17	Baptism	Simeon Crawford		
"	April 17	Baptism	Mrs. Cudney	1855—November 4	Beverley Church.

LIST OF MEMBERS—FIRST BAPTIST CHURCH, BRANTFORD.

When Received	How Received	Names	Date of Leaving	Reason for Leaving
1854—November 3	New York	Mary A. Cowherd		
" November 3	Hamilton	James Cox		
" November 3	Hamilton	Mrs. James Cox		
1855—June 20	Baptism	George C. Connor	1858—August 11	Dropped out.
" June 20	Baptism	Martha A. Clement		
1856—May 3	United States	Cheeney		
1857—March 27	Baptism	ElizabethClement		
" April 3	Baptism	Ruth Clifford	1857—April 17	A letter.
" April 10	Baptism	Jane E. Codwell		
" May 20	Baptism	Ann Clifford		
1858—March 11	First Mention	C. Clement	1858—March 11	Burgessville Church.
" March 25	Baptism	Alfred Cox		
" March 25	Baptism	Sarah M. Cox		
" July 16	Baptism	Rachael Clifford		
1859—June 14	First Mention	Mrs. Cox	1859—June 14	Boston, U. S.
" December 25	Baptism	Sarah J. Cowherd		
1860—January 16	First Mention	Crawford		
" January 26	Baptism	Jane Cowherd		
" February 27	Experience	William Cameron		
" February 27	Experience	Mrs. W. Cameron		
" June 19	First Mention	Elizabeth Crawford	1860—June 19	Dropped out.
" June 19	First Mention	Harriet Crawford	1860—June 19	Dropped out.
1861—March 17	Baptism	Magaret Currie	1870—March 22	A letter.
" July 22	Baptism	Charles Cawley		
" August 27	Baptism	Mrs. Christie		
" October 15	Baptism	Mary Chave	1871—April 26	?
1863—January 27	Baptism	Charlotte Christie	1869—February 23	Waterford Church.
" September 20	Baptism	Edwin Chalcraft		
" September 20	Baptism	Mary M. Chalcraft		

Year	Date	Event	Name	Date 2	Church
1863	September 20	Baptism	Mrs. Cawley		
1866	November 16	Quebec	T. Coles	1880—August 5	Burford Church.
"	November 16	Baptism	Frank Cox		
"	November 16	Baptssm	John Callis	1870—May 26	Tabernacle Church.
"	January 22	Baptism	Isabella Christie		Dropped out.
"	June 16	First Mention	Sister Cowherd	1867—June 16	Scotland Church.
1867	October 22	Experience	Mrs. Cole		
"	December 5	First Mention	Mr. Cawley		
1868	March 29	Baptism	John Cheeseman		
1869	March 5	Baptism	Abel Crawford		
"	March 12	Baptism	James Christopher		
"	March 12	Baptism	Alfred Cowherd	1871—April 26	Buffalo, U. S.
"	March 19	Baptism	Joseph Cawley		
"	March 23	Baptism	Martha Cawley		
"	March 28	Baptism	Mary Cawley		
1870	May 26	First Mention	Mrs. John Callis	1870—May 26	Tabernacle Church.
"	May 26	Baptism	Mr. Chamberlain		
1871	April 26	Blenheim Church	George Chittenden		
"	April 26	Blenheim Church	Mrs. George Chittenden		
"	April 26	Blenheim Church	Andrew Chittenden		
"	April 26	Blenheim Church	Alfred Chittenden	1876—December 3	?
"	April 26	Blenheim Church	Flavius Chittenden		
"	April 26	Blenheim Church	Mary Chittenden		
"	April 26	Blenheim Church	Sarah A. Chittenden		
"	May 9	Blenheim Church	George Chittenden, jr	1880—June 10	Kingsville Church.
"	August 4	Baptism	Miss Callis		
1872	April 5	Baptism	James Cuthbertson	1874—July 14	A letter.
"	May 3	First Mention	John Clark	1872—May 3	Toronto.
"	July 7	First Mention	James Cowherd	1872—July 7	Chatham Church.
"			William Chittenden	1874—October 18	Stratford Church.
1873	November 11	Baptism	William Chittenden	1878—September 19	Wingham Church.

LIST OF MEMBERS—FIRST BAPTIST CHURCH, BRANTFORD.

When Received.	How Received.	Names.	Date of Leaving.	Reason for Leaving.
1873—November 11	Baptism	David Chittenden		
" November 25	Baptism	Augusta Chittenden	1881—December 1	Onondaga Church.
" December 5	Baptism	Lucy Crawford		
" December 9	Baptism	Elmer Crawford		
" January 11	Baptism	Emily Cowherd	1878—May 30	Dropped out.
" April 5	Woodstock Church	Elizabeth Cheyne	1878—October 23	East Ward Church.
1874—May 3	Peterboro' Church	Peter Cunningham	1874—October 18	Woodstock Church.
" July 5	Baptism	Sarah Currie		
" November 1	Chatham Church	James Cowhead		Died.
" November 1	Chatham Church	Mrs. James Cowherd	1881—December 29	Manitoba.
1875—January 7	Baptism	Thomas Champion	1877—March 10	Toronto.
" January 28	Baptism	Jennie Cardwell		
" January 28	Baptism	Annie Craig		
" February 18	Baptism	Miss Cunningham	1875—August 27	East Ward Church.
" March 11	Baptism	Lizzie Cardwell	1881—October 6	East Ward Church.
" August 27	First Mention	Arphelda Cunningham	1875—August 27	East Ward Church.
" October 7	Baptism	John Carter		
" December 5	Tabernacle	W. J. Chalcraft		
1876—April 6	Baptism	Frederick Cowherd		
" April 16	Baptism	Thomas Callis		
" April 27	Baptism	Mary Callis		
" December 3	Letter	Mrs. Cameron		
1877—March 15	Baptism	Alice Cox		
" May 10	Baptism	Ida Cowherd		
" November 29	Baptism	Alexander Clark	1878—May 6	Dropped out.
" December 11	Baptism	Fanny Crawford		
" December 11	Baptism	Nellie Crawford		
" December 11	Baptism	Mary Carter		
1878—January 27	Baptism	J. H. Chatterton	1879—December 11	Dropped out.

Date	Type / Place	Name	Date	Church / Place
1878—April 4	First Mention	John Clifford	1878—April 4	Waterford Church.
" April 4	Experience	James Cox		
" April 7	Drumbo Church	Mrs. James Cox		
" May 23	Letter	Frederick Chalcraft		
" September 12	First Mention	William Chalcraft	1878—September 12	Hamilton Church.
1879—April 1	Baptism	Susia Crawford		
1879—April 6	Baptism	James Cletor		
" April 6	Baptism	Alfred Cawley		
" April 11	Baptism	Ernest Campbell		
" April 11	Baptism	Henry Cheyne	1879—October 23	East Ward Church.
" April 11	Baptism	Joseph Callis		
" April 11	Baptism	William Callis		
" April 20	Baptism	Joseph Clinkhammer		
" May 8	Baptism	Hattie Cameron		
" May 8	Baptism	Charles Cowherd		
1880—August 5	First Mention	Mrs. Frank Cox	1880—August 5	Burford Church.
" December 30	Paris Church	Flavius Chittenden	1881—March 10	Ohio, United States.
1881—January 13	Gobles Church	Adelaide Costin		
" July 7	Baptism	Brother Crinkshank	1881—November 3	Galt Church.
" September 1	Experience	Sister Cochrane		
1882—August 31	Fingal Church	F. K. Chittenden		
" October 24	Baptism	Miss Clement		
1883—January 4	Beamsville Church	Charles C. Haday		
" January 4	Beamsville Church	Mrs. C. Colladay		
" January 4	Beamsville Church	Annie Colladay		
" January 4	Beamsville Church	Susie Colladay		
" May 30	Michigan	Lewis Crandall		
" May 30	St. George Church	Egerton Crandall		
" June 27	East Ward Church	Mrs. H. F. Cawley		
" June 27	Experience	Mr. H. F. Cawley		
" August 1	Onondaga Church	Brother Cowie		

When Received	How Received	Names	Date of Leaving	Reason for Leaving.
1883—August 1	Onondaga Church	Sister Cowie		
" December 16	Baptism	William Clark		
" December 26	Scotland Church	Mrs. F. Chittenden		

D.

When Received	How Received	Names	Date of Leaving	Reason for Leaving.
1842—January 2	First Mention	Hector Dickie	1878—May 8	Died, aged 88 years.
" January 2	First Mention	Ann Dickie	1871—May 21	Died, aged 82 years.
" June 5	First Mention	Hugh Divinney	1855—January 9	Died, aged 72 years.
1843—April 1	Baptism	Elizabeth Dunn		
1845—June 15	First Mention	Mrs. Divinney	1845—August 31	London Church.
" June 15	First Mention	Dora Divinney	1869—September 10	Died.
1849—June 24	Baptism	Mrs. Dalrymple		
" June 24	Baptism	William Dalrymple	1870—May 28	Dropped out
1851—January 3	Markham Church	Rev. T. L. Davidson	1860—June 5	St. George' Church.
" January 3	Markham Church	Mrs. T. L. Davidson	1860—June 5	St. George Church.
1852—January 4	Esquesing	S. K. Dollar	1857—June 6	Died.
" January 4	Esquesing	Mrs. S. K. Dollar		
" July 4	Baptism	Mary Dalton	1861—October 15	Hamilton Church.
" September 5	Baptism	Ann E. Dove	1858—March 25	Simcoe Church.
1853—April 17	Baptism	Dorindah Divinney		
1854—May 22	Baptism	Mrs. Dalton	1856—October 17	Hamilton Church.
1856—May 1	Baptism	Nicholas Dymond		
" May 1	Baptism	M. A. Dymond	1882—June 24	Died.
" May 1	Baptism	Lucy Downs		
1857—April 3	Baptism	Jane Duncan		
" April 3	Baptism	Elizabeth Dimmock	1863—May 24	London Church.
" April 3	Baptism	Jane Dimmock	1860—June 19	Dropped out.
" May 7	Letter	Mary Davis		
" May 7	Perth Church	David Davidson	1860—June 5	Dropped out.

1857—May 7	Perth Church	Elizabeth Davidson		
1858—March 11	Baptism	Wm. Drake		
" March 25	Baptism	Thomas Draper	1868—April 5	Chatham Church.
" April 8	Baptism	Martha Ditty		
" April 8	Baptism	Patience Draper	1868—April 5	Chatham Church.
" July 16	Baptism	Isabella Dalrymple		
" September 10	Baptism	Lydia Dean	1859—February 9	Dundas Church.
" Sept~mber 10	Baptism	Sarah A. Dalton		
1862—April 22	First Mention	Brother Dungey		
" October 19	Baptism	Miss Davis		
" October 19	Baptism	Miss Dickie		
" October 22	Baptism	Evan Davis		
" October 22	Baptism	Mrs. Mary Davis		
1865—January 1	Buffalo	Jennie Dalrymple		
1866—November 16	Quebec Church	Sergeant A. Drake	1867 July 11	A letter.
" November 23	Baptism	Susan Dimmock	1877—April 5	Toronto.
" November 23	Baptism	Rebecca Dymond	1872—February 4	Guelph Church.
1867 July 7	Hamilton Church	Lucy Dalton		
1869—January 3	First Mention	Ruth Davis	1869—January 3	Hamilton Church.
" February 28	Baptism	Mrs. Dengate		
1872 May 3	First Mention	Augusta Dickie	1872—May 3	Fonthill.
1873—November 11	Baptism	Daniel Dengate		
1874—September 6	Tabernacle	Mrs. Thomas Draper		
1875 January 28	Baptism	Cornelia Diaken		
" February 18	Baptism	Louisa Dymond	1879—May 8	East Ward Church.
" February 18	Baptism	Sarah Dunham	1877—April 5	Dropped out.
1877—June 10	Baptism	Lizzie Donovan		
" September 7	Baptism	Mrs. Robert Douglass	1880 March 4	Tabernacle Church.
" October 7	First Mention	Robert Douglass	1880 March 4	Tabernacle Church.
1879—April 6	Baptism	Mrs. William Danskin	1882 March 30	Manitoba.
" April 6	Beamsville	Maggie DeWitt	1879 October 9	Detroit.

LIST OF MEMBERS—FIRST BAPTIST CHURCH, BRANTFORD.

When Received.	How Received.	Names.	Date of Leaving.	Reason for Leaving.
1879—April 11	Baptism	Annie Dawes		
1881—February 3	First Mention	Mrs. Dalton	1880—February 3	Hamilton.
1882—May 25	Baptism	Mrs. Dengate		
1883—December 16	Baptism	Mrs. George Dickinson		

E.

When Received.	How Received.	Names.	Date of Leaving.	Reason for Leaving.
1838—April 3	First Mention	Brother Emerson		
1842—November 19	First Mention	Mrs. Evans	1842—November 19	Paris Church
1848—September 3	First Mention	Brother Edmondson		
1850—September 15	Toronto	John Evans	1852—April 13	A letter
" September 15	Toronto	Rebecca Evans	1852—April 13	A letter
" September 15	Baptism	Thomas Evans	1865—December 5	Dropped out
" September 15	Baptism	Emily Evans	1865—December 5	Dropped out
1851—April 5	Toronto	John Evans, jr	1852—April 13	A letter
1855—May 20	Baptism	Robert Eadie		
" May 20	Baptism	Mrs. Robert Eadie		
1856—July 7	Baptism	Jane Eadie	1860—June 19	Dropped out
1858—March 11	Baptism	Matilda Evans		
1861—February 18	Baptism	Mrs. Jane Excell	1878—May 23	Tabernacle Church
1863—January 18	Baptism	Francis Ellis	1870—May 11	Tabernacle Church
" August 2	Wales	Sarah Edwards	1864—March 20	Ohio, U. S.
1866—November 23	Baptism	James N. Edy	1869—April 23	A letter
1867—March 3	Boston Church	Andrew Edy		
1868—April 5	Wingham Church	Robert Eadie		
" April 5	Wingham Church	Mrs. Robert Eadie		
1869—March 23	Baptism	Mrs. Edy		
" March 23	Baptism	Miss Edy		
1870—June 21	Baptism	——— Evans		
1872—February 4	Zone Church	Hiram Eberle		

Date	Event	Name	Date	Note
1873—April 6	First Mention	Willie Evans	1873 April 6	Buffalo
" November 11	Baptism	Eugene Excell	1877—April 20	Died at Brantford
1874—February 10	Baptism	Jane Edmondson		
" June 7	First Mention	John Eberle	1874—June 7	Bothwell Church
1875—January 10	Guelph Church	John Elliott		
" January 10	Guelph Church	Mrs. John Elliott		
1877—April 19	Baptism	Mr. Eschalman	1879—July 10	Dropped by request.
1881—March 10	Baptism	A. H. Elliot		
1882—November 30	East Ward Church	Sarah Edmundson		
1883—December 26	Baptism	Annie Elliott		

F.

Date	Event	Name	Date	Note
1838—April 3	First Mention	Heman Fitch	1838—June 25	A letter.
" June 25	First Mention	Mrs. H. Fitch	1838—June 25	A letter.
" June 25	First Mention	Mrs Charlotte Forbes	1838—June 25	A letter.
" December 30	First Mention	Harrison Forbes	1838—June 25	A letter.
" December 30	First Mention	Mrs. H. Forbes	1838—June 25	A letter.
1840—June 25	Baptism	Sarah Foster		
1850—September 15	First Mention	Francis Foster	1879—April 3	Died, aged 74 years.
" September 15	First Mention	Mrs. F. Foster	1875—January 2	Died, aged 73 years.
1851—August 31	Baptism	Alice Foster		
" October 31	Baptism	Mary Flynn	1855—March 1	Dropped out.
1852—March 7	Oxford Church	Harrison Forbes		
" July 4	Baptism	Sister Fairman	1856—June 4	Dropped out.
1855—August 14	Baptism	Mary Fletcher		
" June 20	Baptism	Frederick Fawkes	1863—September 20	Ingersoll Church.
1856—January 6	England	Mary Foster		
" April 17	Baptism	Nancy A. Fletcher	1860—June 19	Dropped out.
" May 1	Baptism	Martha Foster	1856—July 19	Died, aged 20 years.
" May 3	Baptism	George Foster	1870—April 14	Tabernacle Church.
" May 16	Baptism	Thomas Foster		

LIST OF MEMBERS—FIRST BAPTIST CHURCH, BRANTFORD.

When Received	How Received	Names	Date of Leaving	Reason for Leaving.
1856—June 4	Baptism	Elizabeth Fysh	1865—December 3	United States.
" November 12	Baptism	Mary Foster		
1857—April 3	Baptism	William Fletcher		
" April 10	Experience	Ann Fletcher		
1858—June 6	Hamilton Church	Mrs. Foreman		
" July 16	Baptism	Catharine Foster	1883—June 28	Died, Aged 38 years.
1859—December 25	Baptism	William Fletcher	1860—April 24	Dropped out.
1860—June 5	Dresden Church	Edmund Foot		Died.
" June 19	First Mention	Dorinda Fysh	1861—January 24	A letter.
" November 27	First Mention	Letitia C. Ferguson	1860—November 27	England.
1861—February 18	Baptism	Sarah A. Fletcher		
" April 16	Baptism	Harriet Fletcher		
" December 15	First Mention	James Fuller	1861—December 15	Caledonia.
1863—September 7	First Mention	Mrs. Fuller	1864—September 7	Lockport, U. S.
1865—February 4	Baptism	Margaret Fletcher		
" February 4	Baptism	Harriet Fletcher		
1866—September 7	Baptism	Alice Furnival		
1867—December —	Boston Church	Mrs. Fairchild		
" July 31	Baptism	Elizabeth Foster		
1868—December 22	Boston Church	Mrs. Fairchild		
1869—March 28	Baptism	Elizabeth Farley	1870—May 26	Dropped out.
1871—January 10	First Mention	Sarah A. Fryer	1871—January 10	Tabernacle Church.
" February 14	Baptism	Emma A. Fletcher		
1872—April 7	Second Onondaga Church	David File	1880—November 11	East Ward Church.
" April 7	Second Onondaga Church	Mrs. D. File	1880—November 11	East Ward Church
1873—November 28	Baptism	Charles Filkins	1879—June 5	A letter.
" October 5	Hamilton	Mr. Freer	1873—December 5	Hamilton Church
" October 5	Hamilton	Mrs. Freer	1873—December 5	Hamilton Church.
1874—January 30	Experience	Mrs. Charlotte Filkins	1879—June 5	A letter.

1874—April 3	Annie Fairchild	Woodstock Church	1880—June 10	Michigan.
" December 6	Francis S. Field	Baptism	1875—August 27	East Ward Church.
1875—January 28	Eugene Fletcher	Baptism		
" February 25	Georgena Fletcher	Baptism		
" April 1	Miss Fitness	Baptism		
" April 1	Miss Fairchild	Baptism		
1876—February 24	Mary Fletcher	Baptism		
1877—October 7	Elizabeth Foster	New Brunswick		
1878—September 26	William Fitness	Baptism		
" September 26	Mrs. William Fitness	Experience		
1879—May 8	Alberta Fairchild	Baptism	1881—September 22	Ingersoll Church.
1881—September 4	Mary Forde	St. Catharines Church	1882—September 28	St. Catharines Church.
1883—June 27	Mary Filer	Montreal		

G.

1845—April 5	William Gardner	Baptism		
1849—June 25	Mary Granville	Baptism		
1851—January 3	Thomas Granville	Baptism		
" October 31	Mrs. Geddes	Baptism	1855—March 1	Dropped out.
1855—July 5	Ellen R. Grey	Baptism		
1856—September 10	Brother Gilpin	First Mention		
1858—March 11	John Goodson	Baptism	1860—February 27	Dropped out.
" March 25	William Goodson	Baptism		
" March 25	Anne Goodson	Baptism		
" May 13	Mary A. Gill	Baptism	1861—August 17	Dropped out.
1860—January 5	Henry Green	Baptism	1879—June 5	Tabernacle.
" April 19	Robert Goodson	United States	1861—May 21	Beachville Church.
1861—April 16	Mrs. Robert Grant	Baptism	1867—August 4	Dundas Church.
1862—March 16	Robert Grant	Baptism	1867—August 4	Dundas Church.
" March 30	George Grantham	Baptism		
" April 6	James Grey	Buffalo	1863—September 13	Buffalo, United States.

LIST OF MEMBERS—FIRST BAPTIST CHURCH, BRANTFORD.

When Received	How Received	Names	Date of Leaving	Reason for Leaving.
1863—May 24	First Mention	Thomas R. Gilpin	1863—May 24	St. Mary's Church.
" June 7	United States	Robert Goodson	1863—June 7	United States.
1869—March 19	Baptism	Sarah J. Griffiths		
1870—May 26	First Mention	Mrs. Grantham	1870—May 26	Dropped out.
" December 4	Guelph Church	Robert Grant		
" December 4	Guelph Church	Mrs. R. Grant		
1871—February 3	Villa Nova	Elizabeth Grey	1872—April 5	United States.
" March 5	Boston Church	Edward Gunston		
" March 5	Boston Church	Mrs. Jane Gunston		
1872—February 4	Experience	Francis Grey	1875—May 27	Dropped out.
" February 4	Experience	Mr. Gibbs	1872—July 9	Dropped out.
" December 1	Beamsville Church	Franklin Grobb		
" December 1	Beamsville Church	Mrs. F. Grobb		
1874—January 11	Baptism	Laura Goatcher		
" March 24	Baptism	Miss Mary Griffith		
" June 7	Beamsville Church	Mary A. Gillmore	1880—May 13	Paris Church.
" November 22	Baptism	Mary Grare		
1875—January 28	Baptism	John Grantham	1881—February 6	Galt Church.
" February 18	Baptism	Ruth Grantham		
" February 21	Baptism	Jesse Gibson	1881—January 13	England.
" March 11	Baptism	Mrs. Gibbs		
" April 11	Baptism	Henry Griffith		
" August 27	First Mention	Edwin Gunston	1875—August 27	East Ward Church.
" August 27	First Mention	Mrs. Jane Gunston	1875—August 27	East Ward Church.
1876—May 11	Baptism	William Grey	1878—May 16	Dropped out.
" February 17	Baptism	Walter Gibson	1876—June 15	Buffalo.
1877—June 3	Baptism	G. H. Girdwood	1882—December 14	Michigan.
" October 7	East Ward Church	Mr. A. Gunston	1880—April 14	East Ward Church.
" October 7	East Ward Church	Mrs. A. Gunston	1880—April 14	East Ward Church.

1877—October 7	First Mention	Fanny Grantham	1878—May 16	Dropped out.
1878—November 7	Baptism	Mrs. Goulding	1880—July 8	Rochester, United States.
" November 28	Baptism	Thomas Goulding	1880—July 8	Rochester, United States.
1879—January 5	Experience	Mrs. George Grantham		
" March 30	Baptism	Romie Gardner		
" April 6	Experience	Mrs. W. Grunstead		
" April 6	Baptism	Annie Godfrey		
" April 11	Baptism	Thomas Goulding	1880—July 8	Rochester, United States.
" April 20	Baptism	Louisa Goulding	1880—July 8	Rochester, United States.
" June 5	First Mention	Mrs. Gardner	1883—August 1	Park Church.
" July 10	First Mention	Mrs. Henry Green	1879—June 5	Tabernacle Church.
1880—January 4	Michigan	Mrs. Grunstead	1879—July 10	St. Thomas Church.
1881—January 13	East Ward Church	Abram Green		
" January 13	East Ward Church	Franklin Grobb		
1882—November 2	Delhi Church	Mrs. F. Grobb		
		Eliza C. Gillespie		

H.

1835—December 4	First Mention	Deacon Hazelton	1835—June 25	A letter.
1836—January 1	First Mention	Brother Hopkins	1838—June 25	Dropped out.
" January 30	First Mention	Hammill's family		
1838—February 6	First Mention	Sister Hopkins	1842—May 21	Dropped out.
" June 25	First Mention	Sister Hazelton	1838—June 25	A letter.
1840—September 19	First Mention	Eliza Hammill	1840—October 17	Dropped out.
1842—February 5	First Mention	Mary A. Henry	1842—February 5	Simcoe Church.
1844—March 16	Baptism	Matilda Hamlin		
1845—January 15	First Mention	Mr. Hartley		
" May 10	Baptism	Selina Hamlin	1851—March 30	Dropped out.
1846—July 4	First Mention	Giles Hartley	1846—July 4	To form a new Church.
" July 4	First Mention	Richard Hartley	1846—July 4	To form a new Church.
" August 1	Baptism	Mary Honeyford	1851—May 23	Dropped out.

LIST OF MEMBERS—FIRST BAPTIST CHURCH BRANTFORD.

When Received	How Received	Names	Date of Leaving	Reason for Leaving.
1850—September 15	Baptism	Sarah Holmes	1853—March 27	Paris Church.
1851—January 3	Oakland Church	Rev. John Harris		
" May 23	First Mention	Mr. A. Honeyford	1851—May 23	Dropped out.
" August 31	Baptism	Mrs. Thomas Huskinson	1861—May 27	Orangeville Church.
" October 5	Woodstock Church	Priscilla Hallam		
" October 5	Baptism	Thomas Huskinson	1861—August 27	Orangeville Church.
1852—February 22	Townsend Church	Allanson Harris	1867—January 29	Beamsville Church.
" April 11	Baptism	John Harrison		
" June 6th	First Mention	Mrs. Harris		
" December 5	Baptism	Martha Hulbert	1860—June 19	Dropped out.
1853—April 11	Baptism	Thomas Harrison	1862—April 22	Dropped out.
1854—July 2	Baptism	Maria Hulbert	1856—January 28	Beamsville Church.
1855—April 1	England	Frederick T. Hill		
" April 15	Baptism	Samuel Hall	1855—December 5	A Letter.
" May 24	First Mention	Mr. Hill		
" May 24	Baptism	Mrs. Thomas Hillis	1865—December 5	Dropped out.
" June 2	Baptism	Thomas Hillis	1865—December 5	Dropped out.
" July 19	Baptism	Eli C. Harris	1859—February 18	Ingersoll Church.
" July 19	Baptism	Mary D. Harriss	1857—February 16	Died, aged 21 years.
" July 26	First Mention	F. E. Hill	1855—July 26	Woodstock Church.
" December 2	Baptism	Lewis Hall	1857—April 17	A Letter.
" December 2	Baptism	Mrs. Lewis Hall	1857—April 17	A Letter.
1856—January 6	Letter Received	F. J. Hill		
" March 28	Baptism	Charlotte Hale		
" March 28	Baptism	Jonathan Hale		
" June 4	Baptism	Mary Hall	1856—August 29	Died, aged 20 years.
1857—January 17	First Mention	Mrs. Alanson Harris	1857—January 29	Beamsville Church.
" April 3	Baptism	Harriet Holland		
" July 8	Baptism	Elmira Hulbert		

Year / Date		Event	Name	Date	Notes
1857	July 8	First Mention	Wm. E. Holbrook	1857—July 21	Dropped out.
"	December 23	First Mention	Rebecca Hallam	1857—December 23	Woodstock Church,
1858	March 11		Henstock		
"	March 25	Baptism	Agnes Hallet		
"	April 8	Baptism	Hartley Hartley		
"	April 8	Baptism	Jane Hartley		
"	April 22	Baptism	William Hardy	1860—March 5	Dropped out.
1859	February 19	Baptism	Miss Myra Holland		
"	December 25	Baptism	Isabella Healley		
1860	January 16	First Mention	Isabella Hartley		
"	January 16	England	Mrs. Holland	1862—July 6	Simcoe Church.
"	January 19	First Mention	Mrs. R. Henstock	1860—January 19	Dropped out.
1861	December 15	First Mention	Sister Hall	1861—December 15	Caledonia Church.
1862	January 5	First Mention	Hannah Hargraves	1862—January 5	Mount Healey Church.
"	March 16	Baptism	George Hunter	1863—January 25	A Letter.
"	May 20	Baptism	Lucy Hickox		
"	June 17	Experience	John Holland	1862—June 17	Simcoe Church.
"	November 7	St. George	Charles Hunter		
"	November 7	St. George	Euphemia Hunter		
"	November 27	West Oxford Church	John Hext		
1865	September 5	First Mention	Elizabeth P. Howell		
"	November 5	Boston	Elizabeth Hazelton	1875—August 27	East Ward Church.
1866	April 27	Baptism	Hazelton		
"	November 23	Baptism	William Hall		
1868	May 26	Baptism	Margaret A. Harrison	1882—February 21	Died, aged 60 years.
"	May 26	Baptism	Grace Harrison	1873—October 2	Died, aged 20 years.
1869	March 5	Baptism	Elizabeth Hext		
"	March 5	Baptism	Emeline Handscomb	1878—May 16	Dropped out.
"	April 23	Baptism	Ezra Hazelton	1880—November 11	East Ward Church.
1870	May 11	First Mention	William C. Hoth	1870—May 11	Park Church.
"	July 12	United States	Dr. J. C. Hurd	1873—April 6	Buffalo, Died

WHEN RECEIVED.	HOW RECEIVED.	NAMES.	DATE OF LEAVING.	REASON FOR LEAVING.
1870—July 12	United States	Mrs. J. C. Hurd	1873—February 26	Died.
" August 4	First Mention	Ann Houlding	1870—August 4	Burtch Corner.
" August 4	England	Joseph Hamlyn	1876—April 27	England.
1871—August 4	Baptism	Miss Hume		
" October 15	Baptism	Sister Howell		
" December 3	Woodstock Church	Adelaide Howell		
" December 17	Burtch Church	Emma Hartley		
1872—January 14	Ingersoll Church	Mrs. Rev. John Harris		
" February 4	Union Church	Lucinda Howell		
" February 4	Union Church	Rachael Howell		
" March 3	Waterdown	Thomas Hill		
" March 3	Waterdown	Mary Hill		
" May 5	Cheddor	George Hill		
" May 5	Cheddor	Mrs. George Hill		
" December 1	Beamsville Church	Alonson Harris		
" December 1	Beamsville Church	Mrs Mary Harris		
" December 1	Beamsville Church	Nellie Harris		
" December 1	Beamsville Church	John Harris	1887—August 25	Died.
" December 1	Beamsville Church	Mrs. John Harris		
1873—November 11	Baptism	Amelia Hazelton	1875—August 27	East Ward Church.
" November 25	Baptism	Bertie Hale	1877—May 29	Dropped out.
" December 26	Beamsville Church	Elmore Harris		
" December 28	Baptism	Susan Hatcher		
1874—January 11	Baptism	Wellington Howell	1887—November 2	Died, aged 36 years.
" January 11	Baptism	Squire Hazelton	1875—August 27	East Ward Church.
" January 11	Baptism	William Hill		
" January 11	Baptism	William Hatcher		
" April 19	Baptism	Mrs. Harrison		
" April 19	Baptism	Elias Hazelton	1878—May 30	Woodstock Church.

—164—

1874	May 3	Baptism	Mrs. Thomas Holden		
"	May 3	Baptism	Rebecca Holden		
"	May 5	Baptism	Mrs. Thomas Hext		
"	July 5	Yarmouth	Annie Hersey		
"	October 25	Baptism	Augustus Howell		
"	November 17	Baptism	Mary A. Holt		
1875	January 28	Baptism	Mary Hume		
"	January 28	Baptism	Elizabeth Handy	1877—May 29	Dropped Out.
"	January 28	Baptism	Hugh Howie		
"	January 28	Baptism	Frederick Hale		
"	January 31	Baptism	Mary A. Hatcher		
"	January 31	Baptism	Thomas Hatcher	1881—June 30	Chatham Church.
"	February 18	Baptism	Hugh Harrison		
"	February 25	Baptism	Robert Hume		
"	February 23	Baptism	Frederick Hill		
"	March 4	Baptism	Thomas Hill		
"	March 7	First Mention	Ada Howell	1875 March 7	Aylmer Church.
"	March 7	England	Mrs. J. A. Hamlyn	1876—April 27	England.
"	March 11	Baptism	Christina Harrison		
"	March 11	Baptism	Mary Harrison		
"	March 11	Baptism	John Harrison		
"	March 25	Baptism	Edward Holmes		Died.
"	April 8	Baptism	Emma Holmes		
"	April 15	Baptism	Mary J. Herron		
"	April 30	Experience	James Hartley		
"	July 4	Wedmore, England	Thomas Hill		
"	July 4	Wedmore, England	Anna Hill		
"	July 4	Letter	Edward Hill	1877—February 15	Tabernacle Church.
"	August 27	First Mention	A. W. Hazelton	1875 — August 27	East Ward Church.
"	August 27	First Mention	Elizabeth Hazelton	" August 27	East Ward Church.
"	August 27	First Mention	S. W. Hazelton	" August 27	East Ward Church.

LIST OF MEMBERS—FIRST BAPTIST CHURCH, BRANTFORD.

When Received.	How Received.	Names.	Date of Leaving.	Reason for Leaving.
1876—March 30	Baptism	Mrs. John Hamlyn	1880—January 29	Woodstock Church.
" April 27	Baptism	George Haddlesay		
" April 27	First Mention	Joseph Hamlyn	1876—April 27	England.
" May 11	Baptism	Ida Holmstead		
" May 18	Baptism	Mrs. George Haddlesay		
" July 6	Baptism	John Hall		
" September 21	Baptism	Emma Harris	1876—November 23	A Letter.
" October 15	Baptism	Mr. Hendry		
" December 3	Baptism	Mrs. Hazelton	1880—November 11	East Ward Church.
1877—April 1	Drumbo Church	Samuel Herbert	1879—May 8	United States.
" April 1	Drumbo Church	Mrs. Samuel Herbert	1879—May 8	United States.
" April 5	First Mention	Sarah Hamlyn	1877—April 5	Dropped out.
" June 10	Baptism	Mrs. Hankinson	1878—June 6	A Letter.
1878—May 30	First Mention	Mrs. Elias Hazelton	1878—May 30	Woodstock Church.
" May 16	First Mention	Emily Hanscomb	1878—May 16	Dropped out.
" May 23	Experience	Edward Hill		
" October 6	Tabernacle Church	Thomas B. Henderson		
" October 6	Tabernacle Church	Sarah Henderson		
1879—March 30	Baptism	Bessie Hill		
" March 30	Baptism	Minnie Harris		
" March 30	Baptism	Annie Holland	1879—April 23	Dropped out.
" April 1	Baptism	Annie Harris		
" April 1	Baptism	Ellen Harrison		
" April 6	Experience	John Holland	1880—April 14	Toronto Church.
" April 6	Baptism	Mabel Harris		
" April 6	Baptism	Lloyd Harris		
" April 6	Baptism	John Hill		
" April 6	Baptism	Newman Hall	1883—March 21	Blenheim Church.
" April 6	Galt Church	Mrs. John Holland		

Year	Date	Type	Name		Note
1879	—April 11	Baptism	Moses Hext	1881—December 29	Onondaga Church.
"	April 11	Baptism	Wallace Hartley		
"	April 15	Baptism	Wm. H. House	1882—June 29	A Manitoba Church.
"	April 15	Baptism	William Hill		
"	April 15	Baptism	Ernest Hill		
"	April 15	Baptism	Eliza Hill		
"	April 15	Baptism	Addie Hext		
"	April 15	Baptism	Effie Hext		
"	April 20	Baptism	Nettie Hamlyn	1880—January 29	Woodstock Church.
"	April 20	Sarnia Church	George W. Holmes	1881—November 17	Toronto.
"	June 1	Baptism	Clara Henry		
"	June 1	Baptism	Cora Henry	1883—May 30	Dropped out.
"	September 7	First Mention (Baptism).	Bella Halcett	1879—September 7	Ottawa Church.
"	October 23	Baptism	Matilda Heath	1879—October 23	Quebec Church.
"	November 2	First Mention	Bro. A. E. Hill	1879 November 2	Emerson Church.
1880	—January 15	First Mention	Brother Hall	1880—January 15	East Ward Church.
"	November 11	First Mention	Brother E. Hazelton	1880—November 11	East Ward Church.
"	November 11	First Mention	Mrs. Hazelton	1880—November 11	East Ward Church.
1881	—February 6	Baptism	G. F. Huskinson	1883—August 1	A Letter.
"	June 30	First Mention	Thomas Hatcher	1881—June 30	Chatham Church.
"	September 1	First Mention	Elizabeth Healey	1881 September 3	A Letter.
"	September 8	Baptism	Thomas M. Harris		
"	September 22	First Mention	Mary Hill	1881—September 22	London Church.
"	December 29	First Mention	Sister Hartley	1881—December 29	Toronto Church.
1882	—May 30	Baptism	James Hately		
"	May 30	Baptism	Mrs. James Hately		
"	August 31	Toronto	John Holland		
"	November 2	St. Catharines Church	Mary Hodgson		
"	December 3	Toronto	Mrs. Hartley		
1883	—May 30	Scotland Church	Perry Handy		
"	May 30	Scotland Church	Mrs. Perry Handy		

LIST OF MEMBERS—FIRST BAPTIST CHURCH, BRANTFORD.

WHEN RECEIVED.	HOW RECEIVED.	NAMES.	DATE OF LEAVING.	REASON FOR LEAVING.
1883—October 31	Baptism	P. Harrison		Died.
" December 16	Baptism	Sarah Harrison		
" December 16	Baptism	Tillie Hill		
" December 16	Baptism	Hattie Hill		
" December 16	Baptism	Mary Hill		
" December 19	Baptism	David Ifill		
" December 19	Baptism	Mary Handy		
" December 19	Baptism	Ida Handy		
" December 16	Baptism	Albert Ifil		
" December 26	Baptism	Matilda Hill		

I.

WHEN RECEIVED.	HOW RECEIVED.	NAMES.	DATE OF LEAVING.	REASON FOR LEAVING.
1855—June 20	Baptism	Elizabeth Iden		
1858—March 11	First Mention	Matilda Ivans	1858—February 9	Dropped out.
" July 16	Baptism	Mercy Iden		
1863—September 20	Baptism	Sarah Iden		
" October 25	Baptism	Abigail Ives		
1879—April 11	Baptism	Ellen Ives.		

J.

WHEN RECEIVED.	HOW RECEIVED.	NAMES.	DATE OF LEAVING.	REASON FOR LEAVING.
1836—November 7	First Mention	Brother Jackson	1857—November 27	Dropped out.
1839—April 18	First Mention	Brother Jones		
1842—January 2	First Mention	Stephen Jones	1851—May 3	Dropped out.
" April 3	First Mention	Mercy Jones		
" May 1	St. Catharines Church	William Jackson	1861—April 16	
" May 1	St. Catharines Church	Mrs. Jackson	1842—May 1	Dropped out.
1844—February 17	Baptism	Lucinda Jones	1851—May 3	Dropped out.
1845—March 15	Baptism	Charles Jarvis	1847—February 6	Dropped out.
1850—July 6	First Mention	Betsey Jex	1850—July 6	Dropped out.

51—February 1	First Mention	Hannah Jones	1851—February 1	
" February 1	First Mention	Mary Jones	1851—May 3	Dropped out.
" March 3	Baptism	Mrs. S. Jones	1851—May 3	Dropped out.
" July 20	Baptism	Jemina Julien	1860—June 19	Dropped out.
1852—November 7	Baptism	Mary A. Jackson		
1853—June 5	Waterford Church	Maria Jarvis		
" August 14	Baptism	Eleanor Jackson		
1854—November 3	Toronto	F. D. Jenkins	1856—June 4	Dropped out.
1855—September 20	Baptism	Mrs. Jex, Sr.		
1856—April 17	Baptism	James Jack		
" June 14	Baptism	Ann Jennings		
" November 12	First Mention	John H. Jack	1850—November 12	Paris Church.
1857—April 3	Baptism	Henry Jarvis	1881—December 29	Paris Church.
" April 3	Experience	Charles Jarvis		
" April 10	Baptism	Walter Jarvis	1858—September 10	Dropped out.
1858—April 8	Baptism	Emily Jones		
" May 13	Baptism	Mrs. Johnston		
" July 16	Baptism	Mrs. Ann Jones		
1861—March 10	Experience	F. D. Jenkins	1862—February 18	Dropped out.
" May 21	Experience	William Jackson		
" July 22	Norwich Church	Henry Jenkinson		
1862—March 2	St. George Church	Mrs. Charlotte Jarvis		
1865—June 7	Baptism	Lydia J. Jackson		
1868—July 28	First Mention	Ann Johnston	1868—July 28	Wingham Church.
" November 10	First Mention	Mrs. Jarvis		
1871—January 10	England	John Jeffries	1879—November 13	East Ward Church.
" January 10	England	Mrs. John Jeffries	1879—November 13	East Ward Church.
1872—May 21	Baptism	Alice Jeffries		
1875—February 25	Baptism	William Jex		
" March 11	Baptism	Homer Johnston	1875—July 22	Dropped out.
" July 2	Baptism	Mrs. Jones		

WHEN RECEIVED.	HOW RECEIVED.	NAME.	DATE OF LEAVING.	REASON FOR LEAVING.
1877—November 9	Baptism	Edward James		
" November 15	Baptism	Mary Jennings		
1878—June 6	Baptism	Brother Jennings		
" October 3	Baptism	Mrs. E. James		
1879—April 6	Baptism	Alfred Jex		
" April 20	Baptism	Edgar Jones		
" May 4	Experience	Lyman Jones	1883—May 30	Dropped out.
1882—March 3	First Mention	Henry Jarvis	1882—March 3	Paris Church.
" May 30	Baptism	Henry Jones		
1883—May 30	First Mention	Mrs. Lyman Jones	1883—May 30	Dropped out.
" December 16	Baptism	Maud Jennings		
" December 19	Baptism	A. Jennings		
" December 19	Baptism	Mary Jennings		

K.

WHEN RECEIVED.	HOW RECEIVED.	NAME.	DATE OF LEAVING.	REASON FOR LEAVING.
1835—December 4	First Mention	Brother Keelar	1836—December 30	Dropped out.
1843—August 19	Letter	F. Keeple.		
1853—April 17	Baptism	Martha Kipp	1864—April 10	Ohio, U. S.
1856—March 28	Baptism	John Knox		
" May 1	Baptism	John Kipp	1858—May 13	Dropped out.
1859—May 3	Baptism	Caroline Kirby		
1860—January 5	Baptism	Esther A. King		
1861—February 18	Baptism	Elizabeth Kennedy	1867—December 5	Dropped out.
1862—January 12	Baptism	William Knox		
1867—September 1	Stratford Church	Rev. A. E. Kitchen		Dropped out.
" September 1	Stratford Church	Mrs. Rev. A. E. Kitchen		
1869—March 23	Baptism	Emily Knox	1872—May 5	Scotland Church.
1870—June 21	Baptism	Agnes Knox		

Year	Date	Event	Name	Date	Status/Church
1875	January 28	Baptism	George Knox	1881—March 17	Tabernacle Church.
"	July 1	Baptism	John Kingswell	1882—May 4	Dropped Out.
1879	April 1	Baptism	Mary Kennedy		
1880	December 5	?	Mrs. Klepper		
1881	September 13	First Mention	Sister Kelly	1881—September 13	Dropped out.

L.

Year	Date	Event	Name	Date	Status/Church
1842	July 16	Beamsville Church	Hannah Lindsay	1842—September 14	Dropped out.
1843	April 1	Baptism	John Liverick		
1845	March 15	Baptism	Ellen Lamont		
"	April 5	Baptism	Francis Lissant	1851 October 5	Paris Church.
"	May 10	Simcoe Church	Henry E. Lee	1851—May 23	Dropped out.
1851	February 1	First Mention	Margaret Lester	1851—May 23	Dropped out.
"	April 5	Baptism	Nelson Laycock	1852—June 18	A letter.
1854	July 2	Baptism	Mrs. John Lake		Died.
1855	March 25	First Mention	Sister Lindzy	1855—March 25	Onondaga Church.
1856	March 28	Baptism	Maria Large		
"	April 17	Baptism	Thomas Large		
"	April 17	Baptism	Eli Lundy	1865—December 5	Dropped out.
"	May 1	Experience	James Lewis	1890 June 19	Dropped out.
"	May 1	Baptism	Mrs Esther Lewis		
"	May 1	Baptism	Ann Jane Lee	1860—May 12	Dropped out.
"	May 1	Baptism	Anna J. Lundy	1865 December 5	Dropped out.
"	May 16	Baptism	George Leaney	1857 October 21	Dropped out.
"	May 16	Baptism	Ann E. Leaney	1857 October 21	A Letter.
1857	April 3	Baptism	Mary A. Logan		
"	April 22	Baptism	Maria Lundy	1865—December 5	Dropped out.
1860	January 16	First Mention	Mary A. Lanzan		
1861	March 19	Baptism	Thomas Lockyer		
"	April 16	Baptism	Robert Lowe		
1862	April 20	Baptism	Mary A. Lowe	1863—January 25	Woodstock Church.

When Received.	How Received.	Names.	Date of Leaving.	Reason for Leaving.
1862—November 7	First Mention	Pardon Latham	1862—November 7	United States.
1868—March 1	First Mention	Lowe	1868—March 1	Chatham Church.
" April 5	Paris Church	Maria Latshaw	1869—May 18	United States.
1869—February 23	Baptism	Ellen Livingstone		
" March 19	Baptism	John Lewis	1870—September 27	Hamilton Church.
" March 19	Baptism	Caroline Lilly		
" March 23	Baptism	Mrs. Ann Livingstone		
" April 23	Baptism	Elizabeth Lake		
" April 23	First Mention	Sister Lester	1869—April 23	Burford Church.
1870—November 13	Baptism	Mrs. Long		
1871—December 3	Woodstock Church	Martha Lee		
1872—December 1	Beamsville Church	Hannah Longmire		
1873—November 11	Baptism	Jane Lanham	1879—December 11	Governor's Road Church.
1875—January 7	Baptism	M. Lindley		
" February 4	Baptism	Sarah Lindley		
" February 4	Baptism	Harriet Lindley		
" February 11	Baptism	Mary A. Livingston		
" February 11	Baptism	Lilly Livingston		
" February 18	Baptism	Mrs. J. Linser		
" February 18	Baptism	Bella Lightbody	1879—September 11	Ottawa Church.
" February 18	Baptism	Jennie Lindsay		
" February 25	Baptism	Jessie Lindsay		
" February 25	Baptism	Ebenezer Lightbody		
" March 4	Baptism	James Linster		
" March 4	Baptism	George Lake	1883—May 30	Dropped out.
" April 11	Baptism	Mrs. Isabella Lightbody	1877—May 29	Dropped out.
" April 30	Baptism	Jennie Lightbody	1880—May 16	Ottawa Church.
" July 2	Baptism	Miss Lightbody	1877—May 29	Dropped out.
1876—April 20	Baptism	Samuel Long	1878—November 7	Dropped out.

1876—December 31	Baptism	Florence Large		
1877—May 6	Baptism	Mary Long	1878 - November 28	A Letter.
" May 16	First Mention	Grace Lightbody	1881—January 13	Tabernacle Church.
" November 15	Baptism	Sister Lester	1878—May 16	Dropped out.
1878—September 26	Experience	Brother Lucas		
" April 1	Baptism	Clara Livingston		
" April 6	Experience	Mrs. George Lindley		
" April 11	Baptism	Mary Lake		
" April 11	Baptism	Lotty Lake		
" April 15	Baptism	Peter Lawn	1879 December 11	United States.
1880—January 25	Baptism	Annie Lindley		
1882—June 29	Michigan	Maggie Likens		
1883—December 10	Experience	E. W. Lockman		
" December 19	Experience	Mrs. Lockman		

M.

1836—June 2	First Mention	Brother Minchel	1836—November 7	Dropped out.
1837—November 1	First Mention	James Martin		
1838—June 25	By Letter	John Moyle		
1844—October 20	First Mention	William Moyle		
1850—November 3	Woodstock Church	Margaret Midgley	1860—June 19	Dropped out.
1851—January 3	Baptism	Elizabeth Miller		
" August 10	Montreal Church	James Morton		
" December 5	New York	Joseph Mitchell	1862—January 12	Governor's Road Church.
1852—November 7	Baptism	Elizabeth Maxwell		
" December 5	Montreal Church	John Alexander Morton	1855—July 26	Dropped out.
1853—January 23	Baptism	Thomas Mordue		
" January 23	Baptism	Nancy A. Mordue		
" January 23	Baptism	Jane Mordue		
" January 23	Baptism	Joseph Mordue		
1854—May 6	Ancaster	Elizabeth Mordue		

WHEN RECEIVED.	HOW RECEIVED.	NAMES.	DATE OF LEAVING.	REASON FOR LEAVING.
1855—March 1	First Mention	Mrs. Mitchell	1855—March 1	Dropped out.
" May 7	First Mention	George Millard		Died.
1856—February 24	Baptism	Robert Mellish	1860—June 19	Dropped out.
" April 17	Baptism	Fanny Montrose		
" May 1	Baptism	Mrs. Robert Maxwell		
" May 16	Baptism	Robert Mitchell		
" June 1	Experience	Jane Maitland	1860—June 19	Dropped out.
" June 4	Baptism	Marion Maxwell		Died.
" July 6	Port Hope	Robert Morton, Sr.	1873—March 27	Died, aged 78 years.
" July 6	Port Hope	Helen Morton	1874—April 17	Died, aged 74 years.
" July 6	Port Hope	Selina Morton		
" September 17	First Mention	Mrs. Anna Moyle	1856—September 19	Paris Church.
1856—November 2	First Mention	Robert Morton, Jr.	1860—April 19	Dropped out.
" November 12	Baptism	Mary Mitchell		
1857—April 3	Baptism	Thomas Mitchell		
" July 8	Baptism	Jane Morton		
" December 23	First Mention	Brother Morgan		
1858—March 25	Baptism	William Morris		
" March 25	Baptism	Thomas Morris	1866—August 21	Toronto Church.
" March 25	First Mention	John Minore, Sr	1875—May 27	Dropped out.
" April 22	Baptism	Susan Minore		
" July 11	Baptism	Sarah A. Miles		
1859—February 9	Baptism	Robert Mathison	1860—November 27	Hamilton Church.
" February 18	First Mention	Margaret Martin	1859—February 18	Woodstock Church.
" December 25	Baptism	John T. Mitchell		
" December 25	Baptism	David J. Mitchell		
" December 25	Baptism	Joseph Mitchell		Dropped out.
1860—January 5	Baptism	Ambrose Mitchell		
" January 5	Baptism	Mary J. Mitchell		

Year — Date	Type	Name	Date	Note
1860—February 27	First Mention	Thomas Morgan		
" June 19	First Mention	Agnes Marshall	1860—June 19	Letter.
" June 19	First Mention	Mrs. Mellish	1860—June 19	Dropped out.
" July 31	Baptism	Ellen Marshall		
" December 16	Baptism	Thomas Muirhead	1862—July 15	Paris Church.
1861—April 15	Baptism	William Muirhead	1863—May 24	St. Mary's Church.
" April 15	Baptism	Robert Muirhead		
1862—January 12	Baptism	William Miles.		
" January 12	Experience	Joseph Mitchell	1862 — January 12	Union Church.
" March 16	Experience	Mrs. Morris.		
" March 23	Baptism	Martha Moyle	1872 — January 14	Paris Church.
" April 8	Baptism	Ellen Muirhead	1862—July 15	Paris Church.
" June 17	Experience	Mrs Canfield Morris.		
" July 15	First Mention	Angus Muirhead	1862—July 15	Paris Church.
" August 28	Letter	Margaret Martin	1860—May 18	United States.
1864—September 7	Experience	Mrs. Andrew Morton	1870—May 11	Tabernacle Church.
1865—June 4	Drummond Church	Andrew Mitchell.		
" June 4	Drummond Church	Mrs. A. Mitchell.		
1867—January 22	Baptism	Elizabeth A. Minturn.		
" December 22	First Mention	Mrs Thomas Morris	1868—December 22	New York.
1868—March 29	Baptism	James Moon.		
1870—November 15	Surgeon's Church	Robert J. Millard	1875 — May 27	Dropped out.
1871—February 14	Baptism	Isabella Muthison		
" December 1	Beamsville Church	William Masales.		
" December 1	Beamsville Church	Mrs. William Misales.		
1872—January 14	Baptism	William Moyle.		
1873—April 6	England	Elizabeth Mather.		
" November 2	Ancaster	S. S. Misner	1875—October 21	Withdrawn.
1875—January 28	Baptism	Emily Murray.		
" January 28	Baptism	Annie Mackie	1875—April 1	Goble's Corners Church.
" January 28	Baptism	Angus Murray.		

LIST OF MEMBERS—FIRST BAPTIST CHURCH, BRANTFORD.

When Received	How Received	Names	Date of Leaving	Reason for Leaving.
1875—January 28	Baptism	J. Murray		
" February 14	Baptism	Angeline Marlett	1875—August 27	East Ward Church.
" February 18	Baptism	Fanny Murray		
" February 18	Baptism	Catharine Myrtle		
" February 25	Baptism	Ella Murray		
" February 25	Baptism	John Minore		
" March 4	Baptism	Diantha Marlett	1880—April 14	East Ward Church.
" March 7	Baptism	Robert M. Murray		
" May 27	First Mention	Ellen Mills	1875—May 27	Dropped out.
" July 1	Baptism	Mary Mordue		
" October 28	Port Burwell Church	Sister Mellish	1878—June 20	Chatham Church.
" December 9	Baptism	Annie Mellish	1879—July 10	Chatham Church.
1876—February 24	Letter	Alfred Mellish	1879—September 11	Dropped out.
" April 2	Baptism	Maria Moss	1879—May 8	Toronto.
" May 7	Baptism	Amy Mellish	1881—June 30	Chatham Church.
" June 22	First Mention	John Minore, jr	1876—June 22	Lindsay.
" September 21	Baptism	Mrs. Mitchell		
1877—April 26	Burgessville Church	J. B. Moore	1883—January 4	United States.
" April 26	Burgessville Church	Mrs. J. B. Moore	1883—January 4	United States.
" April 26	Baptism	Lucy Mills		
" October 7	First Mention	Mrs. Miner	1881—March 17	Guelph Church.
" November 4	United States.	Maggie Mordue		
1878—May 30	First Mention	Brother Morton	1878—May 30	Dropped out.
" July 4	Letter	Mrs. L. Moore		
1879—March 30	Baptism	Matthew Muir		
" April 1	Baptism	Lewis Mehennick	1879—April 23	London Church.
1880—October 3	Guelph Church	Mrs. Mather		
" December 2	Baptism	Lilly Marlatt	1883—June 27	Detroit.
1881—May 12	First Mention	Sister Marshall	1881—May 12	Toronto.

12	1881—November 17	East Ward Church	Ernest Myrtle		
	1882—March 3	Baptism	Mrs. Mitchell		
"	April 2	Baptism	Miss Maybee	1882 August 31	Manitoba.

Mc.

1836	January 20	First Mention	Deacon McDiarmid		
"	March 4	First Mention	James McMichael	1860 September 6	Dropped out.
1837	July 21	First Mention	John McCall		
1845	March 15	Baptism	John McDonald	1856 June 4	Dropped.
1846	July 4	First Mention	Allan McDougall		
"	July 4	First Mention	Mrs McDiarmid		
"	December 4	St. George's Church	William McKenzie		
1847	October 2	First Mention	Mrs. McIntyre		
1849	June 26	Baptism	Mrs. McIntosh	1857 January 5	Beverley Church.
"	June 26	Baptism	Mr. McIntosh	1857 January 5	Beverley Church.
1851	April 5	Baptism	Rosanna McGowen	1855 September 27	United States.
"	October 31	Baptism	William McDonald	1853 June 26	Dropped out.
1852	February 22	Baptism	Mrs. McDonald		
1855	June 20	Baptism	Sarah McCosh		
"	July 5	Baptism	Mary McMeans		
"	July 5	Baptism	Catharine McColl		
"	December 2	St. George's Church	James McMichael	1860 June 10	Dropped out.
1856	March 7	Baptism	Susannah McGuire	1870 October 4	Tabernacle Church.
"	March 7	Baptism	Margaret McGuire		
"	March 7	Baptism	Mrs. McGuire		
"	March 28	Experience	Jane McMichael		
"	May 16	Baptism	John McIntosh	1857 January 29	Beverly Church.
"	June 4	First Mention	Elizabeth McIntyre	1856 June 4	Dropped out.
1857	May 7	Letter	John McIntosh		
"	August 2	Port Hope Church	Thomas McCall	1861 May 21	A letter.
1858	March 11	Baptism	Miss I. McIntosh		

LIST OF MEMBERS—FIRST BAPTIST CHURCH, BRANTFORD.

WHEN RECEIVED	HOW RECEIVED	NAMES	DATE OF LEAVING	REASON FOR LEAVING
1858—March 25	First Mention	Bro. McIntosh	1858—March 25	Dropped out.
" April 8	Baptism	Mary A. McNeil		
" July 16	Baptism	Mrs. Jane McKay		
1859—January 23	Cork, Ireland	Rev'd Robert McClelland		
" December 25	Baptism	Thomas McClelland		
1860—January 5	Baptism	Jane McCaw		
" January 16	Experience	Mrs. Elizabeth McIntyre		
" June 5	First Mention	Jessie McIntosh	1860—June 5	United States.
" June 19	First Mention	Mary McCosh	" June 19	Dropped out.
" June 19	First Mention	Mrs. Duncan McKay	" June 19	Dropped out.
1861—May 21	Baptism	John McAdam		
" May 21	Baptism	Mrs. Mary McAdam		
" May 21	Baptism	James McGregor		
" July 22	Baptism	Mary McGuire		
1862—April 8	Baptism	Sarah McAdam		
" October 19	Baptism	Mrs. McHenry	1883—June 3	Died.
1863—May 24	First Mention	John McDonald	1863—May 24	St. Mary's Church.
1864—November 27	Montreal Church	John McAdam		
" November 27	Montreal Church	Mrs. John McAdam		
" November 27	Montreal Church	Sarah McAdam	1878—February 14	Collingwood Church.
1865—February 4	Baptism	George McDonald		
1866—December 5	Baptism	Isabella McGaw	1880—December 30	Walkerton Church.
1868—March 29	Baptism	Mrs. L. McDougall		
" April 9	Baptism	Isabella McIntosh	1873—September 7	United States.
1869—February 2	?	Jessie McIntosh	1869—February 2	A Letter.
1871—December 3	United States	Bell McIntosh		
1872—February 6	First Mention	David McIntyre		
1873—December 11	Baptism	Annie McDiarmid		
" December 9	Baptism	Lizzie McIntyre	1881—November 3	Burford Church.

Year	Date	Type	Name	Date	Note
1874—	January 11	Baptism	Osborne McIntyre	1881 December 1	Onondaga Church.
"	July 31	Baptism	Sarah McClellan.		
"	November 17	Baptism	Mary McAdam.		
"	November 17	Baptism	George H. McMichael.	1880 February 12	Tabernacle Church.
1875	January 28	Baptism	Mary McClair.		
"	January 28	Baptism	Jacob McMichael	1881—November 17	United States.
"	February 11	Baptism	Robert McHenry.		
"	February 18	Baptism	Minnie McDiarmid.		
"	February 25	Baptism	John McAdam.		
"	February 25	Baptism	John McDiarmid.		
"	March 7	First Mention	Mrs. McDiarmid.	1875—March 7	Aylmer Church.
"	March 7	Baptism	James McHenry.	1878—November 7	Dropped out.
"	March 11	Baptism	Josiah McAdam.		
"	March 11	Baptism	John McDougall.		
"	March 18	Baptism	Nellie McDiarmid.		
"	April 1	Baptism	Mrs. McDiarmid.		
"	September 3	Baptism	Mrs. McIntyre.		
"	October 7	Baptism	Miss McWherter.		
1876	December 28	Baptism	Mary McIntyre.		
1877—	May 16	Baptism	Lizzie McHenry.		
"	June 28	Baptism	Joseph McLean.		
1878	January 6	Letter	Angus McIntosh.		
"	October 6	Waterford Church	George McMichael.	1881—November 17	Buffalo, U. S.
1879—	April 1	Baptism	Nettie McKay.		
"	April 1	Baptism	Minnie McIntyre.		
"	April 6	Baptism	Robert McIntyre.		
"	April 6	Woodstock Church.	Jennie McDiarmid.		
"	April 11	Baptism	Jennie McIntyre.		
"	May 8	Baptism.	Rella McAdam.		
1880—	December 2	Chesley Church.	Jessie McDonald.		
"	December 2	Houghton Church	Martha McDiarmid.		

WHEN RECEIVED.	HOW RECEIVED.	NAMES.	DATE OF LEAVING.	REASON FOR LEAVING.
1881—April 7	Baptism	Annie McLean	1883—June 27	A Letter.

N.

WHEN RECEIVED.	HOW RECEIVED.	NAMES.	DATE OF LEAVING.	REASON FOR LEAVING.
1853—March 13	Baptism	Elizabeth Neir	1856—June 4	Dropped out.
June 26	First Mention	William Norton	1853—June 26	Paris Church.
1857—September 10	First Mention	Eliza Naylor	1857—September 10	St. Mary's Church.
1858—September 10	First Mention	Eliza Naylor	1858—September 10	
" September 10	Baptism	Amelia Naylor		
1872—December 1	Trowbridge Church	William Nutt		
1874—January 4	Experience	William Nott		
1875—February 4	Baptism	Samuel Nixon		
" February 4	Baptism	James Nelson		
" February 11	Baptism	Mrs. T. Nixon		
1876—March 23	Baptism	Mrs. Mary Norwood		
" April 16	Baptism	Charles Norwood		
1879—February 2	Drumbo Church	Sister Near		

O.

WHEN RECEIVED.	HOW RECEIVED.	NAMES.	DATE OF LEAVING.	REASON FOR LEAVING.
1851—May 3	Baptism	Mary Ormerod		
1852—September 5	Baptism	Jane Oliver		
1853—June 5	Baptism	George Oldright	1855—April 5	Dropped out.
1855—September 27	Baptism	Julia Oliver	1860—June 19	Dropped out.
1856—May 1	Baptism	Mrs. Ellen Ormerod		
" June 4	Baptism	Rachael Ormerod		
1857—April 3	Baptism	Daniel Osborne	1870—May 11	Tabernacle Church.
" April 10	Baptism	Marie Osborne	1870—May 11	Tabernacle Church.
1858—April 22	Baptism	John Ormerod	1877—April 5	Dropped out.

1858	September 10	Baptism	William Ocock	1860—June 19 ...... Dropped out.
1860—	December 18	First Mention	Johanna T. Ormerod	1860—December 18 .... Dropped out.
1862—	May 1	Baptism	Rachael Oliver	
1873—	December 26	Baptism	Mrs. Rebecca O'Hara	1878—May 16 ...... Dropped out.
"	December 28	Beamsville Church.	John Oswahl	
1874	July 31	Baptism	Francis Osborne	1878—May 16 ...... Dropped out.
1875—	January 28	Baptism	Mary Oliver	1881—December 20 .... Onondaga Church.
"	January 28	Baptism	Thomas Oliver	" December 20 ...... Onondaga Church.
"	February 11	Baptism	Charles Oakley	" September 1 ...... Ohio, U. S.
1877—	May 4	Baptism	Miss Oakley	" September 1 ...... Ohio, U. S.
"	October 7	Messiah Church.	Jane Oakley	" September 1 ...... Ohio, U. S.

P.

1835—	October 3	First Mention	Thomas Pilsworth	
1836—	June 2	First Mention	Brother Pull	
1837—	September 8	First Mention	Joseph Pilsworth	1845—June 15 ...... Dropped out.
1841—	November 7	First Mention	Charles Pickle	
1842—	March 19	Baptism	Brother Pickard	
"	May 21	Baptism	Hannah Patterson	
1846—	June 6	Letter.	Mrs. Charles Pickle	1851—May 3 ...... Dropped out.
1851—	February 1	First Mention	Mrs. C. Pickle	" May 3 ...... Dropped out.
"	February 1	First Mention	Mary Pickle	" May 3 ...... Dropped out.
"	March 1	Baptism	Miss Phillips	
"	May 3	Baptism	Caleb Poole	
"	May 3	First Mention	Mary Pilsworth	1851—May 3 ...... Dropped out.
"	May 23	Baptism	Mrs. Poole	
1851—	June 8	First Mention	Mrs. Pickles	1851—June 8 ...... Blenheim Church.
"	December 5	Baptism	Mrs Caroline Phillips	1855—November 4 ...... United States.
1852—	April 4	Baptism	Mr. (S. K. ?) Passmore	
1853—	April 17	Baptism	Catharine Passmore	
"	June 5	Toronto Church.	George Pell	

LIST OF MEMBERS—FIRST BAPTIST CHURCH, BRANTFORD.

When Received	How Received	Names	Date of Leaving	Reason for Leaving
1853—June 26	Baptism	Benjamin Plowman	1855—April 5	Dropped out.
1854—July 2	Baptism	Harriet Perry		
1855—July 5	Baptism	George Peters		
" November 4	United States	Harriet A. Phillips		
" November 4	First Mention	E. C. Phillips	1855—November 4	Berlin Church.
1856—March 7	Baptism	O. M. Preston	1864—August 23	Rochester.
" March 28	Baptism	Rhoda Potts	1860—April 19	Scotland Church.
" March 28	Baptism	Samuel Potts	" April 19	Scotland Church.
" April 17	Baptism	Mary A. Patience	" May 15	Scotland Church.
" April 17	Baptism	Benjamin Patience	" May 15	Scotland Church.
" May 1	Baptism	James Perry	" November 27	Dropped out.
" May 1	Baptism	Thomas Pickering	1872—July 7	Chatham Church.
" May 16	Baptism	James E. Perry	1872—July 7	Chatham Church.
" June 1	First Mention	Anna Pickering	1872—July 7	Chatham Church.
" June 4	Baptism	Mary Perry		
1857—April 3	Baptism	Mary Pepper		
" April 10	Baptism	Sarah Passmore	1862—August 3	Hamilton Church.
" May 20	Baptism	William Potts		
" July 8	Baptism	Hannah Plowman		
" July 8	Baptism	Israel Post	1858—July 16	Dundas Church.
1858—March 11	Baptism	Hamlet Pendlebury	1865—September 18	Ingersoll Church.
" March 25	Baptism	Sarah A. Pendlebury		
" March 25	Baptism	Hannah Pendlebury		
" March 25	First Mention	Mrs. Pettit	1858—March 25	Simcoe Church.
" April 6	Baptism	Mary Perry		
" April 22	Baptism	William Pierce		
" April 22	Baptism	Eliza Pearce	1863—January 30	Dropped out.
" June 8	Returned	Thomas Pilsworth		
" June 8	Returned	Mrs. T. Pilsworth		

Year	Date	Type	Name	Date	Church
1859	December 25	Baptism	Elizabeth Popplewell		
1860	January 5	Baptism	William Popplewell		
1860	June 19	First Mention	Henrietta Phillips	1860—June 19	Dropped out.
1861	March 19	Baptism	Albert Peel		
"	December 15	Baptism	Mrs. Parks	1873—January 19	Fredericksburg Church.
1862	March 16	Baptism	Sarah Pilsworth	1868—March 1	Chatham Church.
"	April 6	Scotland	Samuel Potts	1865—June 7	London Church.
"	April 6	Scotland	Rhoda Potts	" June 7	London Church.
"	May 20	Baptism	Sarah Pepper		
1864	December 18	Experience	Mrs. William Pierce	1876 October 12	Tabernacle Church.
1865	February 4	Baptism	Warwick Pierce	1881 June 30	East Ward Church.
1866	November 25	Baptism	Mrs. Charles Powley		
1867	December 5	Baptism	Jane Porter		
1868	March 1	Returned	Thomas Pilsworth	1868—March 1	Chatham Church.
"	March 1	Returned	Mrs. T. Pilsworth	" March 1	Chatham Church.
"	July 31	Baptism	Samuel Passmore		
"	August 30	Baptism	Martha Passmore		
1869	February 5	Baptism	Edwin Poole	1872—January 14	Chatham Church.
"	February 28	Baptism	Eliza J. Poole		
"	April 9	Baptism	Emily Ferry		
1870	May 26	First Mention	Mrs. Parsons		
"	July 12	Baptism	Miss Phillips		
"	November 15	Baptism	Hannah Pierce	1878 May 16	Dropped out.
1871	January 10	First Mention	Sister Phillips	1871—January 10	Tabernacle Church.
"	January 10	Yarmouth Church	Sarah J. Parke		
"	February 19	Baptism	Sister Parsons		
"	March 5	Baptism	William Poole		
1872	April 26	Baptism	Mary Pickering	1872 July 7	Chatham Church.
"	January 14	First Mention	Mrs. Edwin Poole	" January 14	Chatham Church.
"	February 4	Tabernacle Church	Edward Phillips	1873—December 26	Hamilton Church.
"	February 4	Tabernacle Church	Hannah Phillips	" December 26	Hamilton Church.

When Received	How Received	Names	Date of Leaving	Reason for Leaving.
1872—February 4	Tabernacle Church	Mrs. E. Phillips	1873—December 26	Hamilton Church.
" April 7	Ingersoll Church	Thomas Putnam		
" April 7	Ingersoll Church	Mrs. Mary Putnam	1880—October 14	United States.
" October 6	Tabernacle Church	Samuel K. Passmore		
" December 1	Elora Church	Mrs. Fetcher		
" December 1	Elora Church	Mary Fetcher	1878—May 16	Dropped out.
1873—November 2	Nova Scotia	Rev. W. H. Porter	1880—February 5	Rochester, N. Y.
" November 2	Nova Scotia	Mrs. Eliza P. Porter	1876—July 30	Died.
" December 5	Baptism	Grace M. Pearce	" October 12	Tabernacle Church.
" December 5	Baptism	Sarah M. Pearce	" October 12	Tabernacle Church.
" December 9	Baptism	Kate Perrin		
" December 26	Baptism	Emma Poole		
" December 26	Baptism	Lottie Perrin		
1874—January 11	Baptism	Lucy Pierce		
" March 24	Baptism	Hattie Porter	1880—February 5	Rochester, Died Sep. 1, '81
1875—January 28	Baptism	Sarah Peachie	1880—February 5	Rochester, U.S.
" January 28	Baptism	Lottie Porter	1875—December 30	United States.
" January 28	Baptism	Fred Putnam	" October 21	Dropped out,
" February 25	Baptism	Norman Perrin		
" March 4	Baptism	Mary E. Pearce		
" March 11	Baptism	Warren Putnam	1878—April 4	Dropped out.
" March 18	Baptism	Minerva Pearman	1882—May 30	Dropped out.
" July 1	Baptism	Maggie Petrie	" June 29	Rochester U.S.
" December 9	Baptism	Brother Passmore		
1876—January 25	Baptism	Kate Price		
" February 24	Chatham Church	Thomas Pickering	1881—December 29	Manitoba.
" February 24	Chatham Church	Mrs. T. Pickering	" December 29	Manitoba.
" March 16	Baptism	A. Perry	1877—April 5	
" March 30	Baptism	William Perry		Dropped out.

1876 —April 2	Baptism	Henry Poole	1879 —January 30	United States.
" —April 6	Baptism	Mrs. Alfred Pickering	1881 —September 1	Manitoba.
" —April 10	Baptism	Alfred Pickering	" September 1	Manitoba.
" —June 4		William Potts	1876—December 3	?
" —June 1		Mrs. Potts	" December 3	?
1877 —January 7	Baptism	Sister Payne		
" —January 25	Baptism	Priscilla Pool		
" —March 15	Baptism	Joseph Parmenter		
" —March 22	Baptism	Mrs. Amy Parmenter		
" —April 19	Baptism	John B. Poole	1879	April 11	New York.
" —November 4	United States	Jane Phelps		
1878—March 21	East Ward Church	Alfred Popplewell	1886 July 6	Died, aged 29 years.
1879—January 30	First Mention	Mrs. H. Poole	1879—January 30	United States.
1879—March 30	Baptism	Mrs. Alfred Poole	1881—September 29	United States.
" —March 30	Baptism	Alfred Poole	1881—September 29	United States.
" —April 6	Baptism	Frank Passmore		
" —April 11	Baptism	Boardman Porter	1880—February 5	Rochester, U. S.
" —April 15	Experience	Samuel Powell		
" —April 15	Experience	Sarah Potts		
1880—January 25	Baptism	Josephine Potts		
" —November 11	First Mention	Agnes Poole	1880—November 11	United States.
1881 —June 9	Baptism	Harry W. Poole	1883—October 31	United States.
" —June 30	Baptism	Beatrice Parsons		
" —June 30	Experience	Daniel Pine		
1882—November 30	Baptism	Mrs. William Peirce	1881—June 30	Tabernacle Church.
1883—May 2	St. George's Church	Mr. Poole		
		David Papple		

R.

1835—October 2	First Mention	Rev. William Rees	
1836—March 4	First Mention	Brother Robinson	

When Received	How Received	Names	Date of Leaving	Reason for Leaving
1837—May 12	First Mention	Sister Randall	1838—June 25	Dropped out.
1840—June 13	First Mention	Brother Read		
1841—August 1	First Mention	Sister Read	1841—November 7	Beverley Church.
1842—December 5	Baptism	Mrs. Rich	1842—December 25	A Letter.
1844—May 18	First Mention	Martin Robinson	1844—May 18	Boston Church.
1847—February 7	Hamilton Church	Mr. Reynolds		Died.
February 7	Hamilton Church	Mrs Reynolds		Died.
1849—February 2	Montreal Church	Mrs. F. Roy	1851 May 3	Dropped out.
1851—February 1	First Mention	Mrs. Mary Roy		Dropped out.
" March 1	Baptism	Thomas Rainbow	1855—February 25	Dropped out.
" March 1	Baptism	Mrs. Rainbow		
" March 1	United States	Washington Robertson	1856—September 27	Dropped out.
" March 1	United States	Julia Robertson		
" May 3	Baptism	Elizabeth Riley		
1852—May 10	Baptism	Emily Race		
" June 6	London Church	Amanda Ross		
1853—March 6	St. George's Church	Samuel Read		
" June 26	Baptism	Mrs. Roberts		
" August 14	Baptism	William Robinson	1862—September 7	New York.
" November 20	Second Brantford Church	Ann Komain	1860—June 19	Dropped out.
1855—May 6	New York	Abby C. Rich		
" August 5	England	Moses Rediherd		
" November 4	First Mention	Mary A. Rainbow	1855—November 4	United States.
1856—February 24	Baptism	William Rockey	1859—April 14	Died, aged 29.
" March 28	Baptism	Mrs. J. Robinson	1875—May 27	Dropped out.
" May 1	Baptism	Richard Reep	1856—October 17	Dropped out.
" May 16	Baptism	Samuel Root	1861—July 22	Woodstock Church.
" June 4	Baptism	Salem Root		
1857—January 5	Woodstock Church	Mary Rycroft		

Date	Type	Name	Date	Note
1857—April 3	Baptism	George Roy	1868—April 9	Boston Church.
" May 7	Letter	Eliza Rockey		
1858—March 11	Baptism	Robert Roper		
" January 4	Baptism	Andrew Rouse		
1859—December 25	Baptism	William Kushton		
1860 January 5	Baptism	Henry Reid		
" January 5	Baptism	James Kushton		
" January 5	Baptism	Elizabeth Kushton		
" January 5	Baptism	Mary Rushton		
" January 5	Baptism	Hartley Kushton		
" April 10	First Mention	Sophia Rosa	1860—April 10	Buffalo, U. S.
" June 10	First Mention	Mrs. Rycroft		
1861—August 27	Baptism	Cyrus Read		
1863—June 7	Woodstock Church	Saul Read	1865—September 18	Ingersoll Church.
" June 7	Woodstock Church	Sister Riley	1878—May 16	Dropped out.
" October 25	?	Samuel Read		
1854—November 27	Stratford Church	Nancy Riley	1875 May 27	Dropped out.
1860—May 29	Baptism	Perrin E. Runyon		
" November 16	Baptism	Joseph Read		
" November 23	Baptism	Elizabeth Reynolds		
" November 30	Baptism	Anna Rice		
" December 5	Baptism	Miss Randall		
1857 December 5	Baptism	Mrs. Margaret Robertson	1875 May 27	Dropped out.
1858—March 29	Baptism	George Rushton		
" March 29	Baptism	Mrs. George Kushton		
" December 6	Returned Letter	Anna Rice	1870—October 11	Tabernacle Church.
1870—July 12	Baptism	Mary Robson		
1871—August 6	Baptism	Miss Reid		
" October 10	Baptism	Sister Robson	1880—January 15	East Ward Church
1872—April 7	Onondaga Church	Emma Reid	1878—September 26	Wingham Church.
1873—September 7	Boston Church	George Roy	1875 October 21	Dropped out.

LIST OF MEMBERS—FIRST BAPTIST CHURCH, BRANTFORD.

WHEN RECEIVED.	HOW RECEIVED.	NAMES.	DATE OF LEAVING.	REASON FOR LEAVING.
1873—September 7	Boston Church	Eliza Roy	1875—October 21	Dropped out.
" November 2	Hartford Church	Hannah Renner		
1874—October 25	Baptism	Mrs. Riddiford		
" November 1	Bredeicksburg Church	Mrs. A. M. Robbins		
" November 17	Baptism	Elizabeth Keeker		
1875—January 28	Baptism	Emily Riddiford		
" January 28	Baptism	Henry Roy		
" January 28	Baptism	William H. Riddiford		
" February 25	Baptism	George Riddiford	1878—May 16	Dropped out.
" February 25	Baptism	Arthur Riddiford		
" March 28		Sister Roberts	1878—February 7	Stratford Church.
" March 28	Baptism	Mrs. Reid	1876—May 7	East Ward Church
" April 22	Baptism	Mrs. Ramsay		Dropped out.
" April 30	Baptism	George E. Riddiford		
1876—March 16	Baptism	James Rammage	1878—January 31	Simcoe Church.
" March 23	Baptism	Miss Keith		
" April 2	Baptism	Mary A. Kussell		
" April 16	Baptism	Charles Kead		
1877—June 28	Baptism	R. E. Rispin	1877—June 28	Buffalo, U. S.
1878—February 7	Baptism	Thomas Randall		
" February 7	Baptism	Rebecca Randall		
1879—April 11	Baptism	Sarah Rushton		
" April 15	Baptism	Kate Rowland		
" May 4	St. George's Church	Brother Koelofson		
" May 4	St. George's Church	Sister Roelofson		
1880—February 1	Woodstock Church	Mrs. E. J. Koelofson		
" February 1	Woodstock Church	Miss H. Koelofson		
" November 11	East Ward Church	Maggie Robson		
" November 11	East Ward Church	Eugene Robson		

Year	Date	Event	Name	Year	Date	Result
1881	March 10	Tabernacle Church	Alfred Roberts			
"	March 10	Tabernacle Church	Sister Roberts			
"	March 31	Experience	Sister Rich			
"	April 7	Baptism	Daniel Robson			
"	April 7	Baptism	Charles Robson			
"	Dezember 1	Beamsville Church	Frederick Ruth			
1883	May 2	First Mention	F. Root	1883	May 2	Dropped out.

S.

Year	Date	Event	Name	Year	Date	Result
1836	January 1	First Mention	Nancy Shaw	1836	April 1	A Letter.
"	January 1	First Mention	Brother Shaw			
"	March 4	First Mention	Brother Skinner	1836	November 7	Dropped out.
"	September 2	First Mention	Brother Sayles	1855	April 12	Died, aged 67.
1837	March 12	Letter	Sister Spencer			
1839	June 13	Letter	Mary Scott	1855	December 5	A Letter.
1841	September 5	First Mention	Brother Smith	1843	August 19	St. Catharines Church.
1842	July 16	Baptism	Courtland Sanderson	1846	September 5	Dropped out.
1844	March 16	Baptism	Helen Slinger	1851	June 1	Beverley Church.
1849	June 26	Baptism	Emma Skinner	1849	June 26	A Letter.
"	June 26	First Mention	Mr. C. A. Skinner	1851	May 3	Dropped out.
1851	February 1	First Mention	Jacob Sherwood	1851	May 3	Dropped out.
"	February 1	First Mention	Rachel Sherwood	1856	June 4	Dropped out.
"	May 23	First Mention	Matilda Simpson	1856	March 23	Michigan.
"	October 5	Paris Church	Jeremiah Shackleton	1853	November 20	Dropped out.
"	October 31	Baptism	Rebecca Smith			
1852	November 7	Baptism	Mary A. Steel			
1854	January 1	New York	Ellen Stephenson	1860	June 19	Dropped out.
"	May 22	Baptism	Mrs. Sinclte			
"	September 3	Baptism	Thomas Stephenson	1860	June 19	Dropped out.
"	September 3	Baptism	John B. Sharp	1855	December 2	Paris Church.
"	October 6	United States	R. C. Scott			

When Received	How Received	Names	Date of Leaving	Reason for Leaving.
1854—November 3	Woodstock Church	R. W. Sawtell	1855—December 2	Woodstock Church.
" November 3	Woodstock Church	Mrs R. W. Sawtell	1855—December 2	Woodstock Church.
1855—June 3	Baptism	Margaret A. Shackleton	1855—August 6	Paris Church.
" June 20	Baptism	Elizabeth Shackleton	1860—June 19	Dropped out.
" August 14	Baptism	Isabella Sears	1856—February 24	Detroit.
" September 27	Experience	Mrs. C. Scott		
1856—March 28	First Mention	Rachel Shackleton	1856—March 28	United States.
" April 17	Baptism	Mrs. Frances Scott	1860—June 19	Dropped out.
" May 1	Baptism	Mrs. T. S. Shenston		
" May 3	Kingston Church	J. P. Sutton	1875—December 9	East Ward Church.
" May 3	Kingston Church	Ann M. Sutton	1875—December 9	East Ward Church.
" May 3	Baptism	T. S. Shenston		
" May 3	Niagara Church	Daniel Secord	1857—March 12	Accidental Death.
" May 16	Baptism	Margery Silverthorn		
" June 4	First Mention	Matilda Simpson	1856—June 4	Dropped out.
" July 6	Scotland Church	Janet Silverthorn		
" July 6	Niagara Church	Electa Secord		Died.
1857—April 3	Baptism	Robert Smith	1857—November 3	Owen Sound Church.
" April 10	Baptism	Margaret Scanlan	1860—April 19	St. Catharines Church.
" April 10	Baptism	Janet Sisterson	1857—August 4	St. Catharines Church.
" July 8	Baptism	Naomi Shenston		
" July 28	First Mention	Eliza Skinner	1857—July 28	A Letter.
" November 3	First Mention	Annie C. Smith	1857—November 3	Owen Sound Church.
1858—March 25	Baptism	Mrs. Secord	1860—April 19	St. Catharines Church.
" March 25	Baptism	John G. Sisterson	1864—January 24	St. Catharines Church.
" April 8	Baptism	Emily Smithson	1860—June 19	Dropped out.
" June 6	Letter	Robert Smith		
" June 6	Letter	Annie C. Smith		
1859—December 25	Baptism	Joseph Smith	1871—March 5	Burtch Church.

1850—December 25	Baptism	Samuel Smith	1880—November 11	East Ward Church.
" December 25	Baptism	Mrs. Sager	1860 June 10	Boston Church.
1860—January 7	Baptism	Candace Smith		
" January 3	Baptism	Elizabeth Skimings		
1861—May 21	Beamsville Church	William Skelley		
" May 21	Beamsville Church	Amanda Skelley		
" May 21	Beamsville Church	Sarah Skelley		
" August 27	Experience	Mrs. Squire		
" October 20	First Mention	Margaret Showers	1861—October 20	Paris Church.
1862 January 5	Beamsville Church	Augusta Skelley	1864 July 31	Waterford Church.
" March 23	Baptism	Elizabeth Spears		
" March 30	Baptism	Jane Sanderson	1878 —May 16	Dropped out.
1863—August 2	Woodstock Church	Rev. William Stewart		
" August 2	Woodstock Church	Augusta Stewart		
" September 13	Experience	Sister Simpson		
1864—January 24	First Mention	Mrs. Secord	1864—January 24	Blenheim Church.
" August 20	Baptism	Mrs. Jos. Smith	1871—March	Burtch Church.
1865—November 10	Baptism	A. W. Smith	1871—September 1	Chatham Church.
" November 25	Baptism	James Stubbs	1867—March 3	Toronto.
" November 25	Baptism	Mrs. Spencer		
" November 25	Baptism	Miss Spencer		
1867—June 2	United States	Fanny Stockwell		
1868—August 30	Baptism	James Sears	1873 January 28	Hamilton Church.
" December 6	Port Hope	Jemima Shenston	1882 March 30	St. Catharines Church.
1869—January 3	First Mention	Fanny Stockwell	1869—January 3	London Church.
" February 2	First Mention	Mrs. Southers	1869—February 2	Boston Church.
" October 5	(?)	Miss S. Selby		
1870—June 29	Baptism	Ada Sutton	1875 November 5	East Ward Church.
" June 29	Baptism	Miss Sears	1873—October 5	Hamilton Church.
" July 12	Baptism	Miss Spencer		
1871—February 14	United States	Brother Saunders	1873 —April 6	Buffalo.

LIST OF MEMBERS—FIRST BAPTIST CHURCH, BRANTFORD.

When Received	How Received	Names	Date of Leaving	Reason for Leaving.
1871—February 14	United States	Mrs. Saunders	1873—April 6	Buffalo.
" March 5	First Mention	Mary J. Smith	1871—March 5	Burtch Church.
" April 26	Experience	Mrs. W. C. Scott	1878—May 16	Dropped out.
1872—January 14	First Mention	Mrs. A. W. Smith	1871—January 14	Chatham Church.
" November 20	Experience	Mrs. Spriggs		
1873—September 7	Burtch Church	Mrs. Mary Smith		
" October 5	Sarnia Church	Arthur Streeter		
" October 5	England	Mrs. Streeter		
" December 5	Baptism	Josephine Schultz		
" December 26	Baptism	Naomi Spencer		
1874—January 30	Baptism	Ada Stubbs	1883—March 21	Manitoba.
" February 10	Baptism	Rebecca Stubbs		
" May 5	Baptism	Maria Skelwin		
" October 4	Chatham Church	A. W. Smith	1878—August 22	Toronto.
" October 4	Chatham Church	Mrs. A. W. Smith	1878—August 22	Toronto.
" December 4	Baptism	Mary Schultz		
1875—February 11	Baptism	John Spriggs		
" March 25	Baptism	Joseph Swift		
" April 4	Windham Church	Matilda Sipperal		
" April 22	Baptism	Jennie Syrie		
" October 7	Baptism	Susie Strowhill		
1876—April 2	Baptism	Mary A. Sears	1878—May 16	Dropped.
" April 27	Baptism	Mr. Schultz		
" April 27	Baptism	Mrs. Schultz		
" September 21	Baptism	Ruth D. Shenston	1877—September 20	St. Thomas Church.
" November 5	Baptism	Mrs. Smith		
" November 5	Baptism	Nellie Smith		
" November 23	Baptism	Miss Stephenson		
1877—April 19	Baptism	Joseph Smith		

1877—April 26	Chicago	Joseph N. Shenston		
" April 26	St. Catharines Church	Eliza Shenston		
" May 16	Scotland Church	Sarah E. Smith		
" October 7	Mount Forest	John Stewart	1879—May 8	East Ward Church.
" November 7	Baptism	Robert Sanderson		
" November 7	Baptism	Agnes Sanderson		
1878—January 20	Baptism	Mrs. W. W. Smith		
" February 3	Baptism	W. W. Smith		
" February 21	Baptism	Maggie Sanderson		
" May 16	First Mention	Mary Sanderson	1878—May 16	Dropped out.
" November 17	Baptism	Eliza Stewart (Blind)		
" November 28	First Mention	Susie Stronghill	1878—November 28	Fort Edward Church.
" December 1	Simcoe Church	Ellen Stewart		
1879—March 30	Baptism	Alfred Stevens		
" April 1	Baptism	Annie Stockwell	1881—January 13	Toronto.
" April 1	Baptism	Jennie Sanderson		
" April 1	Baptism	Hattie Sanderson		
" April 6	Experience	Mrs. Henry Schultz		
" April 6	Experience	Henry Schultz		
" April 11	Baptism	Maggie Syrie		
" April 11	Baptism	Mary Stockwell		
" June 1	Tabernacle Church	Edward Southwood		
" November 13	First Mention	Brother Streeter	1879—November 13	Dropped out.
" December 11	Baptism	William Southwood	1880—December 2	Paris Church.
1880—October 3	East Ward Church	J. G. Stewart		
" October 3	East Ward Church	Mrs. J. G. Stewart		
1881—January 13	England	Mrs. Clayton Slater	1881—January 13	Toronto.
" January 13	First Mention	Mrs. M. Stockwell	1883—December 2	Detroit.
" January 16	Baptism	Nellie Sanders		
" February 17	Baptism	Brother Sandford (Blind)		
" March 10	Baptism	S. E. Smith	1881—November 10	London Church.

—193—

When Received	How Received	Names	Date of Leaving	Reason for Leaving
1881—March 24	Baptism	George Stubbs		
" April 7	Baptism	Alice Stubbs		
" April 7	Baptism	Lizzie Syrie		
" April 7	Baptism	Robert Seaborn		
" April 28	Woodstock Church	Charles Schofield		
" May 29	Baptism	Mr. Clayton Slater		
" September 15	Baptism	Reuben S. Shenston		
" September 15	Baptism	Mrs. Reuben S. Shenston	1882—February 2	Woodstock Church.
1882—February 2	First Mention	George Schofield	1882—September 28	Paris Church.
" May 4	Baptism	Annie Slater		
" May 18	Baptism	Lucy Stubbs		
1883—December 16	Baptism	Willie Stubbs		
" December 16	Baptism	John Schultz		
" December 16	Baptism	Brother Shawcross		
" December 16	Baptism	Mrs. Shawcross		
" December 16	Baptism	Roy Sanderson		
" December 16	Baptism	Robert Sanderson		
" December 16	Baptism	Fred Sanderson		
" December 16	Baptism	William Sanderson		
" December 19	Baptism	Bessie Stubbs		

T.

When Received	How Received	Names	Date of Leaving	Reason for Leaving
1837—July 21	First Mention	Sister Taylor		Dropped out.
1841—May 15	First Mention	Lucy Taylor	1841—May 23	Dropped out.
" August 1	First Mention	B. G. Tisdale		Dropped out.
1842—July 16	First Mention	Mrs. Thompson	1846—September 5	Dropped out.
1845—March 15	Baptism	James Tutt	1857—July 6	Dropped out.
" March 15	Baptism	Hannah Tutt		
" April 5	Baptism	Nancy Tutt	1846—December 4	Dropped out.

Date	Type	Name	Later Date	Notes
1845 May 10	Baptism	Mrs. Tutt	1870—June 26	Died, aged 69 years.
1840 June 25	Baptism	Jane Tutt		
1851—February 1	First Mention	Mrs. E. P. Tisdale	1821—May 3	Dropped out.
1854 May 22	Baptism	Mrs. Tindale		
1855—June 20	Baptism	Henry C. Tew		
" August 23	Baptism	Ann Tew		
1856—March 28	Experience	Sister E. P. Tisdale		
" March 28	Experience	B. G. Tisdale		
1857 April 3	Baptism	Charles Tutt		
" May 20	Baptism	Jane Todd		
1858 March 11	Baptism	Robert Tutt	1860—June 24	Died, aged 22 years.
" April 8	Baptism	Thomas Thomson		
1859 February 9	Baptism	Joanna Tucker		
" May 3	Baptism	George Tutt	1861 July 6	Died, aged 20 years.
" December 25	Baptism	John Troy		
" December 25	Baptism	Elizabeth Thorn		
1860—January 5	Baptism	Mary Taylor		
" January 5	Baptism	Isabella Taylor		
1865—March 5	Simcoe Church	Mrs. Ann Turner		
1866—May 20	Toronto	Samuel Tapscott	1875—August 27	East Ward Church.
1867 October 28	Baptism	Mrs. Turner		
" October 22	Church	Rev. A. V. Timpany	1885—February 10	Died.
1868 May 26	Baptism	Jane Tanton	1871—November 22	Died.
" July 31	Baptism	Mrs. Mary E. Tutt		
1869 March 23	Baptism	Mrs. Ellen Thom	1874—July 7	St. Thomas Church.
" April 4	Buffalo	Robert Thom	1874—July 7	St. Thomas Church.
1870—June 29	First Mention	Jessie Thompson	1860 April 23	Montreal City.
1871—April 26	Experience	B. G. Tisdale		A Letter.
"	Woodstock Church	Brother Troy		
1873—December 5	Baptism	Rosanna Todd	1882 May 4	Ohio, U.S.
" December 5	Baptism	Adelaide Todd		Ohio, U.S.

WHEN RECEIVED.	HOW RECEIVED.	NAMES.	DATE OF LEAVING.	REASON FOR LEAVING.
1874—January 4	Toronto	Thomas Truss	1883—February 28	A Letter.
" January 4	Toronto	Mrs. Mary J. Truss		
1875—August 27	First Mention	Mrs. S. Tapscott	1875—August 27	East Ward Church.
1876—May 7	Baptism	Mrs. Tiller		
1877—January 7	Yorkville Church	George Teakle	1879—August 7	East Ward Church.
" January 7	Yorkville Church	Mrs. George Teakle	1879—August 7	East Ward Church.
" January 7	Yorkville Church	Sophia Teakle	1879—August 7	East Ward Church.
" August 5	Woodstock Church	Agnes Thompson	1878—March 31	Woodstock Church.
" May 16	First Mention	Mrs. H. Tutt	1878—May 16	Dropped out.
1879—April 6	Baptism	Elizabeth Tanton		
" April 6	Baptism	Louisa Tanton		
" July 10	Baptism	Mrs. Tanton		
1880—December 2	Ohio	Rev. J. B. Tuttle		
" December 2	Ohio	Mrs. J. B. Tuttle		
" December 2	Ohio	Clara M. Tuttle		
" December 2	Ohio	Burton B. Tuttle		
" December 2	Ohio	Ida Tuttle		
1881—November 3	Ohio	Frederick Tuttle		
1883—December 16	Baptism	Mrs. George Tutt		
" December 16	Baptism	Phillip Truss		

U.

WHEN RECEIVED.	HOW RECEIVED.	NAMES.	DATE OF LEAVING.	REASON FOR LEAVING.
1878—July 4	Letter	Mrs. M. Underhill	1880—April 14	A Letter.
1879—April 6	Baptism	John Underhill		
1880—April 14	First Mention	Brother Underhill	1880—April 14	A Letter.

V.

WHEN RECEIVED.	HOW RECEIVED.	NAMES.	DATE OF LEAVING.	REASON FOR LEAVING.
1835—December 4	First Mention	Brother Virginia	1837—April 28	Dropped out.
1837—April 28	First Mention	Sister Virginia		

1850—June 4 .... Baptism ...... George Verrell ...... 1857—May 20 .... Chatham Church.
1860 March 5 .... First Mention ...... Mary Vanevery ...... 1860—March 5 .... St. Georges' Church.
1863—January 30 ..... Letter, U.S. ..... J. P. VanBrocklin ..... 1864—March 8 ...... Dropped out.
" January 30 ..... Letter, U.S. ..... Harriet VanBrocklin .... 1864—March 8 ..... Dropped out.
1867 December 5 .... Baptism ...... Lydia A. Vaughan ....
1871 December 10 ... First Mention ...... Rev. J. Vanton ....
1872—January 17 .... Baptism ...... Sister A. Valentine ....
" July 7 ...... (Dismal). ...... Catharine Vansickle ....
1873 November 23 ... Baptism ...... Elizabeth Vail ....
1875 April 18 ...... First Mention ...... Brother Van Horn ...... 1875—April 18 .... Stouffville Church.
" April 18 ...... First Mention ...... Sister Van Horn ...... 1878 April 18 ...... Stouffville Church.
" September 7 ... First Mention ...... Mrs. Vansickle ...... 1873 September 7 .... Teetersville Church.
1879—April 6 .... Baptism ...... Mary A. Vince ...... 1882 March 30 ...... St. Thomas Church.
" April 11 ...... Baptism ...... Mrs. Jane Vanevery ..... 1882 May 30 .... Dropped out.
" April 15 ...... Baptism ...... Wallace Vanevery ...... 1882 May 30 .... Dropped out.
1883 August 1 ...... Onondaga Church ...... Mrs. H. H. Vansickle ....

W.

1835 December 4 ... First Mention ...... Matthew Whitham ...... 1851—August 3 ..... Dropped out.
1836 September 2 ... First Mention ...... Brother Wm. T. Webster .... 1838 May 12 ...... Dropped out.
1842 July 3 .... First Mention ...... John Winch ...... 1842 July 3 .... Simcoe Church.
" December 17 ... First Mention ...... Rev. John Winterbotham .... Died.
1844 February 17 ... Baptism ...... Geo. Wood ...... 1840—October 26 ... A Letter.
1845 March 15 ..... Baptism ...... Mary Winterbotham ...... 1859 November 2 .... Died at Owen Sound,
1846 May 17 ...... First Mention ...... Mr. Waterhouse .... Aged 71.
" May 17 ...... First Mention ...... Mrs. Waterhouse ....
1847—April 3 ...... Baptism ...... Barthy Whitney ...... 1850—July 6 .... Norwich Church.
1850 July 6 .... First Mention ...... Martha Webster ...... 1850 July 6 .... Dundas Church.
" September 15 ... Baptism ...... Wm. Whitham ....
1851—March 1 ..... Baptism ...... Jane Walker ....
" May 3 .... Baptism ...... Endymiah Wilson ...... 1851—June 8 .... Newmarket Church.

WHEN RECEIVED	HOW RECEIVED	NAMES	DATE OF LEAVING	REASON FOR LEAVING
1851—May 23	First Mention	Mrs. Wheeler	1871—May 30	Dropped out.
" May 23	First Mention	Wm. Webster	1851—May 30	Dropped out.
" September 21	Baptism	Margaret Wright	1856—June 4	Dropped out.
" December 5	Baptism	Mary J. Wright	1855—March 1	Dropped out.
1852—May 10	Baptism	Anna Wright		
" July 4	Experience	Hannah Williams		
1853—January 23	Baptism	Drusilla Waterhouse	1855—July 5	Dropped out.
" April 17	Baptism	Jerome Wadleigh	1855—July 5	Dundas Church.
" April 17	Baptism	Isaac Wallace		
" April 17	Baptism	Rachel Williams		
" April 17	Baptism	Eleanor Wallace		
1854—October 6	Dundas Church	Elizabeth Whitesell	1855—April 5	Dropped out.
" November 3	Woodstock Church	Jerome Wadleigh	1865—December 5	Dropped out.
" November 3	Woodstock Church	Wm. Winter	1863—February 25	Died, Aged 60 years.
1855—March 1	First Mention	Mrs. W. Winter		
" March 1	First Mention	Geo. Ware	1856—September 27	Dropped out.
" May 6	Queenston Church	Mrs. Geo. Ware	1856—June 4	Dropped out.
" May 6	Queenston Church	Wm. Wray		
" June 20	Baptism	Mrs. W. Wray		
" June 20	Baptism	John T. Wallace		
" June 20	Baptism	Ann C. Winter	1861—September 16	Died, Aged 23 years.
" June 20	Baptism	Lucy N. Winter	1858—August 11	Died, Aged 18 years.
" November 4	New York	Edwin E. Warfield	1856—April 17	A Letter.
1856—January 28	First Mention	Isaac Wallis	1856—January 28	Dorchester Church.
" January 28	First Mention	Elona Wallis	1856—January 28	Dorchester Church.
" March 2	Baptism	E. J. Whitham	1856—October 17	Dropped out.
" March 2	Baptism	Elena Whitham	1857—March 3	Dropped out.
" March 7	First Mention	Mary J. Wright	1856—March 7	United States.
" April 17	Baptism	Annie Walden	1858—March 11	Paris Church.

1856	—April 17	Baptism	John Walden	1858	March 11.	Paris Church.
"	April 17	Baptism	Sarah J. Watson			
"	May 16	Baptism	John Whitham	1870	April 27	Tabernacle Church.
"	May 16	Baptism	Benjamin Woods	1858	July 10.	Scotland Church.
"	May 16	Baptism	John Watson			
"	June 4	Baptism	Euphemia West			
"	July 6	Baptism	Albina West			
"	November 12	Baptism	Elizabeth White	1863	August 2	Hamilton Church.
1857	February 1	England	Margaret Williams			
"	April 10	Baptism	Mary A. Wray			
"	April 17	Baptism	Wm. West			
"	July 8	Baptism	Isabella Wray			
1858	—June 6	Westport	Catherine Webster			
"	July 10	Baptism	Eliza Winter	1858	October 10	Died, Aged 14 years.
"	September 10	First Mention	Mary Williams	1858	September 10	St. Mary's Church.
1859	—February 9	First Mention	Jane Walker	1859	February 9	Second Onondaga Church
"	June 19	Blenheim Church	James Winter			
"	December 25	Baptism	Elizabeth Waddington			
1860	January 16	First Mention	Mrs. Wyatt			
"	July 31	Baptism	Mrs. Wright			
1861	—January 24	First Mention	Samantha Warren	1861	January 24	A Letter.
"	August 27	Baptism	James White	1862	August 3	Hamilton Church.
"	October 20	First Mention	Mrs. Weir	1861	October 20	Chatham Church.
"	October 20	Baptism	Hugh Williams			
"	December 15	Baptism	Andrew Wright			
1862	March 2	Paris Church	John Walden	1862	July 15	Paris Church.
"	March 2	Paris Church	Ann Walden	1862	July 15.	Paris Church.
"	March 30	Baptism	Elizabeth White			
"	May 20	Baptism	Lydia Wells	1875	May 27	Dropped out.
1863	April 7	First Mention	Sister Wadleigh	1863	April 7.	Caledonia Church
"	May 3	Onondaga Church	Mary A. Warfield	1867	October 10	Dropped out.

WHEN RECEIVED	HOW RECEIVED	NAME	DATE OF LEAVING	REASON FOR LEAVING
1864—February 24	First Mention	Dr. Walrath		
" April 27	Baptism	Mrs. Walton		
" August 16	Baptism	Catherine Webb	1867 October 22	United States.
" November 27	West Oxford Church	John West		
1867—February 26	Baptism	Mary Watson	1867—October 22	United States.
" December 5	First Mention	Robert Webster		
1858—March 1	First Mention	Brother Williams	1868 March 1	Chatham Church.
" March 1	First Mention	Mrs. Williams	1868 March 1	Chatham Church.
" May 26	Baptism	Mrs. Elizabeth Webster	1875—August 27	East Ward Church.
1869—June 7	Detroit	Mary Watson		
" February 9	First Mention	Mary Welsh	1869—February 9	Wingham Church.
" April 2	Kingston Church	Thomas Webster	1875—August 27	East Ward Church.
1870—April 27	First Mention	Mrs. Whitham	1870—April 21	Tabernacle Church.
1871—April 11	England	George Whelpton	1880—March 4	Doe Lake.
" April 11	England	Mrs. George Whelpton	1880—March 4	Doe Lake.
" April 11	England	Caroline Whelpton		
" April 26	First Mention	Eliza West	1871—April 26	Park Hill Church.
" August 4	Baptism	Mrs. Webster		
" December 3	Simcoe Church	Mrs. Laura Wilson		
1873—January 14	Park Hill Church	Eliza West		
1872—March 4	Parkhill Church	William West		
1873—December 26	Baptism	Mrs. Emily Wickham		
" December 28	Baptism	Henry Whelpton	1880—March 4	Doe Lake Church.
1874—February 8	Baptism	William Whelpton	1880—March 4	Doe Lake Church.
" May 17	Baptism	Ettie Wyatt		
" August 9	Baptism	Ellen Wilson		
" November 22	Baptism	Ransom Williams		
1875—January 28	Baptism	Albert Webster		
" January 28	Experience	Martha Webster		

Year	Date	Type	Name	Year	Date	Note
1875	February 4	Baptism	George Winter			
"	February 25	Baptism	Amelia Wallace			
"	February 25	Baptism	Robina Wallace			
"	March 4	Baptism	W. T. Webster			
"	March 18	Baptism	Albert Westover			
"	March 25	Baptism	A. E. Westover	1875	August 27	East Ward Church.
"	April 8	Baptism	Fanny L. Wyatt	1878	May 30	Dropped out.
"	April 11	Baptism	Elizabeth M. Weir			
1876	March 23	First Mention	William T. Wickham	1876	December 3	?
"	April 2	First Mention	Phillip Wardell.			
"	April 2	Baptism	Mrs. P. Wardell.			
"	April 6	Baptism	Miss Webster.			
"	September 21	Baptism	A. E. Webster	1876	September 21	Woodstock Church.
"	December 3	First Mention	Mrs. W. Wickham	1876	December 3	?
"	December 21	Baptism	Miss A. West.			
1877	October 7	New Brunswick Church	Mrs. A. T. Waterous.			
"	December 11	Baptism	Mrs. A. Wall			
"	December 11	Baptism	Allen Wall			
1878	January 20	First Mention	Mrs. White	1878	January 20	Waterford Church.
"	February 14	First Mention	Emily Webster	1878	February 14	St. Catharines Church.
"	February 21	Baptism	Mary Wilson			
"	March 3	Baptism	Brother Wilson			
"	August 22	First Mention	Mrs. Henry Wilson	1878	August 22	Dropped out.
"	August 22	First Mention	Mr. Henry Wilson	1878	August 22	Dropped out.
1879	March 30	Baptism	Minnie Winter			
"	March 30	Baptism	Della White			
"	March 30	Baptism	Edith White			
"	March 30	Baptism	Arthur White			
"	April 1	Baptism	Eva Webster			
"	April 1	Baptism	Mena Wall			
"	April 1	Baptism	Lillie Wall			

LIST OF MEMBERS—FIRST BAPTIST CHURCH, BRANTFORD.

WHEN RECEIVED.	HOW RECEIVED.	NAMES.	DATE OF LEAVING.	REASON FOR LEAVING.
1879—April 1	Baptism	Eva Wilson		
" April 1	Baptism	Thomas Winter		
" April 6	Baptism	William Winter		
" April 11	Baptism	Alice Watson		
" April 11	Baptism	Mary Wood		
" April 11	Experience	Mrs. Elizabeth Wilson		
" April 15	Baptism	Emma Whelpton	1880—March 4	Doe Lake Church.
" April 15	Baptism	Sarah Whelpton	1880—March 4	Doe Lake Church.
" April 20	Baptism	Mrs. David Winter		
" July 30	Baptism	Mrs. Williams		
" July 30	Baptism	Blanche Williams		
" November 2	Waterford Church	Elizabeth White		
" December 11	Baptism	Emily Whitaker		
1880 August 5	First Mention	N. Wardell	1880—August 5	Grimsby Church.
" October 3	East Ward Church	W. T. Wickham		
" October 3	East Ward Church	Mrs. W. T. Wickham		
" December 30	Baptism	Matilda Wallace		
1881 March 10	Baptism	Annie Winter		
" March 10	Baptism	Bessie Webster	1882—May 4	Paris Church.
" March 31	Experience	A. E. Williams	1882—November 2	Dropped out.
" June 9	Onondaga Church	Jennie Wheting		
" June 9	Baptism	Mrs. A. E. Williams		
" September 22	First Mention	Sister Wall	1881—September 22	London Church.
1882—February 2	Letter	W. M. Watson		
" February 2	Letter	Mrs. W. M. Watson		
" March 3	Stouffville Church	Frank Wixon	1883—October 31	Ingersoll Church.
" March 3	Stouffville Church	Mrs. Frank Wixon	1883—October 31	Ingersoll Church.
1883—May 2	First Mention	Mrs. C. Wilson	1883—May 2	Dropped out.
" August 1	First Mention	Mrs. Westover	1883—August 1	Park Church.

—202—

1883—December 10 .... Baptism .... George Winter, jr ....
  "   December 10 .... Baptism .... ? Wells ....
  "   December 20 .... Toronto .... Mrs. O. White ....

Y.

1845—May 10 .... Baptism .... Thomas Young ....
1853—July 3 .... Paris Church .... William Young ....
  "   July 3 .... Paris Church .... Mrs. Young ...... 1858 — February 10 .... Died, aged 39 years.
1855—June 20 .... Baptism .... Eliza S. Young .... 1864—March 22 .... Paris Church.
1850—April 17 .... Baptism .... Edward Young .... 1869—April 19 .... Dropped out.
  "   June 4 .... Baptism .... Frank Young ....
  "   June 4 .... Baptism .... Mary Young ....
1860—June 19 .... First Mention .... Thomas Young .... 1860—June 19 .... Dropped out.
  "   June 19 .... First Mention .... Elizabeth Young ..... 1860—June 19 .... Dropped out.
1862—April 8 .... Baptism .... Winifred C. Young ....
  "   November 7 ...... First Mention .... Sister Young .... 1862 — November 7 ..... A Letter.
1864—March 22 .... First Mention .... Eliza Young .... 1864—March 22 .... Ohio, United States.
1867—January 22 ...... First Mention .... John Yule ....
  "   January 27 ...... Baptism .... Barbara Yule .... 1868—September 6 ...... Toronto.
  "   August 4 .... Almonte Church ...... James. C. Yule ...... 1868—September 6 ...... Toronto.
  "   September 6 ..... First Mention .... Pamelia Yule .... 1868—September 6 ...... Toronto.
1870—May 7 .... First Mention .... Mrs. Ann Young ...... 1870—May 7 .... Tabernacle Church.
1874—July 5 .... Mrs. Young ....
  "   July 5 .... Miss Young ....
1875—February 18 ..... Baptism .... Amelia Young ....
  "   August 27 .... John Yule .... 1875—August 27 .... East Ward Church.
  "   August 27 .... Mrs. John Yule ...... 1875—August 27 .... East Ward Church.

Z

1872—May 31 .... Baptism .... Brother Zealand ....

APPENDIX.

Thy word is truth. All scripture is given by inspiration of God, and is profitable for doctrine. To the law and to the testimony: if they speak not according to this word it is because there is no light in them. But though we, or an angel from heaven, preach any other gospel unto you, let him be accursed. They received the word with all readiness of mind and searched the scriptures daily, whether these things were so. If any man shall add unto these things, God shall add unto him the plagues that are written in this book. *God's word.*

BRANTFORD, ONT.
PRESS OF THE EXPOSITOR.
1890.

"And the Lord said unto Moses, Make thee a fiery serpent, and set it upon a pole: and it shall come to pass, that every one that is bitten, when he looketh upon it, shall live. And Moses made a serpent of brass, and put it upon a pole, and it came to pass, that if a serpent had bitten any man, when he beheld the serpent of brass, he lived."—*Numbers* xxi 8, 9.

"And as Moses lifted up the serpent in the wilderness, even so must the Son of man be lifted up: that whosoever believeth in him, should not perish, but have eternal life. For God so loved the world, that he gave his only begotten Son, that whosoever believeth in him should not perish, but have everlasting iife."—*John* iii, 14, 15, 16.

Declaration of Faith.

I, OF THE SCRIPTURES.

We believe that the Holy Bible was written by men divinely inspired, and is a perfect treasure of heavenly instruction ;* that it has God for its author, salvation for its end,† and truth without mixture for its matter ;‡ that it reveals the principles by which God will judge us ;§ and therefore is, and shall remain till the end of the world, the true centre of Christian union, and the supreme standard by which all human conduct, creeds and opinions should be tried.*

PLACES IN THE BIBLE WHERE TAUGHT.

*Tim. iii, 16, 17.—All scripture is given by inspiration of God, and is profitable for doctrine, for reproof, for correction, for instruction in righteousness ; that the man of God may be perfect thoroughly furnished unto all good works. Also 2 Pet. i, 21. 2 Sam. xxiii, 2. Acts i. 16 ; iii, 21 John x, 35. Luke xvi, 29-31. Ps. cxix, 111. Rom. iii, 1, 2.

†2 Tim. iii, 15—Able to make thee wise unto salvation. Also 1 Pet i, 10-12. Acts xi. 14. Rom. i, 16. Mark xvi, 16. John v, 38-39.

‡Proverbs xxx, 5, 6—Every word of God is pure.—Add thou not unto his words, lest he reprove thee, and thou be found a liar. Also John xvii, 17. Rev. xxii, 18, 19. Rom. iii, 4.

§Romans ii, 12—As many as have sinned in the law shall be judged by the law. John xii, 47, 48. If any man hear my words—the word I have spoken, the same shall judge him in the last day. Also 1 Cor. iv, 3, 4. Luke x, 10-16 ; xii, 47, 48.

Phil iii, 16—Let us walk by the same rule ; let us mind the same thing. Also Ephes. iv. 3-6. Phil. i, 1, 2. 1 Cor. i, 10. 1 Pet. iv, 11.

* John iv, 1—Beloved, believe not every spirit, but try the spirits whether they are of God. Isaiah viii, 20—To the law and to the testimony ; if they speak not according to this word, it is because there is no light in them. 1 Thes. v, 21—Prove all things. 2 Cor. xiii, 5—Prove your own selves. Also Acts xvii, 11. 1 John iv, 6. Jude iii, 5. Eph. vi, 17. Ps. cxix, 59, 60. Phil. ii, 9-11.

II, OF THE TRUE GOD.

We believe that there is one, and only one, living and true God, an infinite, intelligent spirit, whose name is JEHOVAH, the Maker and Supreme Ruler of Heaven and Earth;† inexpressibly glorious in holiness,† and worthy of all possible honor, confidence and love;‡ that in the unity of the Godhead are three persons, the Father, the Son, and the Holy Ghost;§ equal in every divine perfection, and executing distinct but harmonious offices in the great work of redemption.*

PLACES IN THE BIBLE WHERE TAUGHT.

John iv, 24 God is a spirit. Ps. cxlvii His understanding is infinite. Ps. lxxxiii, 18 Thou whose name alone is JEHOVAH, art the Most High over all the earth. Heb. iii, 4 Romans i, 20. Jer. x, 10.

†Ez. xv, 11 Who is like unto thee, glorious in holiness? Isa. vi, 3. 1 Pet. i, 15, 16. Rev. iv, 6-8

‡Mark xii, 30 Thou shalt love the Lord thy God with all thy heart, and with all thy soul, and with all thy mind, and with all thy strength. Rev. iv, 11 Thou art worthy, O Lord, to receive glory and honor and power, for thou hast created all things, and for thy pleasure they are and were created. Mat. x, 37. Jer. ii, 12, 13.

§Mat. xxviii, 19 Go ye therefore and teach all nations, baptizing them in the name of the Father, and of the Son, and of the Holy Ghost. John xv, 26 When the Comforter is come, whom I will send you from the Father, even the Spirit of Truth, which proceedeth from the Father, he shall testify of me. 1 Cor. xii, 4-6. 1 John, v, 7.

John x, 30 I and my Father are one. John v, 17 ; xiv, 23 ; xvii, 10. Acts v, 3, 4. 1 Cor. ii, 10, 11. Phil. ii, 5, 6.

* Ephes. ii, 19 For through him (the Son) we both have an access by one Spirit unto the Father. 2 Cor. xiii, 14 The grace of our Lord Jesus Christ, and the love of God, and the communion of the Holy Ghost, be with you all. Rev. i, 4, and 5. Comp. ii, 7.

III, OF THE FALL OF MAN.

We believe that man was created in holiness, under the law of his Maker,* but by voluntary transgression fell from that holy and happy state,† in consequence of which all mankind are now sinners,‡ not by constraint but choice;§ being by nature utterly void of that holiness required by the law of God, positively inclined to evil, and therefore under just condemnation to eternal ruin without defence or excuse.*

PLACES IN THE BIBLE WHERE TAUGHT.

*Gen. i, 27 God created man in his own image. Gen. i, 31 And God saw everything that he had made, and behold it was very good. Eccles. vii, 20. Acts xv, 26. Gen. ii, 16.

†Gen. iii, 6-24—And when the woman saw that the tree was good for food, and that it was pleasant to the eyes, and a tree to be desired to make one wise, she took of the fruit thereof and did eat, and gave unto her husband with her and he did eat.—Therefore the Lord God drove out the man; and he placed at the east of the Garden of Eden cherubims and a flaming sword which turned every way to keep the way of the tree of life. Rom. v, 12.

Rom. v, 19—By one man's disobedience many were made sinners. John iii, 6. Ps. li, 5. Rom. v, 15-19; viii, 7.

§Isa. liii, 6—We have turned every man to his own way. Gen. vi, 12. Rom. iii, 9-18.

Eph. ii, 1-3—Among whom also we had our conversation in times past in the lusts of our flesh, fulfilling the desires of the flesh and of the mind; and were by nature the children of wrath even as others. Rom. i, 18—For the wrath of God is revealed from heaven against all ungodliness and unrighteousness of men, who hold the truth in unrighteousness. Rom. i, 32: ii, 1-16. Gal. iii, 10. Mat. xx, 15.

* Ez. xviiii, 19, 20—Yet ye say, Why? doth not the son bear the iniquity of the father?—The soul that sinneth it shall die. The son shall not bear the iniquity of the father, neither shall the father bear the iniquity of the son: the righteousness of the righteous shall be upon him, and the wickedness of the wicked shall be upon him. Rom. i, 20 —So that they are without excuse. Rom. iii, 19—That every mouth may be stopped and all the world may become guilty before God. Gal. iii, 22.

IV, OF THE WAY OF SALVATION.

We believe that the salvation of sinners is wholly of grace* through the Mediatorial offices of the Son of God,† who by the appointment of the Father freely took upon him our nature, yet without sin;‡ honored the divine law by his personal obedience;§ by his death made full atonement for our sins: that having risen from the dead he is now enthroned in Heaven;* and uniting in his wonderful person the tenderest sympathies with divine perfection, he is every way qualified to be a suitable, a compassionate, and an all-sufficient Saviour.**

PLACES IN THE BIBLE WHERE TAUGHT.

*Eph. ii, 5—By grace ye are saved   Mat. xviii, 11. 1 John iv, 10. 1 Cor. iii, 5-7. Acts xv, 11.

†John iii, 16—For God so loved the world that he gave his only begotten Son, that whosoever believeth in him should not perish, but have everlasting life. John i, 1-14. Heb. iv, 14; xii, 24.

‡Phil. li, 6, 7—Who being in the form of God, thought it not robbery to be equal with God; but made himself of no reputation, and took upon him the form of a servant, and was made in the likeness of men. Heb. ii, 9; ii, 14. 2 Cor. v, 21.

§Isa. xli, 21—The Lord is well pleased for his righteousness' sake;

he will magnify the law and make it honorable. Phil. ii, 8. Gal. iv,
4, 5 Rom. iii, 21.

Isa. liii, 4, 5—He was wounded for our transgressions, he was
bruised for our iniquities ; the chastisement of our peace was upon
him ; and with his stripes we are healed. Mat. xx, 28. Rom. iv, 25 ;
iii, 21-26. 1 John iv, 10 ; ii, 2. 1 Cor. xv, 1-3. Heb. ix, 13-15.

* Heb. i, 8—Unto the Son he saith, Thy throne, O God, is for ever
and ever. Heb. i, 3 ; viii, 1. Col. iii, 1-4.

** Heb. vii, 25—Wherefore he is able also to save them to the
utmost that come unto God by him, seeing he ever liveth to make in-
tercession for them. Col. ii, 9 For in him dwelleth all the fulness of
the Godhead bodily. Heb. ii, 18—In that he himself hath suffered,
being tempted, he is able to succor them that are tempted. Heb. vii,
26. Ps. lxxxix, 19. Ps. xlv.

V, OF JUSTIFICATION.

We believe that the great Gospel blessing which Christ secures to
such as believe in him is Justification ;† that Justification includes the
pardon of sin‡ and the promise of eternal life on principles of righteousness ;§ that it is bestowed, not in consideration of any works of righteousness which we have done, but solely through faith in the Redeemer's
blood ; by virtue of which faith his perfect righteousness is freely im-
puted to us of God ;* that it brings us into a state of most blessed
peace and favor with God and secures every other blessing needful for
time and eternity.**

PLACES IN THE BIBLE WHERE TAUGHT.

*John i, 16 – Of his fulness have all we received. Eph. iii, 8.

†Acts xiii, 39—By him all that believe are justified from all things.
Isaiah iii, 11, 12. Rom. viii, 1.

‡Rom. v, 9—Being justified by his blood we shall be saved from
wrath through him. Zech. xiii, 1. Mat. ix, 6. Acts x, 43

§Rom. v, 17—They which receive the abundance of grace and of
the gift of righteousness shall reign in life by one. Jesus Christ. Titus
iii, 5, 6. 1 Peter iii, 7. 1 John ii, 25. Rom. 5, 21.

Romans iv, 4, 5—Now to him that worketh is the reward not
reckoned of grace, but of debt. But to him that worketh not, but believeth on him that justifieth the ungodly, his faith is counted for
righteousness. Romans v, 21 ; vi, 23. Phil. iii, 7 9.

* Romans v, 19—By the obedience of one many shall be made
righteous. Romans iii, 24-26 ; iv, 23-25. 1 John ii, 12.

**Romans v, 1, 2—Being justified by faith, we have peace with God
through our Lord Jesus Christ ; by whom also we have access by faith
into this grace wherein we stand, and rejoice in hope of the glory of
God. Romans v, 3—We glory in tribulation also. Romans v, 11 We
also joy in God. 1 Cor. i, 30, 31. Mat. vi, 33. 1 Tim. iv, 8.

VI, OF THE FREENESS OF SALVATION.

We believe that the blessings of salvation are made free to all by the Gospel ;* that it is the immediate duty of all to accept them by a cordial, penitent and obedient faith,† and that nothing prevents the salvation of the greatest sinner on earth but his own inherent depravity and voluntary rejection of the Gospel ;‡ which rejection involves him in an aggravated condemnation.§

PLACES IN THE BIBLE WHERE TAUGHT.

*Isaiah lv, 1—Ho, every one that thirsteth, come ye to the waters. Rev. xxii, 17—Whosoever will, let him take the water of life freely. Luke xiv, 17.

†Romans xvi, 26—The Gospel—according to the commandment of the everlasting God, made known to all nations for the obedience of faith. Mark i, 15. Romans i, 15-17.

‡John v, 40—Ye will not come to me that ye might have life. Mat. xxiii, 37. Rom. ix, 32. Prov. i, 24. Acts xiii, 46.

§John iii, 19—And this is the condemnation, that light is come into the world, and men loved darkness rather than light because their deeds were evil. Mat. xi, 20. Luke xix, 27. 2 Thess. i, 8.

VII, OF GRACE IN REGENERATION.

We believe that in order to be saved sinners must be regenerated or born again ;* that regeneration consists in giving a holy disposition to the mind ;† that it is effected in a manner above our comprehension by the power of the Holy Spirit, in connection with divine truth,‡ so as to secure our voluntary obedience to the Gospel,§ and that its proper evidence appears in the holy fruits of repentance, and faith, and newness of life.

PLACES IN THE BIBLE WHERE TAUGHT.

*John iii, 3—Verily, verily, I say unto thee, except a man be born again, he cannot see the kingdom of God. John iii, 6, 7. 1 Cor. i, 14. Rev. viii, 7-9; xxi, 27.

†2 Cor. v, 17—If any man be in Christ he is a new creature. Ez. xxxvi, 26. Deut. xxx, 6. Rom. ii, 28, 29; v, 5. 1 John iv, 7.

‡John iii 8—The wind bloweth where it listeth, and thou hearest the sound thereof, but canst not tell whence it cometh and whither it goeth : so is every one that is born of the Spirit. John i, 13—Which were born not of blood, nor of the will of flesh, nor of the will of man, but of God. James i, 16-18—Of his own will begat he us with the word of truth. 1 Cor. i, 30. Phil. ii, 13.

§1 Peter i, 22 25—Ye have purified your souls by obeying the truth through the Spirit. 1 John v, 1—Whosoever believeth that Jesus is the Christ is born of God. Eph. iv, 20-24. Col. iii, 9-11.

Eph v, 9—The fruit of the Spirit is in all goodness and righteousness and truth. Rom viii, 9. Gal. v, 16-23. Eph. iii, 14-21. Mat. iii, 8-10 ; vii, 20. 1 John v, 4-18.

VIII, OF REPENTANCE AND FAITH.

We believe that Repentance and faith are sacred duties, and also inseparable graces wrought in our souls by the regenerating Spirit of God,* whereby, being deeply convinced of our guilt, danger and helplessness, and of the way of salvation by Christ,† we turn to God with unfeigned contrition, confession and application for mercy ;‡ at the same time heartily receiving the Lord Jesus Christ as our Prophet, Priest and King, and relying on Him alone as the only and all-sufficient Saviour.§

PLACES IN THE BIBLE WHERE TAUGHT.

*Mark i, 15—Repent ye and believe the Gospel. Acts xi, 18— Then hath God also to the Gentiles granted repentance unto life. Eph. ii, 8—By grace ye are saved through faith, and that not of yourselves : it is the gift of God. 1 John v, 1—Whosoever believeth that Jesus is the Christ is born of God.

†John xvi, 8—He will reprove the world of sin, and of righteousness, and of judgment. Acts ii, 37, 38—They were pricked in their heart and said, Men and brethren, what shall we do ? Then Peter said unto them, Repent, and be baptized every one of you in the name of Jesus Christ for the remission of your sins. Acts xvi, 30, 31.

‡Luke xviii, 13—And the publican smote upon his breast, saying, God be merciful to me, a sinner. Luke xv, 18-21. James iv, 7-10. 2 Cor. vii, 11. Rom. x, 12, 13. Ps. li.

§Rom. x, 9-11—If thou shalt confess with thy mouth the Lord Jesus, and shalt believe in thy heart that God hath raised him from the dead, thou shalt be saved. Acts iii, 22, 23. Heb. iv, 14. Ps. ii, 6. Heb. i, 8 ; viii, 25. 2 Tim. i, 12.

IX, OF GOD'S PURPOSE OF GRACE.

We believe that Election is the eternal purpose of God, according to which he graciously regenerates, sanctifies and saves sinners ;* that being perfectly consistent with the free agency of man, it comprehends all the means in connection with the end,† that it is a most glorious display of God's sovereign goodness, being infinitely free, wise, holy and unchangeable ;‡ that it utterly excludes boasting, and promotes humility, love, prayer, praise, trust in God, and active imitation of his free mercy ;§ that it encourages the use of means in the highest degree ;

that it may be ascertained by its effect in all who truly believe the Gospel* ; that it is the foundation of Christian assurance,†† and that to ascertain it with regard to ourselves demands and deserves the utmost diligence.

PLACES IN THE BIBLE WHERE TAUGHT.

*2 Tim. i, 8, 9—Be not thou therefore ashamed of the testimony of our Lord, nor of me his prisoner ; but be thou partaker of the afflictions of the Gospel, according to the power of God ; who hath saved us and called us with an holy calling, not according to our works, but according to his own purpose and grace, which was given us in Jesus Christ before the world began. Eph. i, 3-14. 1 Peter i, 1, 2. Rom. xi, 5, 6. John xv, 16. 1 John iv, 19. Hos. xii, 9.

†2 Thes. ii, 13, 14—But we are bound to give thanks always to God for you, brethren beloved of the Lord, because God hath from the beginning chosen you to salvation, through sanctification of the Spirit and belief of the truth ; whereunto he called you by our Gospel, to the obtaining of the glory of our Lord Jesus Christ. Acts xiii, 48. John x, 16. Mat. xx, 16. Acts xv, 14.

‡Ex. xxxiii, 18, 19—And Moses said, I beseech thee, show me thy glory. And he said, I will cause all my goodness to pass before thee, and I will proclaim the name of the Lord before thee, and I will be gracious to whom I will be gracious, and will show mercy on whom I will show mercy. Mat. xx, 15—Is it not lawful for me to do what I will with my own? Is thine eye evil, because I am good? Eph. i, 11. Rom. ix, 23, 24. Jer. xxxi, 3. Rom. xi, 28, 29. Jam. i, 17, 18. 2 Tim. i, 9. Rom. xi, 32-36.

§1 Cor. iv, 7—For who maketh thee to differ from another? and what hast thou that thou didst not receive? Now if thou didst receive it, why dost thou glory as if thou hadst not received it? 1 Cor. i, 26-31. Rom. iii, 27 ; iv, 16. Col. iii, 12. 1 Cor. iii, 5-7 ; xv, 10. 1 Peter v, 10. Acts i, 24. 1 Thes. ii, 13. 1 Peter ii, 9. Luke, xviii, 7. John xv, 16. Eph. i, 16. 1 Thes. ii, 12.

2 Tim. ii, 10—Therefore I endure all things for the elect's sake, that they also may obtain the salvation which is in Christ Jesus with eternal glory. 1 Cor. ix, 21.—I am made all things to all men, that I might by all means save some. Rom. viii, 28-30. John vi, 37-40. 2 Peter i, 10.

* 1 Thes. i, 4-10—Knowing, brethren beloved, your election of God ; for our Gospel came unto you, not in word only, but in power, and in the Holy Ghost, and in much assurance, &c,

**Rom. viii, 28-30—Moreover, whom he did predestinate, them he also called, and whom he called, them he also justified, and whom he justified, them he also glorified. What shall we then say to these things? If God be for us, who can be against us? Isaiah xiii, 16. Romans xi, 29.

††2 Peter i, 10, 11—Wherefore the rather, brethren, give diligence to make your calling and election sure ; for if ye do these things ye shall never fall ; for so an entrance shall be ministered unto you abundantly into the everlasting kingdom of our Lord and Saviour Jesus Christ. Phil. iii, 12. Heb. vi, 11.

X, OF SANCTIFICATION.

We believe that Sanctification is the process by which, according to the will of God, we are made partakers of his holiness ;* that it is a progressive work ;† that it is begun in regenerating,‡ and that it is carried on in the hearts of believers by the presence and power of the Holy Spirit, the Sealer and Comforter, in the continual use of the appointed means—especially the Word of God, self-examination, self-denial, watchfulness and prayer.§

PLACES IN THE BIBLE WHERE TAUGHT.

*1 Thes. iv 3—For this is the will of God, even your sanctification. 1 Thes. v, 23—And the very God of Peace sanctify you wholly. 2 Cor. vii, 1 ; xiii, 9. Eph. , 4

†Prov. iv, 18—The path of the just is as the shining light, which shineth more and more unto the perfect day. 2 Cor. iii, 18. Heb. vi, 1. 2 Peter i, 5-8. Phil. iii, 12-16.

‡John ii, 29—If ye know that he [God] is righteous, ye know that every one that doeth righteousness is born of him. Rom. viii, 5—They that are after the flesh do mind the things of the flesh ; but they that are after the Spirit, the things of the Spirit. John iii, 6. Phil. i, 9-11. Eph. i, 13, 14.

§Phil ii, 12, 13—Work out your own salvation with fear and trembling, for it is God which worketh in you both to will and to do his good pleasure. Eph. iv, 11, 12. 1 Peter ii, 2. 2 Peter iii, 18. 2 Cor. xiii, 5. Luke xi, 35 ; ix, 23. Mat. xxvi, 41. Eph. vi, 18 ; iv, 30.

XI, OF THE PERSEVERENCE OF SAINTS.

We believe that such only are real believers as endure unto the end ; that their persevering attachment to Christ is the grand mark which distinguishes them from superficial professors ;† that a special providence watches over their welfare,‡ and they are kept by the power of God through faith unto salvation.§

PLACES IN THE BIBLE WHERE TAUGHT.

*John viii, 31—Then said Jesus, If ye continue in my word then are ye my disciples indeed. 1. John ii, 27, 28 ; iii, 9 : v, 18.

†1 John ii, 19—They went out from us, but they were not of us : for if they had been of us, they would no doubt have continued with us ; but they went out that it might be made manifest that they were not all of us. John xiii, 18. Mat. xiii, 20, 21. John vi, 66-69. Job xvii, 9.

‡Rom. viii, 28—And we know that all things work together for good unto them that love God, to them that are the called according to his purpose. Mat. vi, 30-33. Jer. xxxii, 40. Ps. cxxi, 3 ; xci, 11, 12.

§Phil. i, 6—He who hath begun a good work in you will perform
it until the day of Jesus Christ. Phil. ii, 12, 13. Jude 24, 25. Heb.
i, 14. 2 Kings vi, 16. Heb. xiii, 5. 1 John iv, 4

XII, OF THE HARMONY OF THE LAW AND THE GOSPEL.

We believe that the Law of God is the eternal and unchangeable
rule of his moral government;* that it is holy, just and good,† and
that the inability which the Scriptures ascribe to fallen men to fulfill
its precepts arises entirely from their love of sin ;‡ to deliver them
from which and to restore them through a Mediator to unfeigned
obedience to the holy Law is one great end of the Gospel, and of the
means of grace connected with the establishment of the visible church.§

PLACES IN THE BIBLE WHERE TAUGHT.

*Rom. iii, 31—Do we make void the law through faith? God for-
bid. Yea, we establish the law. Mat. v, 17. Luke xvi, 17. Rom.
iii, 20 ; iv, 15.

†Rom. vii, 12—The law is holy and the commandment holy, and
just, and good. Rom. vii, 7, 14, 22. Gal. iii, 21. Ps. cxix.

‡Rom. viii, 7, 8—The carnal mind is enmity against God ; for it
is not subject to the law of God, neither indeed can be. So then they
that are in the flesh cannot please God. Josh. xxiv, 19. Jer. xiii, 23
John vi, 44 ; v, 44.

§Rom. viii, 2-4—For the law of the Spirit of Life in Christ Jesus
hath made me free from the law of sin and death. For what the law
could not do, in that it was weak through the flesh, God sending his
own Son in the likeness of sinful flesh, and for sin, condemned sin in
the flesh, that the righteousness of the law might be fulfilled in us, who
walk not after the flesh but after the Spirit. Rom. x, 4. 1 Tim. i, 5.
Heb. viii, 10. Jude 20, 21. Heb. xii, 14. Mat. xvi, 17, 18. 1 Cor.
xii, 28.

XIII, OF A GOSPEL CHURCH.

We believe that a visible church of Christ is a congregation of baptized believers ;* associated by covenant in the faith and fellowship of
the Gospel ;† observing the ordinances of Christ ;‡ governed by his
laws,§ and exercising the gifts, rights and privileges invested in them
by his word ; that its only scriptural officers are Bishops, or Pastors,
and Deacons ;* whose qualifications, claims and duties are defined in
the Epistles to Timothy and Titus.

PLACES IN THE BIBLE WHERE TAUGHT.

*1 Cor. i, 1-13—Paul unto the church of God which is at Corinth Is Christ divided? Was Paul crucified for you? Or were ye baptized in the name of Paul? Mat. xviii, 17. Acts v, 11; viii, 1; xi, 31. 1 Cor. iv, 17; xiv, 23. 3 John, 9. 1 Tim. iii, 5.

†Acts ii, 41-42—Then they that gladly received his word were baptized, and the same day there were added to them about three thousand souls. 2 Cor. viii, 5—They first gave their ownselves to the Lord, and unto us by the will of God. Acts ii, 47. 1 Cor. v, 12, 13.

‡1 Cor. xi, 2—Now I praise you, brethren, that ye remember me in all things, and keep the ordinances as I delivered them unto you. 2 Thes. iii, 6. Rom. xvi. 17-20. 1 Cor. xi, 23. Mat. xviii, 15-20. 1 Cor. v, vi. 2 Cor. ii, vii. 1 Cor. iv, 17.

§Mat. xviii, 20—Teaching them to observe all things whatsoever I have commanded you. John xiv, 15; xv, 12. 1 John iv, 21. John xiv, 21. 1 Thes. iv, 2. 2 John, 6. Gal. vi, 2. All the Epistles.

Eph. iv, 7 Unto every one of us is given grace according to the measure of the gift of Christ. 1 Cor. xiv, 12 Seek that ye may excel to the edifying of the church. Phil. i, 27 That I may hear of your affairs, that ye stand fast in one spirit, with one mind, striving together for the faith of the Gospel. 1 Cor. xii, xiv.

* Phil. i, 1—With the Bishops and Deacons. Acts xiv, 23; xv, 22. 1 Tim. iii, Titus i.

XIV, OF BAPTISM AND THE LORD'S SUPPER.

We believe that Christian Baptism is the immersion in water of a believer;* into the name of the Father, and Son, and Holy Ghost ;† to show forth, in a solemn and beautiful emblem, our faith in the crucified, buried and risen Saviour, with its effect, in our death to sin and resurrection to a new life ;‡ that it is pre-requisite to the privileges of a church relation, and to the Lord's Supper ;§ in which the members of the church, by the sacred use of bread and wine, are to commemorate together the dying love of Christ, preceded always by solemn self-examination. *

PLACES IN THE BIBLE WHERE TAUGHT.

Acts viii, 36-39—And the eunuch said, See, here is water, what doth hinder me to be baptized? And Philip said, If thou believest with all thy heart thou mayest.—And they went down into the water, both Philip and the eunuch, and he baptized him. Mat. iii, 5, 6. John iii, 22, 23; iv, 1, 2. Mat. xviii, 19. Mark xvi, 16. Acts ii, 38; viii, 12; xvi, 32-34; xviii, 8.

†Mat. xxviii, 19 Baptizing them in the name of the Father, and of the Son, and of the Holy Ghost. Acts x, 47, 48. Gal. iii, 27, 28.

‡Rom. vi, 4 Therefore we are buried with him by baptism into death; that like as Christ was raised from the dead by the glory of the Father, even so we also shall walk in newness of life. Col. ii, 12. 1 Pet. iii, 20, 21. Acts xxii. 16.

§Acts ii, 41, 42—Then they that gladly received his word were baptized, and there were added to them the same day about three thousand souls. And they continued steadfastly in the Apostles' doctrine and fellowship, and in breaking of bread and in prayers. Mat. xxviii, 19, 20. Acts and Epistles.

1 Cor. xi, 26—As often as ye eat this bread and drink this cup ye do show the Lord's death till he come. Mat. xxvi, 26-29. Mark xiv, 22-25. Luke xxii, 14-20.

* 1 Cor. xi, 28—But let a man examine himself, and so let him eat of that bread and drink of that cup. 1 Cor. v. 1-8; x, 3-32; xi, 17-32. John vi, 26-71.

XV, OF THE CHRISTIAN SABBATH.

We believe that the first day of the week is the Lord's Day, or Christian Sabbath,* and is to be kept sacred to religious purposes :† by abstaining from all secular labor and sinful recreations ;‡ by the devout observance of all the means of grace, both private§ and public ; and by preparation for that rest that remaineth for the people of God.*

PLACES IN THE BIBLE WHERE TAUGHT.

*Acts xx, 7—On the first day of the week, when the disciples came together to break bread, Paul preached to them. Gen. ii, 3. Col. ii, 16, 17. Mark ii, 27. John xx, 19. 1 Cor. xvi, 1, 2.

†Ex. xx, 8—Remember the Sabbath Day, to keep it holy. Rev. i, 10—I was in the spirit on the Lord's Day. Ps. cxviii, 24—This is the day which the Lord hath made ; we will rejoice and be glad in it.

‡Isa. lviii, 13, 14—If thou turn away thy foot from the Sabbath, from doing thy pleasure on my holy day ; and call the Sabbath a delight, the holy of the Lord honorable ; and shalt honor him, not doing thine own ways, nor finding thine own pleasure, nor speaking thine own words ; then shalt thou delight thyself in the Lord, and I will cause thee to ride upon the high places of the earth, and feed thee with the heritage of Jacob. Isa. lxi, 2-8.

§Ps. cxviii, 15—The voice of rejoicing and salvation is in the tabernacle of the righteous.

Heb. x, 24, 25—Not forsaking the assembling of yourselves together, as the manner of some is. Acts xi, 26.—A whole year they assembled themselves with the church and taught much people Acts xiii, 44—The next Sabbath day came almost the whole city together to hear the word of God. Lev. xix, 30. Ex. xlvi, 3. Luke iv, 16. Acts xvii, 2, 3. Ps. xxvi, 8 ; lxxxvii, 3.

* Heb. iv, 3-11—Let us labor therefore to enter into that rest.

XVI, OF CIVIL GOVERNMENT.

We believe that Civil Government is of Divine appointment for the interests and good order of human society,* and that magistrates are to be prayed for, conscientiously honored and obeyed,† except only in things opposed to the will of our Lord Jesus Christ,‡ who is the only Lord of the conscience, and the Prince of the kings of the earth.§

PLACES IN THE BIBLE WHERE TAUGHT.

*Rom. xiii, 1-7—The powers that be are ordained of God. For rulers are not a terror to good works, but to the evil. Deut. xvi, 18. 2 Sam. xxiii, 3. Ex. xviii, 23. Jer. xxx, 21.

†Mat. xxii, 21 Render therefore unto Cesar the things that are Cesar's, and unto God the things that are God's. Titus iii, 1, 1 Peter ii, 13. 1 Tim. ii, 1-8.

‡Acts x, 29 —We ought to obey God rather than man. Mat. x, 28 Fear not them which kill the body, but are not able to kill the soul. Dan. iii, 15-18; vi, 7-10. Acts iv, 18-20.

§Mat. xxiii, 10 —Ye have one Master, even Christ. Rom. xiv, 4 Who art thou that judgest another man's servant. Rev. xix, 16—And he hath on his vesture and on his thigh a name written, KING OF KINGS AND LORD OF LORDS. Ps. lxxii, 11; ii. Rom. xiv, 9-13.

XVII, OF THE RIGHTEOUS AND THE WICKED.

We believe that there is a radical and essential difference between the righteous and the wicked;* that such only as through faith are justified in the name of the Lord Jesus and sanctified by the Spirit of our God are truly righteous in his esteem;† while all such as continue in impenitence and unbelief are in His sight wicked, and under the curse,‡ and this distinction holds among men both in and after death.§

PLACES IN THE BIBLE WHERE TAUGHT,

*Mal. iii, 18 — Ye shall discern between the righteous and the wicked; between him that serveth God and him that serveth him not. Prov. xii, 26. Isa. v, 20. Gen. xviii, 23, Jer. xv, 19. Acts x, 34, 35. Rom. vi, 16.

†Rom. i, 17—The just shall live by faith. Rom. vii, 6—We are delivered from the law, that being dead wherein we were held, that we should serve in newness of spirit and not in the oldness of the letter. 1 John ii, 29 If ye know that he is righteous, ye know that every one that doeth righteousness is born of him. 1 John iii, 7. Rom. vi, 18-22. 1 Cor. xi, 32. Prov. ii, 31. 1 Peter iv, 17, 18.

‡1 John v, 19—And we know that we are of God, and the whole world lieth in wickedness. Gal. iii, 10—As many as are of the works of the law are under the curse. John iii, 36. Isa. lvii, 21. Ps. x, 4. Isa. lv, 6, 7.

§Prov. xiv, 32—The wicked is driven away in his wickedness, but the righteous hath hope in his death. (See also the example of the rich man and Lazarus.) Luke xvi, 25 Thou in thy lifetime receivedst thy good things and likewise Lazarus evil things; but now he is comforted and thou art tormented. John viii, 21-24. Prov. x, 24. Luke xii, 4, 5; ix, 23-26. John xii, 25, 26. Eccl. iii, 17. Mat. vii, 13, 14.

And as they went on their way, they came unto a certain water, and the Eunuch said, See, here is water; what doth hinder me to be **baptised (immersed, sprinkled)**? And Philip said, if thou believest with all thine heart thou mayest.

We give now, without a note or comment, every text in God's Word in which the words **Baptize, Baptism, Baptized, Baptizeth, Baptizest** and **Baptizing** occur.

And were **baptized (immersed. sprinkled)** of him in Jordan, confessing their sins.—Mat. iii, 6.

But when he saw many of the Pharisees and Saducees come to his **baptism (immersion, sprinkling)**, he said unto them, O generation of vipers, who hath warned you to flee from the wrath to come?—Mat. iii, 7.

I indeed **baptize (immerse, sprinkle)** you with water unto repentance; but he that cometh after me is mightier than I, whose shoes I am not worthy to bear: he shall **baptize (immerse, sprinkle)** you with the Holy Ghost and with fire.—Mat iii, 11.

Then cometh Jesus from Galilee to Jordan unto John, to be **baptized (immersed, sprinkled)** of him.—Mat. iii, 13

And he answered and said, I believe that Jesus Christ is the Son of God. * * * * * And they went down into the water, both Philip and the Eunuch, and he **baptized (immersed, sprinkled)** him. And when they were come up out of the water, &c.—Acts viii, 37.

But John forbad him, saying, I have need to be **baptized (immersed, sprinkled)** of thee, and comest thou to me ?—Mat. iii, 14.

And Jesus answering said unto him, Suffer it to be so now ; for thus it becometh us to fulfil all righteousness. Then he suffered him —Mat. iii, 15.

And Jesus, when he was **baptized (immersed, sprinkled)**, went up straightway out of the water ; and lo, the heavens were opened unto him, and he saw the Spirit of God descending like a dove, and lighting upon him —Mat. iii, 16.

But Jesus answered and said, Ye know not what ye ask. Are ye able to drink of the cup that I shall drink of, and to be **baptized (immersed, sprinkled)** with the **baptism (immersion, sprinkling)** that I am **baptized (immersed, sprinkled)** with ? They say unto him, We are able.— Mat. xx, 22

Know ye not that as many of us as were baptized (immersed, sprinkled) into Jesus Christ were baptized (immersed, sprinkled) into his death? Therefore we are buried with him by baptism (immersion, sprinkling) into death; that like as Christ was raised from the dead by the glory of the Father, even so we also should walk in newness of life. For if we have been planted together in the likeness of his death, we shall be also in the likeness of his resurrection.—Rom. vi, 3, 4, 5.

And he saith unto them, Ye shall indeed drink of my cup and be baptized (immersed, sprinkled) with the baptism (immersion sprinkling) that I am baptized (immersed, sprinkled) with, but to sit on my right hand and on my left is not mine to give, but it shall be given to them for whom it is prepared of my Father—Mat. xx, 23.

The baptism (immersion, sprinkling) of John, whence was it? from heaven or of men? And they reasoned with themselves, saying, If we shall say, From heaven, he will say unto us, Why did ye not then believe him? —Mat. xxi, 25.

And brought them out and said, Sirs, what must I do to be saved? And they said, Believe on the Lord Jesus Christ and thou shalt be saved, and thy house. And they spoke unto him the word of the Lord and to all that were in his house. And he took them the same hour of the night and washed their stripes; and was **baptised (immersed, sprinkled)**, he and all his, straightway * * * * * rejoiced, believing in God with all his house. (Acts xvi, 31.)

Go ye therefore, and teach all nations, **baptizing (immersing, sprinkling)** them in the name of the Father, and of the Son, and of the Holy Ghost. - Mat xxviii, 19.

Teaching them to observe all things whatsoever I have commanded you; and lo, I am with you always, even unto the end of the world. Amen.—Mat. xxviii, 20.

John did **baptize (immerse, sprinkle)** in the wilderness, and preach the **baptism (immersion, sprinkling)** of repentance for the remission of sins.—Mark i, 4.

And there went out to him all the land of Judea, and they of Jerusalem, and were all **baptized (immersed, sprinkled)** of him in the river of Jordan, confessing their sins.—Mark i, 5.

I have a **baptism (immersion, sprinkling)** to be
baptised (immersed, sprinkled) with, and how am I
straightened till it be accomplished.—(Luke xii, 50). He
fell on his face, saying, O, my Father, if it be possible let
this cup pass from me. And being in an agony he prayed
more earnestly, and his sweat was as it were great drops
of blood falling down to the ground.—(Luke xxii, 42).
My God, my God, why hast thou forsaken me?—Mark
xv, 34.

———

I indeed have **baptized (immersed, sprinkled)** you
with water, but he shall **baptize (immerse, sprinkle)**
you with the Holy Ghost.—Mark i, 8.

And it came to pass in those days that Jesus came
from Nazareth of Galilee, and was **baptized (immersed
sprinkled)** of John in Jordan.—Mark i, 9.

But Jesus said unto them, Ye know not what ye ask;
can ye drink of the cup that I drink of? and be **baptized
(immersed, sprinkled)** with the **baptism (immersion,
sprinkling)** that I am **baptized (immersed, sprinkled)**
with?—Mark x, 38.

And they said unto him, We can. And Jesus said unto them, Ye shall indeed drink of the cup that I drink and with the **baptism (immersion, sprinkling)** that I am **baptized (immersed, sprinkled)** withal shall ye be **baptized (immerseed, sprinkled)**.—Mark x, 39.

The **baptism (immersion, sprinkling)** of John, was it from heaven, or of men ? answer me —Mark xi, 30.

And he said unto them, Go ye into all the world and preach the gospel to every creature.—Mark xvi, 15.

He that believeth and is **baptized (immersed, sprinkled)** shall be saved ; but he that believeth not shall be damned.—Mark xvi, 16.

And he came into all the country about Jordan, preaching the **baptism (immersion, sprinkling)** of repentance for the remission of sins.—Luke iii, 3.

Then said he to the multitude that came forth to be **baptized (immersed, sprinkled)** of him, O generation of vipers, who hath warned you to flee from the wrath to come ?—Luke iii, 7.

Then came also publicans to be **baptized (immersed, sprinkled)**, and said unto him, Master, what shall we do ?—Luke iii, 2.

John answered, saying unto them all, I indeed **baptize (immerse, sprinkle)** you with water ; but one mightier than I cometh, the latchet of whose shoes I am not worthy to unloose. He shall **baptize (immerse, sprinkle)** you with the Holy Ghost and with fire.— Luke iii, 16.

Now when all the people were **baptized (immersed, sprinkled)**, it came to pass, that Jesus also being **baptized (immersed, sprinkled)**, and praying the heaven was opened.— Luke iii, 21.

And all the people that heard him, and the publicans, justified God, being **baptized (immersed, sprinkled)** with the **baptism (immersion, sprinkling)** of John. —Luke vii, 29.

But the Pharisees and lawyers rejected the counsel of God, being not **baptized (immersed, sprinkled)** of him. —Luke vii, 30.

The **baptism (immersion, sprinkling)** of John, was it from heaven, or of men ?—Luke xx, 4.

And they asked him, and said unto him, Why baptizest (immersest, sprinklest) thou then, if thou be not that Christ, nor Elias, neither that prophet?—John i, 25.

John answered them, saying, I baptize (immerse, sprinkle) with water ; but there standeth one among you, whom ye know not.—John i, 26.

These things were done in Bethabara beyond Jordan, where John was baptizing (immersing, sprinkling).—John i, 28.

And I knew him not, but that it might be made manifest to Israel, therefore I am come baptizing (immersing, sprinkling) with water.—John i, 31.

And I knew him not ; but he that sent me to baptize (immerse, sprinkle) with water, the same said unto me, Upon whom thou shalt see the Spirit descending, and remaining on him, the same is he which baptizeth (immerseth, sprinkleth) with the Holy Ghost.—John i, 33.

After these things came Jesus and his disciples into the land of Judea ; and there tarried with them and baptized (immersed, sprinkled).—John iii, 22.

And John also was baptizing (immersing, sprinkling) in Ænon near to Salim, because there was much water there ; and they came and were baptized (immersed, sprinkled).—John iii, 23.

For John was not yet cast into prison.—John iii, 24.

And they came unto John and said unto him, Rabbi, he that was with thee beyond Jordan, to whom thou bearest witness, behold, the same baptizeth, (immerseth, sprinkleth) and all men come unto him.—John iii, 26.

When therefore the Lord knew how the Pharisees had heard that Jesus made and baptized (immersed, sprinkled) more disciples than John—John iv, 1.

(Though Jesus baptized (immersed, sprinkled) not, but his disciples.)—John iv, 1.

And went away again beyond Jordan into the place where John at first baptized (immersed, sprinkled); and there he abode.—John x, 40.

For John truly baptized (immersed, sprinkled) with water ; but ye shall be baptized (immersed, sprinkled) with the Holy Ghost not many days hence.—Acts i, 5.

Beginning from the baptism (immersion, sprinkling) of John, unto that same day that he was taken up from us, must one be ordained to be a witness with us of his resurrection.—Acts i, 22.

Then Peter said unto them, Repent, and be baptized (immersed, sprinkled), every one of you in the name of Jesus Christ for the remission of sins, and ye shall receive the gift of the Holy Ghost.—Acts ii, 38.

Then they that gladly received his word were baptized (immersed, sprinkled); and the same day there were added unto them about three thousand souls.—Acts ii, 41.

But when they believed Philip preaching the things concerning the kingdom of God, and the name of Jesus Christ, they were baptized (immersed, sprinkled), both men and women.—Acts viii, 12.

Then Simon himself believed also; and when he was baptized (immersed, sprinkled), he continued with Philip, and wondered, beholding the miracles and signs which were done.—Acts viii, 13.

(For as yet he was fallen on none of them: only they were baptized (immersed, sprinkled) in the name of the Lord Jesus.)—Acts viii, 16.

And immediately there fell from his eyes as it had been scales: and he received sight forthwith, and arose, and was baptized (immersed, sprinkled).—Acts ix, 18.

That word, I say, ye know, which was published throughout all Judæa, and began from Galilee, after the baptism (immersion, sprinkling) which John preached.—Acts x, 37.

And he commanded them to be baptized (immersed, sprinkled) in the name of the Lord. Then prayed they him to tarry certain days.—Acts x, 48.

Then remembered I the word of the Lord, how that he said, John indeed baptized (immersed, sprinkled) with water, but ye shall be baptized (immersed, sprinkled) with the Holy Ghost.—Acts xi, 16.

When John had first preached before his coming the baptism (immersion, sprinkling) of repentance to all the people of Israel.—Acts xiii, 24.

And when she was baptized (immersed, sprinkled), and her household, she besought us, saying, If ye have judged me to be faithful to the Lord, come into my house, and abide there. And she constrained us.—Acts xvi. 15.

And Crispus, the chief ruler of the synagogue, believed on the Lord with all his house ; and many of the Corinthians hearing believed, were baptized (immersed, sprinkled) —Acts xviii, 8.

This man was instructed in the way of the Lord ; and being fervent in the spirit, he spake and taught diligently the things of the Lord, showing only the baptism (immersion, sprinkling) of John.— Acts xviii, 25.

And he said unto them, Unto what then were ye baptized (immersed, sprinkled)? And they said, Unto John's baptism (immersion, sprinkling).—Acts xix, 3.

Then said Paul, John verily baptized (immersed, sprinkled) with the baptism (immersion, sprinkling) of repentance, saying unto the people, that they should believe on him which should come after him, that is, on Jesus Christ,—Acts xix, 4.

When they heard this, they were baptized (immersed, sprinkled) in the name of the Lord Jesus.—Acts x x, 5.

And now why tarriest thou? arise, and be baptized immersed, sprinkled). and wash away thy sins, calling on the name of the Lord.—Acts xxii, 16.

Is Christ divided? was Paul crucified for you? or were ye baptized (immersed, sprinkled) in the name of Paul?—1 Cor i, 13.

I thank God that I baptized (immersed, sprinkled) none of you but Crispus and Gaius.—1 Cor. i, 14.

Lest any should say that I had baptized (immersed, sprinkled) in mine own name.—1 Cor. i, 15.

And I baptized (immersed, sprinkled) also the household of Stephanas; besides, I know not whether I baptized (immersed, sprinkled) any other.—1Cor. i. 16.

For Christ sent me not to baptize (immerse, sprinkle) but to preach the gospel ; not with wisdom of words, lest the cross of Christ should be made of none effect.—1 Cor. i, 17.

And were all **baptized (immersed, sprinkled)** unto Moses in the cloud and in the sea.—1 Cor. x. 2.

For by one Spirit are we all **baptized (immersed, sprinkled)** into one body * * * *—1 Cor. xii, 13.

Else what shall they do which are **baptized (immersed, sprinkled)** for the dead * * why are they then **baptized (immersed, sprinkled)** for the dead?—1 Cor. xv, 29.

For as many of you as have been **baptized (immersed, sprinkled)** into Christ have put on Christ·—Gal. iv, 27.

One Lord. one faith, one **baptism (immersion, sprinkling.**—Eph. iv, 5,

Buried with him in **baptism (immersion, sprinkling)** wherein also ye are risen with him * * —Col. iii 12.

Of the doctrine of **baptisms (immersions, sprinklings)**, * * * —Heb. vi. 2.

The like figure whereunto even **baptism (immersion, sprinklng)** doth also save us * * —1 Peter iii, 21.

The following are the only places in the New Testament where **water** is mentioned in connection with the rite of **Baptism**:

And Jesus when he was **baptized (immersed, sprinkled)** went up straightway **out of the water.**—Mat. iii, 16 and Mark i, 10.

John truly **baptized (immersed, sprinkled)** with **water**; but ye shall be **baptized (immersed, sprinkled)** with the Holy Ghost not many days hence.—Acts i, 5.

Therefore am I come **baptizing (immersing, sprinkling)** with **water.**—John i, 31.

I indeed **baptize (immerse, sprinkle)** you with **water**, but ye shall be **baptized (immersed, sprinkled)** with the Holy Ghost. Mat. iii, 11. Mark i, 10, Luke iii, 16 and John i, 25. (And **filled all the house** where they were sitting.—Acts ii. 2)

Was **baptizing (immersing, sprinkling)** in Enon, near to Salem because there was **much water** there.—John iii, 23.

They came to a certain **water**, and the Eunuch said, See, here is **water**, what does hinder me to be **baptized (immersed, sprinkled)**? * * * And **they went down both into the water**, both Philip and the Eunuch, and he **baptized (immersed, sprinkled)** him. And when they were come up **out of the water**, etc —Acts viii, 38.

Who can forbid **water**, that these should not be **baptized (immersed, sprinkled)** * * —Acts x, 47.

And were all baptized of him IN THE RIVER JORDAN, confessing their sins.—Mark i, 5.   And it came to pass in those days that Jesus came from Nazareth of Galilee, and was baptized of John IN JORDAN, and Jesus when he was baptized went up straightway OUT OF THE WATER.—Mark i, 9.

I indeed baptize you with water, but he shall baptize you with the Holy Ghost.—Mark i, 8.   (And suddenly there came a sound from heaven as of a mighty rushing WIND, and it FILLED ALL THE HOUSE WHERE THEY WERE SITTING.—Acts ii, 2.)

John was also baptizing in Enon, near to Salim, BECAUSE there was MUCH WATER THERE.—Acts iii, 23.

Know ye not that as many of us as were baptized INTO Christ, were baptized INTO HIS DEATH? THEREFORE, we are BURIED WITH HIM BY BAPTISM INTO HIS DEATH.—Rom. vi, 3.   They went down both INTO THE WATER, both Philip and the eunuch; and he baptized him, and when they were COME UP OUT OF THE WATER, etc.—Acts viii, 38.

He that hath my commandments and keepeth them, he it is that loveth me.—John xiv, 21.

There shall be for every male child to be baptized two Godfathers and one Godmother * * * must be ready at the Font. And the priest coming up to the Font shall take the child into his hands * and then naming it after them, he SHALL DIP IT IN THE WATER, discreetly and warily. BUT IF THEY CERTIFY that the child is weak, it shall suffice to pour water upon it.

(Of Adults.) Standing at the FONT   then shall the Priest take each person to be baptized by the right hand, and placing him conveniently near the FONT, shall then DIP HIM IN THE WATER, or pour water upon him. --Extracts from Book of Common Prayer.

No parent shall be urged to be present, nor be admitted to answer as Godfather for his own child. Church of England Canon, No. 29.

The Holy Scriptures speak only of Baptism by immersion. The dogma of the Church is to sprinkle, and we should in this, as in everything else, follow the Church. Roman Catholic Catechism.

Suffer the little CHILDREN to come unto me. and forbid them not. * * * * And he took them up in his arms, put his hands on them and BLESSED them.— Mat. 10, 15.

Jesus himself BAPTIZED NOT, but his disciples.—John 4, 2.

The following are the only places in the New Testament where t .e words " CHILD," " CHILDREN " and " BABE " occur, according to Dr. Robert Young's " Analytical Concordance."

2 Tim. 3, 15—That from a CHILD thou hast known the
1 Cor. 13, 11—When I was a CHILD I spake as a CHILD.
  "   13, 11—I understood * CHILD, I thought * CHILD.
Gala.   4, 1—The heir, as long as he is a CHILD, differeth
Mark   9, 24—Straightway the father of the CHILD cried.
  "   9, 36—He took a little CHILD and set him in the
Luke   1, 59—They came to circuscise the CHILD, and
  "   1, 66—What manner o[CHILD shall this be ? and
  "   1, 76—Thou, CHILD, shalt be called the Prophet.
  "   1, 80—The CHILD grew, * waxed strong in spirit.
  "   2, 17—Which was told * concerning this CHILD.
  '   2, 21—days * * for the circumcising of the CHILD.
  "   2, 27—The parents brought in the CHILD Jesus.
  "   2, 40—The CHILD grew, * waxed strong in spirit.

Luke	9, 47—And Jesus * took a CHILD and set him by
"	9, 48—Whosoever shall receive this CHILD in my
John	4, 49—Saith * Sir, come down ere my CHILD die
"	16, 21—As soon as she is delivered of the CHILD.
Heb.	11, 23—Because they saw he was a proper CHILD.
Mat.	17, 18—The CHILD was cured from that very hour.
Luke	2 43—The CHILD Jesus tarried behind in Jerus'lem
"	9, 12—Healed the CHILD and delivered him again
Acts	4, 27—Of a truth against thy holy CHILD Jesus.
"	4, 30—Done by the name of thy holy CHILD Jesus.
Mat.	10, 21—to death, and the father the CHILD ; and
Luke	1, 7—They had no child because that Elisabeth
Acts	7, 5—To his seed * * when * * he had no CHILD.
Rev.	12. 4—Devour her CHILD as soon as it was born.
"	12, 5—Her CHILD was caught up unto God.
Mat.	23, 15—Make him twofold more the CHILD of hell.
Acts	13, 10—Thou CHILD of the devil, thou enemy of
Rev.	12, 5—And she brought forth a man CHILD, who
1 Cor.	14, 20—Howbeit in malice be ye CHILDREN, but in
1 Tim.	2, 15—She shall be saved in CHILD bearing, if
Heb.	11, 11—Was delivered of a CHILD when she was
Luke	2, 5—Mary his * * wife being great with CHILD.
Mark	9, 21—How long * ago ? * * he said, Of a CHILD.
Mat.	18, 2—Jesus called a little child unto him, and
"	18, 3—Except ye be converted * * as * CHILDREN
"	18, 4—Shall humble himself as this little CHILD.
"	18, 5—Whoso shall receive one such little CHILD
"	19, 13—Then were there brought * little CHILDREN.
"	19. 14—Suffer little CHILDREN and forbid them not.
Mark	10, 14—Suffer the little CHILDREN to come unto me
"	10, 15—Receive the kingdom * * as a little CHILD
Luke	18, 16—Suffer little CHILDREN to come unto me.
"	18, 17—Receive the kingdom * * as a little CHILD
1 John	2, 18—I write unto you, little CHILDREN, because
"	2, 18—Little CHILDREN, it is the last time ; and as
John	13, 33—Little CHILDREN, yet a little while I am
Gala.	4, 19—My little CHILDREN, of whom I travail in
1 John	2, 1—My little CHILDREN, these things write I
"	2, 12—Little CHILDREN, * * your sins are forgiven
"	2, 28—And now, little CHILDREN, abide in him.
"	3, 7—Little CHILDREN, let no man deceive you.
"	3, 18—My little CHILDREN, let us not love in word
"	4, 4—Ye are of God, little CHILDREN, and have
"	5, 21—Little CHILDREN, keep yourselves from idols

Luke	9, 28—I beseech thee * * he is mine only CHILD.
Mat.	2, 8—Go and search * * * for the young CHILD.
"	2, 9—It * * * stood over where the young CHILD
"	2, 11—They saw the young CHILD with Mars his
"	2, 12—Arise, and take the young CHILD, and
"	2, 13—Herod will seek the young CHILD to destroy
"	2, 14—He took the young CHILD and his mother
"	2, 20—They are dead * sought the young CHILD.
"	2, 21—He arose, and took the young CHILD and
"	1, 18—She was found with CHILD of the Holy
"	1, 23—Behold, a virgin shall be with CHILD, and
"	24, 19—Woe unto them that are with CHILD, and
Mark	13, 17—But woe to them that are with CHILD.
Luke	21, 23—But woe unto them that are with CHILD
1 Thes.	5, 3—Upon them * * upon a woman with CHILD.
Rev.	12, 2—And she being with CHILD cried, travailing
Acts	7, 19—They cast out their young CHILDREN.
Gala.	4, 3—Even so we, when we were CHILDREN, were
Eph.	4, 14—Tnat we henceforth be as mere CHILDREN.
Mat.	14, 21—Five thousand men besides * * * CHILDREN
"	15, 38—Four thousand men besides * * * CHILDREN
Mark	7, 28—Yet the dogs * * * eat of the CHILDREN's
"	9, 37—Receive one of such CHILDREN in my name.
"	10, 13—They brought young CHILDREN to him that
Luke	7, 22—They are like unto CHILDREN sitting in the
"	11, 7—and my CHILDREN are with me in bed.
John	21, 5—Jesus saith * CHILDREN, have ye any meat ?
1 Cor.	14, 20—Brethren, be not CHILDREN in understanding
Heb.	2, 13—And the CHILDREN which God hath given
"	2, 14—Forasmuch then as the CHILDREN are part
Mat.	2, 16—Slew all the CHILDREN that were in Beth.
"	21, 15—CHILDREN crying in the temple, and saying
"	2, 18—Rachel weeping for her CHILDREN, and
"	3, 9—God is able * to raise up CHILDREN unto A.
"	7, 11—How to give good gifts unto your CHILDREN
"	10, 21—CHILDREN shall rise up against * parents.
"	11, 19—But wisdom is justified of her CHILDREN.
"	15, 26—It is not meet to take the CHILDREN's bread.
"	18, 25—His wife and CHILDREN and all that he had.
"	19, 29—Every one that hath forsaken * CHILDREN
"	22, 24—If a man die, having no CHILDREN, his
"	23, 37—Often would I have gathered thy CHILDREN
"	27, 25—His blood be on us and on our CHILDREN.
Mark	7, 27—Let the CHILDREN first be filled : for it

Mark	7, 27	Is not meet to take the CHILDREN's bread.
"	10, 24	CHILDREN, how hard it is for them that
"	10, 29	There is no man that hath left * CHILDREN
"	10, 30	He shall receive * * CHILDREN and lands.
"	12, 19	If a man's brother * * leave no CHILDREN
"	13, 12	CHILDREN shall rise up against their parents
Luke	1, 17	Turn the hearts * fathers to the CHILDREN
"	3, 8	God is able * to raise up CHILDREN unto A.
"	7, 35	But wisdom is ?ustified of all her CHILDREN.
"	11, 13	How to give good gifts unto your CHILDREN
"	13, 34	Often would I have gathered thy CHILDREN
"	14, 26	Hate not his father * * and CHILDREN and
"	18, 29	There is no man that hath left * CHILDREN
"	19, 44	Shall lay * thy CHILDREN within thee ; and
"	20, 31	And they left no CHILDREN, and died.
"	23, 28	Weep for yourselves and for your CHILDREN
John	8, 39	If ye were Abranam's CHILDREN ye would
"	11, 52	The CHILDREN of God that were scattered
Acts	2, 39	Promise is unto you and to your CHILDREN.
"	13, 33	Fulfilled the same unto us their CHILDREN.
"	21, 5	Brought us on our way with * CHILDREN:
"	21, 21	Ought not to circumcise their CHILDREN
Rom.	8, 16	Beareth witness that we are the CHILDREN
"	8, 17	If CHILDREN, then heirs ; heirs of God, and
"	8, 21	Into the glorious liberty of the CHILDREN.
"	9, 7	They are the seed * are they all CHILDREN ?
"	9, 8	They which are the CHILDREN of the flesh
"	9, 8	Are not the CHILDREN of God * * CHILDREN
1 Cor.	7, 14	Else were your CHILDREN unclean ; but
2 Cor.	6, 13	I speak as unto my CHILDREN, be ye also
"	12, 14	for the CHILDREN ought not to lay up for
"	12, 14	But the parents for the CHILDREN.
Gala	4, 25	Which * is in bondage with her CHILDREN
"	4, 27	The desolate hath many more CHILDREN
"	4, 28	Now we * as Isaac was, are the CHILDREN
"	4, 31	We are not CHILDREN of the bond woman.
Eph	2, 3	Were by nature the CHILDREN of wrath.
"	5, 1	Be * followers of God, as dear CHILDREN
"	5, 8	But now * walk as CHILDREN of the light.
"	6, 1	CHILDREN, obey your parents in the Lord.
"	6, 4	Ye fathers, provoke not your CHILDREN to
Col	3, 20	CHILDREN, obey your parents in all things.
"	3, 21	Fathers, provoke not your CHILDREN * lest
1 Thes.	2, 7	Even as a nurse cherisheth her CHILDREN.

"	2, 11 —We exhorted * as a father doth his CHILD.
1 Tim.	3, 4—Having his CHILDREN in subjection with
"	3, 12—Ruling their CHILDREN and their own house
"	5, 4—If any widow have CHILDREN or nephews
Titus	1, 6 —Having faithful CHILDREN, not accused of
1 Peter	1, 14—As obedient CHILDREN, not fashioning
2 Peter	2, 14—Having eyes * adultery * cursed CHILEREN.
1 John	3, 10—In this the CHILDREN of God are manifest.
"	3, 10—And the CHILDREN of the devil; whosoever
"	5, 2—By this we know that we love the CHILDREN
2 John	5, 1—Unto the elect lady and her CHILDREN
"	5, 4 —That I found of thy CHILDREN walking in
"	5, 13 – The CHILDREN of thy elect sister greet thee.
3 John	5, 4—To hear that my CHILDREN walk in truth.
Bev.	2, 23—I will kill her CHILDREN with death, and
Mat.	5, 9—They shall be called the CHILDREN of
"	5, 45—That ye may be the CHILDREN of your
"	8, 12—CHILDREN of the kingdom shall be cast
"	9, 15 – Can the CHILDREN of the bride chamber *
"	12, 27 – By whom do your CHILDREN cast * out ?
"	13, 38—The good seed are the CHILDREN of the
"	13, 38 – The tares are the CHILDREN of the wicked.
"	17, 25—Of their own CHILDREN or of strangers ?
"	17, 26—Jesus saith * Then are the CHILDREN free
"	20, 20—Then came * mother of Zebedee's CHILDREN
"	23, 31—CHILDREN of them which killed the prophets
"	27, 9—Whom they of the CHILDREN of Israel did
"	27, 56—And the mother of Zebedee's CHILDREN·
Mark	2, 19—Can the CHILDREN of the bride chamber
Luke	1, 16—Many of the CHILDREN of Israel shall he
"	5, 34—Can ye make the CHILDREN of the bride
"	6, 35—Ye shall be the CHILDREN of the Highest
"	16, 8—CHILDREN of this * * wiser than the CHILD
"	20, 24—The CHILDREN of this world marry, and are
"	20, 36—Are the CHILDREN of God, being the CHILD
John	4 12—Drank thereof himself and his CHILDREN.
"	12, 36—That ye may be the CHILDREN of light.
Acts	3 25—Ye are the CHILDREN of the prophet, and
"	5, 21 – All the senate of the CHILDREN of Israel.
"	7, 23—To visit his brethren, the CHILDREN of Israel
"	7, 37 —Which said unto the CHILDREN of Israel
"	9, 16 – And kings, and the CHILDREN of Israel
"	20, 36—Which God sent unto the CHILDREN of Israel
"	13, 26—CHILDREN of the stock of Abraham, and

Rom.	9, 26—They shall be called the CHILDREN of
"	9, 27—Though the number of the CHILDREN of
2 Cor.	3, 7—So that the CHILDREN of Israel could not
"	3, 13—CHILDREN of Israel could not steadfastly
Gala	3, 7—The same are the CHILDREN of Abraham.
"	3, 13—For ye are all the CHILDREN of God by faith
Eph.	2, 2—Worketh in the CHILDREN of disobedience.
"	5, 6—The wrath of God upon the CHILDREN of
Col.	3, 6—Cometh on the CHILDREN of disobedience.
1 Thes.	5, 5—CHILDREN of the light and the CHILDREN of day
Heb.	11, 22—Of the departing of the CHILDREN of Israel.
"	12, 5—Which speaketh unto you as unto CHILDREN
Rev.	2, 14—Cast a stumbling block before the CHILDREN
"	7, 4—All the tribes of the CHILDREN of Israel.
"	21, 12—Twelve tribes of the CHILDREN of Israel.
Mat.	11, 16—It is like unto CHILDREN sitting in the
Eph.	1, 5—The adoption of CHILDREN by Jesus Christ.
1 Tim.	5, 14—The younger women marry, bear CHILDREN.
2 Tim.	5, 10—If she have brought up CHILDREN, if she
Titus	2, 4—Teach * women * to love their CHILDREN
Luke	20, 28—Having a wife, and he die without CHILDREN
"	20, 29—Took a wife, and died without CHILDREN.
Mat.	11, 25—Thou hast revealed them unto BABES.
Rom.	2, 20—An instructor * foolish, a teacher of BABES
1 Cor.	3, 1—But as unto carnal, even as unto BABES.
1 Peter	2, 2—As new-born BABES, desire the sincere *

The following are the only places in the New Testament where POUR, POURED, POURING, POURETH or POUREDST are found :

And I heard a great voice out of the temple saying to the seven angels, Go your ways and POUR out the vials of the wrath of God upon the earth.—Rev. 16, 1.

There came unto him a woman having an alabaster box of very precious ointment, and POURED it on his head as he sat at meat.—Mat. 26, 7.

And when he had made a scourge of small cords, he drove them all out of the temple, and the sheep and the oxen ; and POURED out the changers' money, and overthrew the tables.—John 2, 19.

On the Genti'es also was POURED out the gift of the Holy Ghost.—Acts 10, 45.

The same shall drink of the wine of the wrath of God, which is POURED out without mixture into the cup of his indignation ; and he shall be tormented with fire and brimstone in the presence of the holy angels, and in the presence of the Lamb.—Rev. 14, 10.

And the first went and POURED out his vial upon the earth ; and there fell a noisome and grievous sore upon the men which had the mark of the beast, and upon them which worshipped his image.—Rev. 15, 2.

After that he POURETH water into a bason, and began to wash the disciples' feet, and to wipe them with the towel wherewith he was girded.—John 13: 5.

And went to him, and bound up his wounds, POURING in oil and wine, and set him on his own beast, and brought him to an inn and took care of him.—Luke 10. 34.

The word SPRINKLE does not appear in the New Testament. The following are the only places where the words SPRINKLING, SPRINKLED or SPRINKLETH occur :

For when Moses had spoken every precept to all the people according to the law, he took the blood of calves and of goats, and water, and scarlet wool, and hyssop, and SPRINKLED both the book, and all the people.—Heb. 9, 19.

Let us draw near with a true heart in full assurance of faith, having our hearts SPRINKLED from an evil conscience, and our bodies washed with pure water.—Heb 10, 22.

For if the blood of bulls and of goats, and the ashes of an heifer SPRINKLING the unclean, sanctifieth to the purifying of the flesh.—Heb. 9, 13.

Through faith he kept the passover, and the SPRINKLING of blood, lest he that destroyed the firstborn should touch them.—Heb 11, 28.

And to Jesus the mediator of the new covenant, and to the blood of SPRINKLING, that speaketh better things than that of Abel.—Heb. 11, 14.

Elect according to the foreknowledge of God the Father, through sanctification of the Spirit, unto obedience and SPRINKLING of the blood of Jesus Cnrist : Grace unto you, and peace, be multiplied.—1 Peter, 1, 2.

AN OUTLINE

OF THE

INDIA TELUGU MISSION

OF THE

Baptist Foreign Missionary Society

OF

ONTARIO AND QUEBEC.

NOTE. Being anxious, for various reasons, to have this book out before the close of the year (1890), the binder, by request, had the covers ready by the time the last sheet was printed, but in consequence of the paper not being of a uniform thickness it was found necessary, in order to fill the covers, to add a few more pages hence this addition.

I a

Burhampoor
Nagpoor
Sunnagur
Burgur
ORISSA
Akola
RAJAH
Ganjam
OF
BERAR
Bobilli
Chicacole
NIZAM'S
HANAMAKONDA
Binliapatam
Vizagapatam
SECUNDERABAD
Hyderabad
Igui
Palnur
NERSIPAVPETTA
DOMINIONS
Kamah R.
Guntoor
Coconada
Akbur
VINUKONDA
Masulipatam
CUMBUM
BAPTLA
KURNOOL
ONGOLE
RAMAPATAM
T. Nagar GUDAVAGIRI
Pennar
NELLORE
Cuddapah
MADRAS
MYSORE
Arnee
Arcot
Mysore
Pondicherry
Coimbatoor
Coleroon R.
Tanjore
TELUGU
COUNTRY

Scale of Miles.
50   100   150   200

TRAVANCORE
Cochin R.
Ramnad
Gulf of
Manaar
CEYLON
Trincomalee
Madahpaud
C. Comorin

BAY OF BENGAL

Seymour, Boston

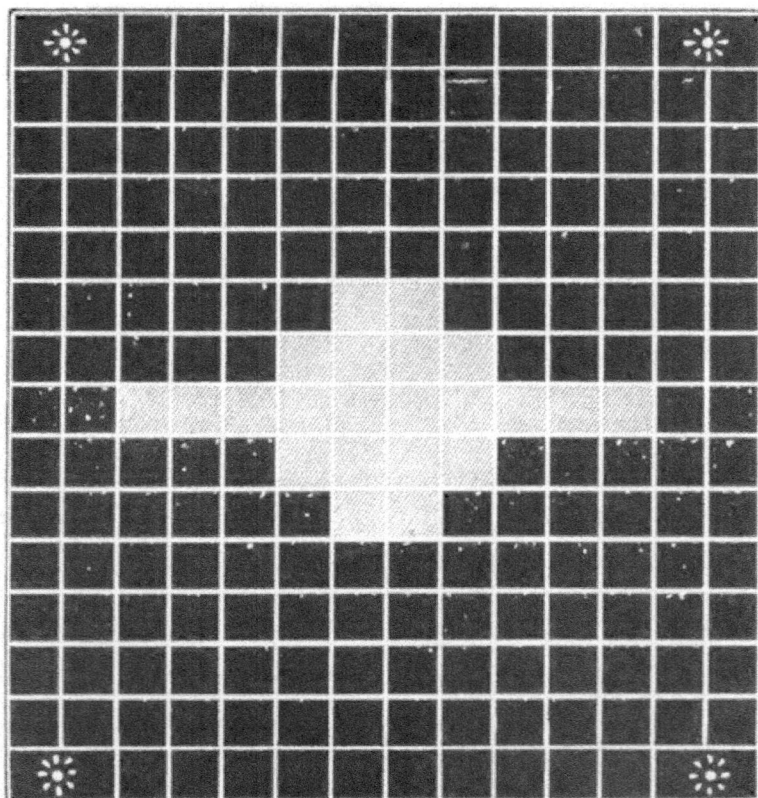

The Telugu's number 18,000,000 souls, but inasmuch as they form only the 41st part of the vast population of Asia, they appear, by some at least, to be regarded as too insignificant a people to have so much money expended on them.   In order to dispel such erroneous impression the above diagram has been prepared.   The population of Ontario is, say 2,200,000, each block in the above represents 100,000 population.   The 22 light colored squares represents the Ontarions, and the 180 dark ones the Telugus.

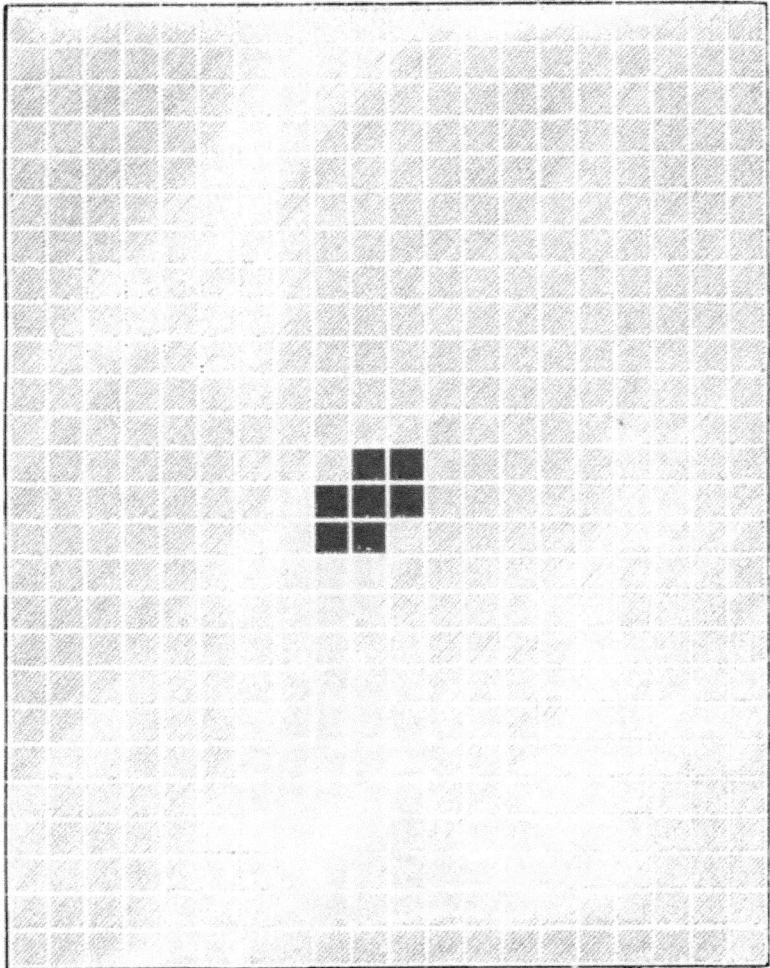

Each of the 513 light colored squares on the foregoing represents 5 Protestant ministers (2,555) who are caring for the 2,200,000 of Ontario's population, and the 7 dark colored squares represent the 35 Protestant missionaries who are caring for 18,000,000 of Telugus. In Ontario there is 1 minister to every 858 of the population, while in Teluguland there is only 1 to every 500,000.

1835.

The location of the Telugu mission is clearly shown on the accompanying map. The mission was commenced by the American Foreign Missionary Society, now called *The Baptist Missionary American Union*. The first missionaries sent out were Rev. S. S. Day and wife, who took passage for Calcutta on the 22nd September, 1835, in the ship *Louvre*. Mr. Day was a Canadian.

1836.

Mr. and Mrs. Day arrived safely at Calcutta early in February of this year. The report says: "The Board was first directed to the people who speak the Telugu tongue by the Rev. Mr. Sutton, an English Baptist minister. He described the country as stretching along the coast south westerly from Orissa 600 miles, and transversely into the interior 400 miles, and a population of 13,000,000."

1837.

Rev. Levi Hall and wife are reported as colleagues of Mr. and Mrs. Day.

1838.

Missionaries on the field, Rev. S. S. Day and wife.

The report alludes to the death, in India, of Rev. Levi Hall and wife.

1839.

Missionaries on the field, Rev. S. S. Day and wife.

The report says: "The Board regrets that they have not yet been able to reinforce this mission owing to various untoward circumstances. Mr. Day has been laboring alone during the whole period since the mission was established."

Rev. Stephen Van Husen and wife sailed for Madras, October 22nd of this year.

1840.

Mr. and Mrs. Day still in charge of the mission. Rev. Stephen Van Husen and wife arrived at Madras March 9th of this year as aids to Mr. Day.

1841.

Missionaries in charge, Mr. and Mrs. Day and Rev. S. Van Husen and wife.

1842.

Mr. and Mrs. Day and Mr. and Mrs. Van Husen reported as the only missionaries in charge, their residence being in Nellore.

1843.

The same missionaries as last year. The report says: "The missionaries were expecting shortly to organize a mission church. Besides the missionaries there were nine natives who cherished a hope in Christ."

1844.

The missionaries the same as last year. The report says: "Thousands begin to doubt as to the divinity of their idols."

1845.

The missionaries the same as last year. A mission church has been organized composed of the two missionaries and their wives, Elizabeth Jackson, Christian Nursa, James Cay and Elisha.

Some time during the year Mr. Van Husen (and wife I assume) was obliged to return to America on account of ill health, arriving in America 1st October. On the 3rd December, Mr. Day was taken suddenly and alarmingly sick and was obliged to leave the mission hurriedly. Arrived in London April 11th, and in America June 2nd.

1846.

Without any missionaries. Report says: "Mr. Day found the Executive Committee discussing the propriety of abandoning the Telugu mission. Mr. D. entered his most emphatic determined protest to the abandonment of the Telugu field."

1847.

Missionaries in charge, none. The report says: "The Telugu mission established ten years ago has had, for the most of that period, the services of only one missionary and is now left with native helpers only."

1848.

Missionaries all in America. At the meeting of the American Board held in the City of Troy, New York, the report states that the meeting "was opened by prayer by the Rev. John Bates, from Ireland." This is the father of our Canadian missionaries Mrs. Timpany and Mrs. McLaurin. The report says: "For more than two years the Telugu mission has been left in charge of native assistants * * * If missionaries are not to be sent it can hardly be expected to protract the existence of the mission. * * * No mission in the Union, in comparison with the work to be performed, has been sustained by us so feebly as this."

"The population is immense, they are a noble race, the country always accessable, the government favorable, the language beautiful, expense moderate, intercourse with the people unrestrained and a beginning made. * * * There is no mission but our own in the Nellore district containing over 2,000,000 souls."

1849.

Rev. S. S. Day is reported as back to his mission. Mrs. Day remaining in America. Mr. and Mrs. Jewett arrived at Madras on their way to Nellore in February, and at Nellore October 10th. Mr. Day writes: " * * * how changed! The sanctuary of the Lord where the name of our God and Saviour was proclaimed and where prayer was wont to be made, has for a long time been forsaken and closed up, so that the heathen passer-by might tauntingly say: 'where is now thy God?'"

1850.

Mr. Day and Mr. Jewett and wife are the missionaries in charge. The report says : " The Telugu mission was re-established too recently to add to or change materially the views expressed last year."

1851.

The missionaries in charge the same as last year. Mr. Day writes: " The general aspect is more encouraging than at any time since the commencement of the mission."

1852.

The missionaries in charge the same as last year. Rev. F. L. Douglass and wife were designated for the Telugu mission.

1853.

The missionaries in charge the same as last year. At the meeting of the American Board, held in the city of Albany, N. Y., May 17th, whether or not the Telugu mission should or should not be continued came up for discussion. The report says: " What a critical moment this was ! How evenly poised the scale beam ! Thousands do now and perhaps millions will yet have cause to rejoice throughout eternity that the beam was brought down in favor of the Telugu mission."

In consequence of ill health Mr. Day was again obliged to return to America. He sailed from Madras June 22nd, and arrived in America in September. He never was able to again return to the mission.

Rev. Mr. F. L. Douglass and wife sailed for Teluguland December 1st.

1854.

Missionaries in charge, Mr. and Mrs Jewett. Extract from report : " Your committee feel that the question of *relinquishment* is now no longer one for discussion."

1855.

Missionaries in charge. Mr. and Mrs. Jewett and Mr. and Mrs. Douglass. Mr. Jewett pleads most earnestly for more men. He says: "What can we do who are but dust and ashes? *Give us men.*"

1856.

Missionaries in charge the same as last year. Nine were baptized during the year and two native preachers employed. Mr. Jewett writes: "We labor under the deep impression that we are doing a work which, in its ultimate results, will affect the welfare of millions by turning them from the worship of idols to the living God." Christian Nursa, a much devoted Telugu, died Nov. 12th.

1857.

Missionaries in charge the same as last year. Two were baptized during the year, making the Nellore church 12.

1858.

Missionaries in charge the same as last year. The " Indian Meeting " greatly embararssed the mission.

1859.

Missionaries in charge the same as last year. Mr. Douglass writes in relation to a revival: " It is a day of great trembling and rejoicing among us. We firmly believe that this 'lone star' will be the centre of a cluster of brighter stars."

1860.

Missionaries in charge the same as last year. Five were baptized during the year.

1861.

Missionaries in charge the same as last year. Mr. Douglass writes: " In the evening we went again to the village.

After I had read a few verses from the Bible and made a few remarks, Lydia, sitting, and before unobserved, in the crowd, numbering perhaps 100 people, began in a very simple way to speak of Jesus. All the head men of the village were present. No sooner had she risen to her feet, with her staff in her hand, than the company divided and stood for more than an hour with eyes fixed on this aged disciple of Jesus as she poured forth in the sweetest and most stirring language and imagery the truth of God—such a display of the sins and folly of heathenism to which she had been devoted for fifty years, its entire emptiness and unsurpassed cruelty, then the glorious gospel of the Son of God, in its fulness and saving power. There was a deep feeling and interest in the assembly, no interruption, except to say, as many did, "yes, mother, what you say is true.'"

1862.

Missionaries in charge the same as last year until Mr. and Mrs. Jewett were obliged to return to America for their health.

1863.

Missionaries in charge Mr. and Mrs. Douglass. The report says: "When we look at upwards of 14,000,000 of heathen so accessible, and their character as among the most intelligent and elevated of the Hindoos * * * we are convinced that there are no fields from which we might expect better returns if the stations were only properly manned."

1864.

Missionaries in charge the same as last year, but in consequence of bad health they were obliged to absent themselves from the mission for several months in order to be aside the sea.

1865-1866.

Missionaries in charge, Mr. Douglass and wife and Mr. Jewett (Mrs. Jewett in America), and Rev. J. E. Clough and wife. The report says: "Rev. A. V. Timpany, of Ontario, Canada West, has been appointed a missionary of the Union." Mr. and Mrs. Clough arrived on the mission field in February. Eleven were baptized during the year, making their entire native membership 38.

1866.

The Canada Auxiliary to the American Baptist Missionary Union was virtually formed on the 16th October, 1866, in the Beamsville parsonage house, the only two officers being Rev. Wm. Stewart, B.A., Secretary, and T. S. Shenston, Treasurer.

1867.

The first annual meeting was held in the Thames Street Baptist Church in the town of Ingersoll, October 17th of this year. The two officers the same as last year. Receipts for the year, $1169.27. At this meeting there were present who took part thereat, Rev. Dr. Murdock, of Boston, U. S.; Rev. Dr. Fyfe, of Woodstock; Rev. C. Walker, of St. Catharines; Rev. H. Lloyd, M.A., of Toronto; Rev. John Bates, of Woodstock; Rev. Dr. Davidson, Secretary of the Home Missionary Society; Rev. A. V. Timpany, the first Canadian Foreign Missionary; Rev. J. C. Hurd, of Brantford; Rev. Wm. Pixley, of New York, etc.

1868.

The second annual meeting was held in the Alexander Street Baptist Church, Toronto, on the 22nd of October. Officers the same as last year. Receipts for the year, $2056.93. Mr. Timpany and wife reached Madras 4th of May.

1869.

The third annual meeting was held in the town of Woodstock, on the 21st of October. Secretary and Treasurer the same as last year, and an Executive Committee: Rev. John Bates, Rev. H. Lloyd, M. A., and H. E. Buchan, M. D. Receipts for the year $3180.46. Rev. John McLaurin reports the result of his 4000 miles travel in behalf of the mission.

1870.

The fourth annual meeting was held in the Queen Street Baptist Church, St. Catharines, on the 20th of October. Secretary and Treasurer the same as last year. Rev. John Bates, President, and H. E. Parsons and W. Craig, Vice-Presidents. Receipts for the year, $2853.35.

Mr. and Mrs. McLaurin sailed from New York 29th December, 1869, and arrived safe in India in due time in the early part of this year.

1871.

The fifth annual meeting was held in the John Street Methodist Church, Hamilton, in consequence of the Park Street Baptist Church being enlarged. The Secretary and Treasurer and President being the same as last year. Vice-Presidents, Wm. Craig and C. A. Morse. Receipts for the year, $3994.10.

Nov. 1st, Mr. McLaurin moved with his family to Ongole.

1872.

The 6th annual meeting was held in the Aylmer Baptist Church on the 17th October. Rev. John Bates, President; Wm. Craig and H. E. Parsons, Vice-Presidents; Rev. J. L. Campbell, Secretary; T. S. Shenston, Treasurer. Receipts for the year, $2136.08.

In February, Mr. Timpany was acting as President of the Theological Seminary at Ramapatam.

1873.

The 7th annual meeting was held in the First Baptist Church, Brantford, October 16th. Officers the same as last year. Receipts for the year, $3341.10.

At this meeting there were present who took part therein: Rev. T. Dyall, Rev. Theo. H. Porter, Rev. M. Sanders from N. S., and Rev. G. H. Brigham from the Union. Bro. McLaurin reported as at Ongole. At the close of the platform meeting (10.30 p.m.) the Board of Directors met at the house of T. S. Shenston, at which meeting were present Wm. Craig (in the chair), Rev. John Dempsey, Rev. R. A. Fyfe, D. D., Rev. James Cooper, Rev. James Coutts, Rev. Mr. Saunders, Rev. J. L. Campbell, J. E. Wells, A. R. Pratt, Rev. Theo. H. Porter and T. S. Shenston. The object of the meeting was the formation of an independent mission of our own at Cocanada, at the recommendation of missionaries Timpany and McLaurin. It was decided to form such a mission at once, Dr. Fyfe was delegated to wait on the American Baptist Missionary Union at Boston, and arrange as to the matters of detail respecting our missionaries leaving them for the purpose named. This was arranged satisfactory to all the parties concerned, and Dr. Fyfe telegraphed from Boston on Tuesday, 28th October, 1873, at 4 o'clock, p.m., to Mr. McLaurin "go to Cocanada on basis of your letter, send in your resignation," which reached Madras in nine and one quarter hours; then by mail to Ongole.

1874.

The 8th annual meeting was held in the York Street Church, London, on the 22nd October. Officers the same as last year with the exception of A. A. Ayre, Esq., occupying Mr. Parson's place. At this meeting Mr. L. Jewett and wife were present and Mrs. Jewett sang several Telugu hymns. Receipts for the year, $4580.88.

On March 12th, Mr. McLaurin took possession of Cocanada, our first missionary field.

1875.

The 9th annual meeting was held in the Baptist Chapel, Guelph, Oct 21st. The society was now called the "*Baptist Missionary Society of Ontario and Quebec.*" Among those who took part at this meeting were Dr. Fyfe, Rev. Mr. Travers of Oswego, N. Y., Rev. D. A. Steele of Amherst, N. S., Dr. Davidson and G. F. Currie (who was designated for the Telugu field). Officers the same as last year with the exception of Mr.

C. Raymond, President, instead of Mr. Bates.   Receipts for the year, $6012.

1876.

The 10th annual meeting was held in the Jarvis Street Baptist Church, Toronto, October 19th.   Among those who took part at this meeting were Dr. Fyfe, Rev. E. Edmonds, Rev. John Craig (under appointment of the Board), Rev. A. A. Cameron, Rev. J. Gordon of Montreal, Dr. W. S. McKenzie, of Boston, Mass., and Rev. A. V. Timpany, returned missionary.   Officers the same as last year excepting Dr. Fyfe, President, instead of Mr. Raymond.   Receipts for the year, $4914.88.

1877.

The 11th annual meeting was held in the Jarvis Street Baptist Church, Toronto, October 17th.   Among those who took part were Dr. Fyfe, Rev. G. M. W. Carey, Rev. A. H. Monro, Rev. J. W. A. Stewart, Rev. A. V. Timpany (missionary), Rev. George Richardson, Rev. Wm. Stewart, Rev. Dr. J. H. Castle, Rev. John Craig (who was at this meeting designated for the Telugu field).   Officers: Rev. R. A. Fyfe, President; Wm. Craig and A. A. Ayer, Vice-Presidents ; T. S. Shenston, Treasurer ; Rev. J. L. Campbell and Rev. James Coutts, Secretaries.   Receipts for the year, $7921.37.

1878.

The 12th annual meeting was held in the First Baptist Church, Brantford, on the 17th October.   Among those who took part were Rev. Wm. Stewart, Rev. John Torrance, Rev. J. L. Campbell, Rev. A. A. Cameron, Rev. J. D. King, Rev. T. L. Davidson, Rev. E. J. Stobo.   Officers : President, T. S. Shenston ; Vice-Presidents and Secretaries the same as last year : T. Dixon Craig, Treasurer.   Receipts for the year, $6,699.65.

1879.

The 13th annual meeting was held in the Queen Street Baptist Church, St. Catharines, December 16th.   Among those who took part thereat were Rev. Wm. Stewart, Rev. W. H. Porter, A. P. McDiarmid, Rev. E. J. Stobo, Rev. John McLaurin. Officers the same as last year. Receipts for the year, $9145.21.

1880.

The 14th annual meeting was held in the Jarvis Street Baptist Church, Toronto, 22nd October. Among those who took part thereat were Rev. J. H. Castle, D.D., Rev. J. E. Hooper, Rev. John McLaurin, Rev. J. L. Campbell and Rev. A. M. Douglass of New York. The officers the same as last year. Receipts for the year, $8948.51.

1881.

The 15th annual meeting was held in the Olivet Baptist Church, Montreal, October 28th. Among those who took part thereat were Rev. A. H. Monro, Rev. Wm. Stewart, Rev. W. N. Clark, Rev. John McLaurin and Rev. W. S. McKenzie of Boston, U. S. Receipts for the year, $7687.53.

1882.

The 16th annual meeting was held in the James Street Baptist Church, Hamilton, October 19th. Among those present who took part thereat were, Rev. D. Hutchison, Rev. W. Dawley, Rev. F. A. Douglass and Rev. B. D. Thomas. Receipts for the year, $10,596.78.

1883.

The 17th annual meeting was held in the Talbot Street Church, London, October 18th. Officers: Chas. Raymond, President; Wm. Craig and A. A. Ayer, Vice-Presidents; Rev. J. W. A. Stewart, Secretary; T. S. Shenston, Treasurer. Among those present who took part thereat were Rev. J. L. Campbell, Rev. Dr. B. D. Thomas, Rev. W. N. Clark and Rev. Wm. Stewart. Receipts for the year, $9600.94.

1884.

The 18th annual meeting was held in the St. Thomas

2a

Baptist Church, October 16th. Officers the same as last year. Among those who took part thereat were, Rev. Dr. Castle, Rev. Mr. McDiarmid, Rev. John Craig, Rev. Mr. Hallum and Mrs. Churchill. Receipts for the year, $12,657.29.

1885.

The 19th annual meeting was held in the church at Guelph, October 22nd. Officers the same as last year. Among those present who took part thereat were Mr. Smith of Tiverton, Rev. J. W. A. Stewart, Rev. G. M. W. Carey and Rev. F. W. Auvache. Receipts for the year, $13,820.18.

1886.

The 20th annual meeting was held in the Paris Baptist Church, October 21st. Officers the same as last year. Among those present were Mr. Wm. Craig, Mr. and Mrs. McLaurin, Miss Frith and Mr. Stillwell. Receipts for the year, $14,653.65.

1887.

The 21st annual meeting was held in the Jarvis Street Baptist Church, Toronto, October 17th. Officers: Wm. Craig, President; Chas. Raymond and A. A. Ayer, Vice-Presidents; Rev. James Grant, Secretary, and T. Shenston, Treasurer. Addresses were made by Rev. W. S. McKenzie, U. S., Rev. John McLaurin and Robert Garside. Receipts for the year, $15,583.67.

1888.

The 22nd annual meeting was held in the city of St. Catharines, October 18th. Officers: President, Wm. Craig; Vice-Presidents: Rev. Elmore Harris and D. Bentley; Treasurer, T. S. Shenston; Secretary, Rev. John McLaurin. Bro. McLaurin, in a very brief note, tendered his resignation as a missionary of the Board, without one word in allusion to the past or the future. It was, however, stated by a member of the Board, which statement was not questioned, that Bro. McLaurin's reason for resigning was that when he was able to return to India he wished to do so as the missionary of such society as suited him best. The matter was referred to a committee who reported: "we find that the Board has acted towards our returned missionary not only in strict conformity with the constitution of the society, but beyond this, in our judgment, wisely and generously," which report was adopted unanimously.

At a subsequent meeting, "after full discussion" the following resolution was passed unanimously: all the circumstances of the case being fully considered, *resolved:* "that in the best interest of Bro. McLaurin himself, and the denomination, his resignation be accepted." Subsequently, at the close of the last day, Bro. McLaurin was requested to withdraw his resignation, which he did. This, and what subsequently grew out of it, occasioned the alienation of some old and warm friends of the mission. Receipts for the year, $19,238.33.

1889.

The 23rd annual meeting was held in the city of Ottawa, October 18th. Officers the same as last year. Receipts for the year, $19,040.86.

1890.

The 24th annual meeting was held in the town of Woodstock, October 18th. Officers: President, Rev. S. Bates, B.A.; Vice-President, Wm. Craig; Secretary, Rev. John McLaurin; Treasurer, John Firstbrook. Receipts for the year, $20,042.45.

Dr. Murdoch writes, Feb. 3, 1891: "The Lord has given another Telugu revival. The joyful intelligence has been received from Ongole that two thousand and twenty-three were baptized in the last quarter of 1890, of whom sixteen hundred and seventy-one were baptized Sunday, December 28. Two thousand were waiting for baptism. Let all the people praise the Lord. The mission calls for twenty-five new men. Will not the Lord's people arise and send them?" *Standard*, Feb. 12, '91

Total Annual Receipts.

	Members.	Ontario and Quebec Foreign Missionary Society.	Women's F. M. Society. West.	Women's F. M. Society. Eass.
1867		$1,169 27		
1868		2,056 93		
1869		3,180 46		
1870		2,853 35		
1871		3,994 09		
1872		2,136 08		
1873		3,341 10		
1874		4,580 88		
1875		6,012 00		
1876		4,914 85		
1877		7,921 57	$590 44	$434 37
1878		6,699 65	898 78	598 44
1879		9,145 21	1,424 55	978 81
1880		8,948 51	1,535 95	590 57
1881	638	7,687 52	1,625 10	825 30
1882	914	10,596 75	2,223 92	958 45
1883	925	9,690 94	2,678 99	1,018 91
1884	1024	12,657 29	3,897 45	1,138 22
1885	No report	13,820 82	3,416 78	1,069 30
1886	1872	14,653 65	4,104 49	1,107 07
1887	1805	15,209 22	4,636 74	1,158 71
1888	1947	19,238 33	5,766 06	1,399 88
1889	2030	19,940 84	4,924 36	1,255 90
1890	2393	20,042 45	5,838 06	1,530 68
Totals -		$191,253 43	$37,796 51	$12,664 73

(In the Members column, spanning 1867–1880: "Until 1874, we were only auxiliary to the American Baptist Missionary Union.")

The American Baptist Missionary Union Report of the Telugu Mission for the last three years.

	Baptised.	Membership.	Amount Paid.
1888	2321	26,629	$63,679 48
1889	2849	30,659	58,369 87
1890	3340	33,838	64,778 38

REV. ROBERT ALEXANDER FYFE, D.D.

The first President of the Baptist Foreign Missionary Society of Ontario and
Quebec. Born Oct. 20, 1816. Died at Woodstock, Ont., Sept. 4, 1878

REV. JOHN BATES.

Father of Mrs. Timpany and Mrs. McLaurin. Born Jan.
1805. Died at St. George, Ont., May 8, 1875.

MRS. BATES.

The wife of the Rev. John Bates and the mother of Mrs. Timpson and Mrs. McLaurin, our first Missionaries.

REV. A. V. TIMPANY.

Our first Foreign Missionary. Born Dec. 21, 1840. Died at Cocanada India, Feb. 19, 1885.

MRS. JANE TIMPANY.
(Nee Bates).

The wife of Missionary Rev. A. V. Timpany, our first
Missionary to India.

REV. JOHN McLAURIN.

Our first Missionary to Cocanada.

MRS. MARY McLAURIN.
(Nee Bates).
Wife of Missionary Rev. John McLaurin.

REV. LYMAN JEWETT, D.D.

A Telugu Missionary of the American Baptist Missionary Union.

MRS. JEWETT.

The wife of Missionary Rev. Dr. Lyman Jewett

REV. G. F. CURRIE, M.A.

He was the youngest son of Zebula and Lovinia Currie, was born in Fredericton, N. B., in 1844. Was designated at Guelph, Oct, 1875. Died at Cocanada, July 31, 1886.

MRS. MARIA E. CURRIE.

(Nee Armstrong.)

Wife of Missionary Rev. G. F. Currie.

REV. JOHN CRAIG, B.A.

Sailed for India as one of our Missionaries in 1877,
and arrived in India, Jan., 1888.

MRS. JOHN CRAIG.
(Nee Perry).

Wife of Missionary Rev. John Craig. Born Feb. 13,
1873. Died at Akidu, India, April 2, 1881.

MRS. JOHN CRAIG.
(Née Summers).

The wife of Missionary Rev. John Craig, B.A.

COLOMBO MISSION HOUSE.

F. J. Anderson

6a

SAMULCOTTA SEMINARY BUILDINGS.

THE SANTO OPEN SEMINARY NEW BUILDING.

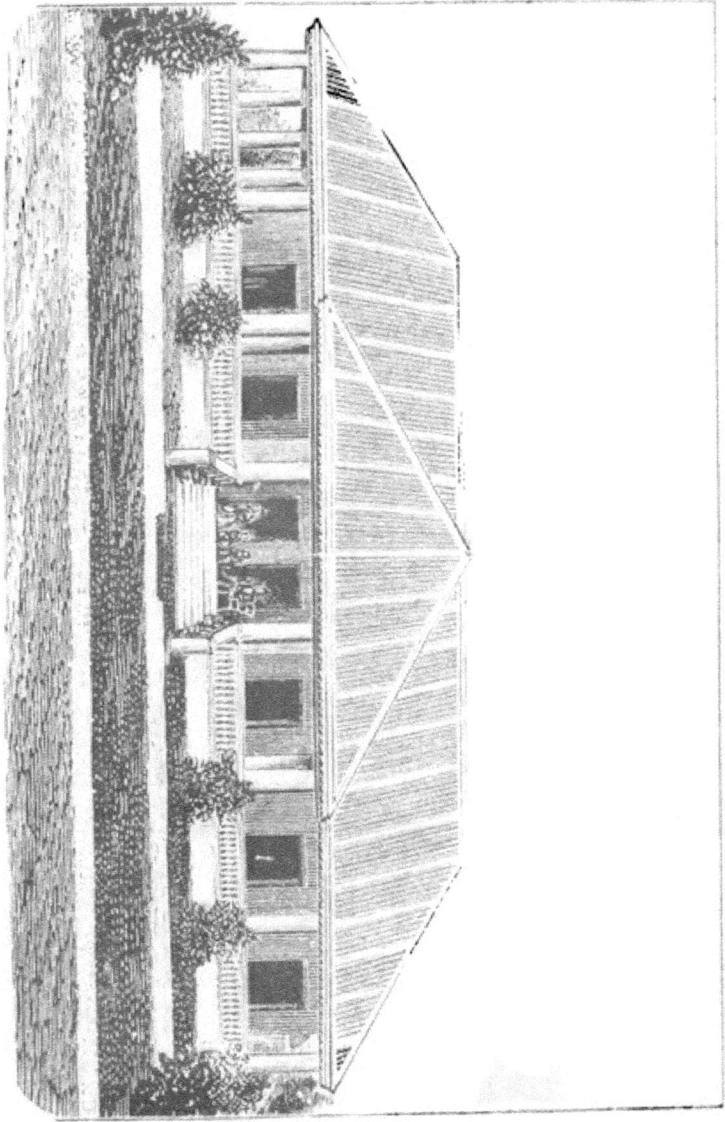

ZÜRICH.

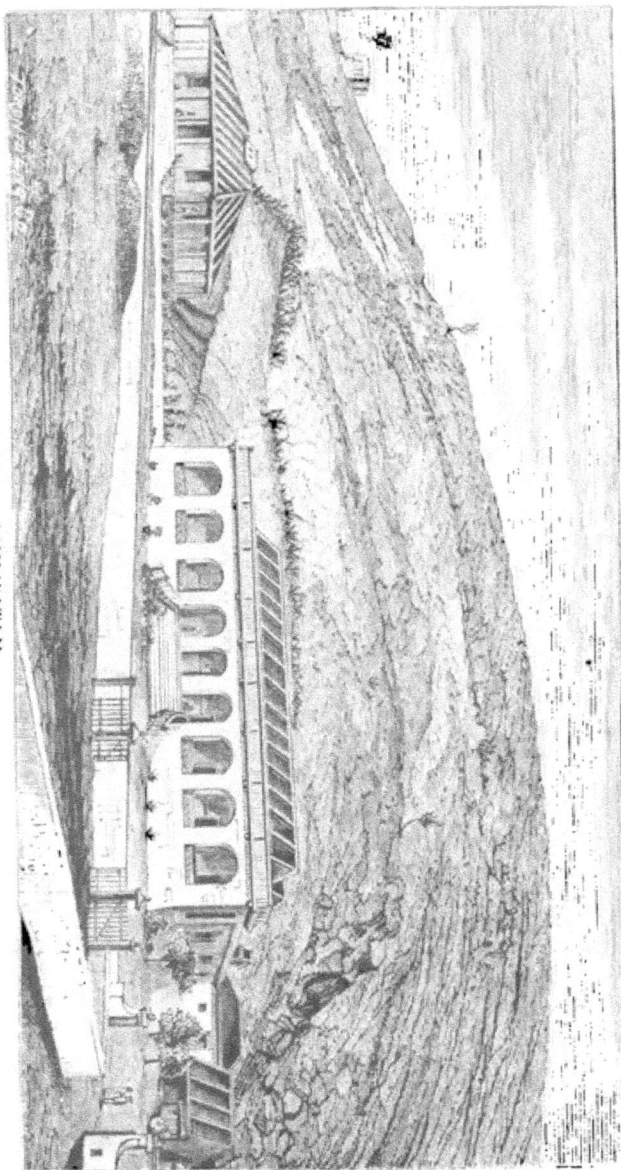

BALBI-YALA.

7a

THE FIRST GRADUATING CLASS OF THE SAMULCOTTA SEMINARY.

The first graduating class of the Samulcotta Seminary. Who can estimate the power for good that these four men, carefully trained and consecrated to Christ's service, represent? We hope to hear of these men from time to time as leaders in Christian work, and we trust that year by year gradually increasing classes will go forth into the great harvest field. We are doing no more important work in India than that of training native preachers and teachers. Through these chiefly must India be evangelized.

THE COANADA MISSION BOAT "CANADA."

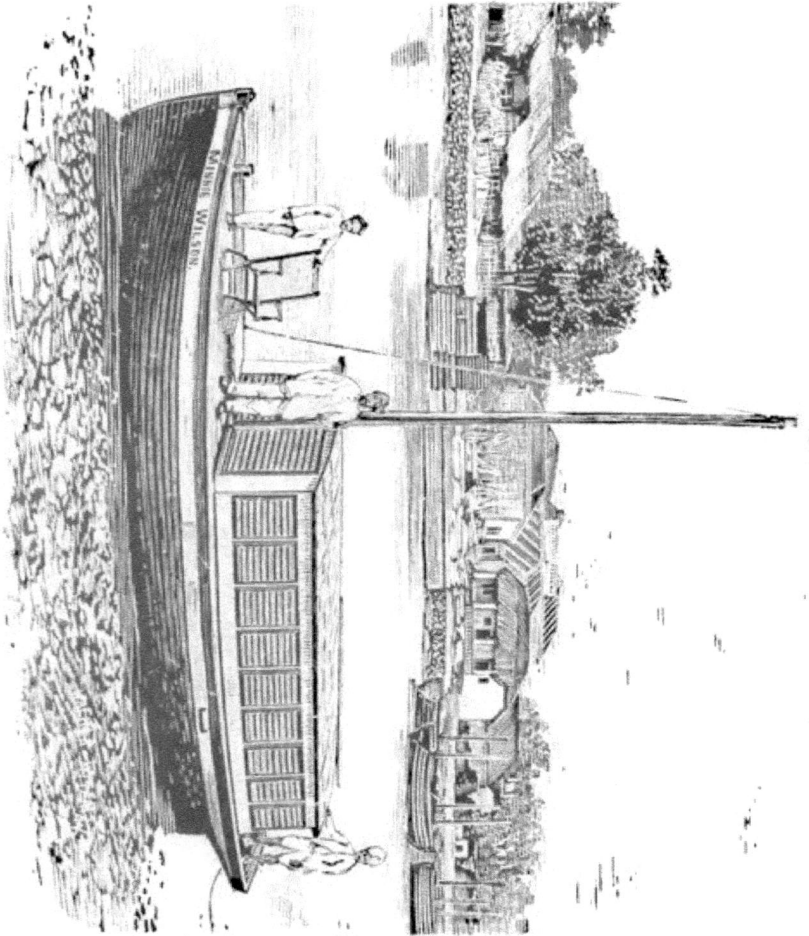

This boat was purchased April, 1874, and cost with the repairs about $100, and was paid for by the Oliver Baptist Church Sunday School, Montreal City. It was named after a young lady of that school who had been most active in securing the money. In 1879, it was broken up and a part of it used in the building of the "Canadian."

Sa

MISS FRITH.

Arrived in Cocanada, Nov. 13, 1882, as a Missionary
of the Women's Foreign Missionary Society.

REV. F. W. AUVACHE.

Arrived in India March 2, 1886, as one of our Missionaries and returned on account of his health, May 3, 1888.

MRS. F. W. AUVACHE.
(Nee Owen.)

Wife of Missionary Rev. F. W. Auvache, sailed for
India with her husband from Quebec, Nov. 21, 1885.

REV. J. R. STILLWELL, B.A.

He was ordained and designated in the First Church, Brantford, in July, 1885, and in company with Rev. John Craig and wife sailed for India in August 1st following.

MRS. J. R. STILLWELL.
(*Nee* Delahey).

Wife of Missionary Rev. J. R. Stillwell, arrived in
India, August 1st, 1885.

REV. H. F. LAFLAMME.

One of our Missionaries. He landed in Cocanada,
November 12, 1887.

MISS S. ISABEL HATCH.

Sailed from Boston, U. S., October 14th, 1886, as one of
our Missionaries to India.

REV ROBERT GARSIDE.

He sailed for India with his wife Dec. 7th, 1887, as one
of our Missionaries.

10a

MRS. GARSIDE.

She sailed for India with her husband December 7th,
1887, as one of our Missionaries.

REV. J. E. DAVIS, B.A.

He with his wife reached India as our Missionaries,
November 12, 1887.

MRS. J. E. DAVIS.

She with her husband reached India as our Missionaries, November 12, 1887.

MISS STOVEL.

One of our Missionaries. She sailed in company with Miss Baskerville and Miss Simpson, arriving at Madras October 22nd, 1888, and at Cocanada four days afterwards.

Ha

MISS. MARTHA ROGERS.

REV. JOHN G. BROWN, B.A.

Mr. Brown and wife sailed from New York, Oct. 9th, 1889, as
our Missionaries for Teluguland.

REV. JAMES A. K. WALKER.

Mr. Walker and wife sailed from New York October 9th, 1889,
as our Missionaries for Teluguland.

www.ingramcontent.com/pod-product-compliance
Lightning Source LLC
Chambersburg PA
CBHW021117270326
41929CB00009B/915